Ethics:

The Study of Moral Values

By
Mortimer J. Adler
and
Seymour Cain

Preface by
William Ernest Hocking
Alford Professor Emeritus, Harvard University

ENCYCLOPÆDIA BRITANNICA, INC.

Chicago • London • Toronto • Geneva

PREFACE

Our topic is ethics—one of the greatest ventures, and adventures, of the human mind. Why "adventures"? Because ethics is an attempt to make a science of what is in reality an art, the art of right living. Every art has had its traditional precepts and techniques, not so much reasoned out as felt out and handed on to beginners dogmatically, often as sacred mysteries. This is eminently true of the art of right living: its codes have been transmitted rather than explained; and anyone who undertakes to replace authority by a reasoned system takes a long risk. Can there be a strict science of duty, of the distinction between right and wrong, of the "You ought"?

Let me illustrate the difficulty from a contemporary case. Not long ago, a professor of ethics in an American university found himself in doubt about the value of his teaching. He put the question directly to his students in a mid-term examination, assuring them that he wanted a hard and honest answer, and that no one would be either penalized or praised for his comment. One able and candid student replied that the teaching had had no noticeable effect on behavior; and, further, that in the nature of the case it could not have, for

> You cannot *prove* that a man ought to love
> his neighbor; and if you could, that proof
> would *not in the least* help him to do so.

The professor, impressed by this answer, read it to his class, and raised the following question: does ethics attempt to prescribe what we ought to *feel*, or solely what we ought to *do?* We cannot help what we feel, but we can help what we do. The phrase "You ought," which announces a duty, usually applies to action and implies a sharp contrast with what we feel like doing; whereas the more militant injunction "You've got to do this *and like it*" seems to demand more than good morals requires. Is it perhaps the case that the rule "Thou shalt love thy neighbor as thyself" is a religious rather than an ethical duty?

This question suggests that ethics may be bounded on one side by religion and on the other side by law. For law is definitely concerned with what we do, not with what we feel. Paying one's accepted debts is a legal duty; but whether one does so from a sense of justice or from good business policy, law does not inquire. Immanuel Kant makes this the precise difference between law and ethics. Law, he says, makes the demand "Act *externally* so that your freedom can coexist with the freedom of all others . . ." whereas ethics requires a right *motive* as well as a right *act*.

In the ancient codes, rules of law, religion, and ethics went together. "Thou shalt not steal"—a rule of action—stood with "Thou shalt not covet"—a rule for feeling (the institution of property was thus doubly protected)—and both were considered religious obligations. But for pure ethics, the question remains whether the "You ought" applies to feeling: if for good and sufficient reasons I dislike my neighbor, is there a moral duty to love him? We can, indeed, stand ready to help him—a pragmatic equivalent of love; but our actual sentiments are what they are, and the "You ought"—the whole subject matter of ethics—means nothing unless we are able and free to conform or not to conform to the alleged duty. This issue is fundamental to the entire enterprise in which we are here engaged.

We find codes of ethics, the world over, demanding not acts alone, but feelings. They call for courage, for fidelity, for benevolence; for the fellow feeling (Li) of Confucius; for the unperturbed poise (Tao) of Lao Tze and the Stoics; for sympathy, or for the beyond-sympathy of Nietzsche's will to power—a kindly concern well blended with pugnacity, but still a state of feeling. Do these codes, then, assume that we are free to feel as we ought to feel—that we can somehow achieve right feeling?

ETHICS:

The Study of Moral Values

The great ethical thinkers in the Western tradition have taken different views on this issue.

Plato's Socrates assumes a desire to control desire, and that, with due attention, due discipline *(paideia)*, and due indoctrination (not excluding a bit of mythology deliberately invented for the purpose), the motivation of life can be altered, until all ranks in the state accept their divergent lots gladly, including the grim communism of the guardians.

Spinoza, however, while putting up the strongest plea for the "intellectual love of God" as an ideal blessedness, excludes any role for freedom of the will. For under the divine necessity, states of mind-and-feeling vary strictly with states of body-and-action: we can be freed from the bondage of passion only by accepting the divine inevitability of being what we are and of striving to preserve that being.

Nothing in the whole history of thought seems to me more remarkable than the completeness and enthusiasm with which this lonely and battered and nobly courageous thinker entered into the spirit of the physical science which was just then beginning that conquest of men's minds we call "modernity," and beyond which we are now passing. It was not until two hundred years after Spinoza that Herbert Spencer, spurred by Darwin's picture of man's evolution, gave clear expression to the same paradox. "If you mean by freedom of the will doing what we wish," he said, "we are always free. The point is, we cannot do otherwise; and we *cannot wish what we wish.*" There Nature has its necessary control: determining our wishes, Nature determines our "free" acts.

Thus one ideal threatens to displace another: the ideal of mathematical perfection in the processes of physical change—including human behavior—tends to exclude the ethical ideal that *we desire what we ought to desire,* and—as all our great ethical thinkers call on us to do—put away our trivial, sense-bound, egocentric, contentious cravings in behalf of a durable and universal love. This ethical ideal assumes as within our power what religion has commonly described as a "change of heart," and has called on God to effect ("Create in me a clean heart, O God, and renew a right spirit within me"). It would seem that Spinoza's genius, realizing this clash, had deliberately placed him *on both sides of the issue,* without being fully capable of resolving the impasse.

At the present moment of human history, the two poles of this dilemma have reached their maximum tension. What Spinoza and Kant were forecasting, in treating human nature as an integral part of total Nature, we are now confirming with the widest experimental verification. Ethics no longer ignores what the empirical sciences—physical, biological, and social— have to say about the factors of human behavior, the chemistry and dynamics of bodily metabolism, organic balances and heredities. The arts of psychosomatic medicine and psychiatry have all but replaced *ethical exhortation* by a *therapy* which assumes that wrongness of deed and sentiment is a disease rather than a moral fault. (At the same time, anomalies in alien ideology or economic theory are often judged with a rigor of moral condemnation which assumes the alien's complete freedom to feel as one ought to feel and think as one ought to think.)

Little as Spinoza and Kant could foresee all this, they were not without inklings of the answers which are now emerging. Montaigne already, in his quiet way, little concerned with the niceties of speculation, had noted that "the *relish* of good and evil depends in a great measure upon the opinion we have of them"; *i.e.,* the motive power of a desire is not a fixed physical quantity but is changeable with changes in our thinking—especially with the thinking which *makes an object of that desire itself.* For (as Montaigne did not observe) what we make an object of, that we have already in principle detached from ourselves. Under the living spell of desire (or "libido"), we are vividly aware of *its object,* but not of *it as object:* once it is observed as an object, an external force (especially if ticketed with a scientific label), we are so far loosed from its power as to be able either to reject its claim or to accept it without compulsion. In that posture we are concretely free—Spencer to the contrary notwithstanding—free not simply *to do as we wish* but *to wish as we wish,* meaning free to throw our weight on the desire we believe we *ought* to entertain.

To speak more exactly, in this radical freedom to change our own motivation, what occurs is that our *total aim* suspends the realization of any partial aim proposed by desire. Ethical theory, concerned as it must be with particular deeds and feelings, tends to neglect the overall directive of the will. From the first, the human being has some enveloping sense of the *total nisus* of his being, which he seeks to define and to give a governing authority. This growing total aim confronts particular desires with a demand for agreement—"integration"—as between whole and part. The terms of this required integration are not preordained; the solution must be *made.* The self, called on for creativity, must act as artist, devising particulars of action that may realize the adopted desire. Our ethics becomes literally an *art of living.*

And, as in all true art, this power to determine our own motivation, to change ourselves, is not unattended with suffering: it calls for that deepest effort, the *will to suffer* in creation. No one who has known an alcoholic in the fight with his own appetites can be ignorant of the reality, and the cost, of the grim and concrete freedom to mold one's desire to the "I ought."

With this insight, our present ethical outlook may join hands with a much older conception of the total good which human life may achieve, that of fulfilling an appointment with Destiny. Recall the Stoic lines,

> Lead me, O Zeus, and Thou, O Destiny,
> The way I am bid by Thee to go.
> To follow I am willing.
> For were I recusant
> I do but make myself a slave
> And still must follow.

The all-embracing good is thus seen—not with Aristotle as happiness, nor with Plotinus as merging with the One, but as fulfilling a personal mission or task, in cooperation with the world process of continuing creation.

Such a total aim lends a new significance to the detailed

choices of life. And the metaphysical world view which assures the validity and pertinence of such an aim—disposing of the split substances and certitudes of Descartes—marks our emergence from the "modern" period, and the beginning of a new era.

And the possibility of *changing men's motives*—of changing ourselves, and of changing the motivations of others (including those of our enemies) by inducing them to change themselves—this possibility, made use of, may well be the most important single item in our labors for world peace.

In these readings we realize the immense enrichment, through the ages, of the treasury of ethical thought, and the steady, long-time unveiling of the true meaning of early intuitions. As we see that true meaning, the validity of those intuitions is equally impressive, and a sense of fellowship with our origins grows strong. The moral search has its felt identity throughout: we are joined with our beginnings in a new rapport. And we realize that we can hardly appreciate the present without the search itself, traced not from near the end, but from the recorded beginning.

WILLIAM ERNEST HOCKING

FOREWORD

I

This Reading Plan is an aid to the understanding of ethics, or moral philosophy. You need not have done the readings in other Reading Plans to follow the discussions in this one. Sometimes a reference is made to another Reading Plan, in order to provide additional understanding of the reading under discussion. For instance, in the Guide to the Seventh Reading, which consists of selections from Hobbes's *Leviathan,* we refer to the discussion of his psychological theory in the forthcoming Reading Plan *Biology, Psychology, and Medicine.*

How to Use the Reading Plan. This Plan contains three parts: a list of readings, guides to each of the readings, and suggestions for additional readings.

1. *The Reading List.* There are fifteen readings. The reading time will vary with the selection and the reader. The First Reading, Plato's *Laches,* will require much less time than the Ninth Reading, on Spinoza's *Ethics,* or the Eleventh Reading, Kant's *Fundamental Principles of the Metaphysic of Morals.* The whole course of readings should take about thirty weeks, or an average of two weeks per reading. The reader, however, is well advised to pursue each reading at his own pace, proceeding faster or slower in accordance with his rate of comprehension.

2. *The Guides.* These should prove most helpful to the reader of *Great Books of the Western World* who is going it alone, without teacher, discussion leader, or other study aids. The

purpose of the guide is to help you get started on an assignment by providing you with background material and by stimulating your thinking about the reading. Background material may include information about the particular historical setting —tradition, culture, and contemporary conditions—in which the book was written. It may also include remarks on the form and style of the readings, which range from a Platonic dialogue to a biological treatise.

A major portion of each guide describes the content and analyzes the meaning of the reading. Significant and difficult passages are cited and discussed. Where a whole work is being studied, we try to show how the parts fit together in the whole. We consider especially the basic ethical ideas and problems discussed in the reading and try to relate them to perennial ethical concerns.

The final section of each guide raises questions that are suggested by the reading. You cannot answer such questions merely by repeating what the text says, or by an unqualified "yes" or "no," or by a flat "true" or "false." Hence, a brief discussion follows the statement of a problem, in order to indicate its significance and suggest some of the possible answers. You may be satisfied simply to read the questions and give them a little thought. Or you may want to delve more deeply into them and write out considered answers. The discussions following the questions are intended to stimulate your own inquiry and thought. They are not meant to provide the final or "right" answers. Try to answer the questions yourself.

Each guide concludes with a section entitled SELF-TEST-ING QUESTIONS. These are quite distinct from the discussion questions. They are factual questions about the reading that can be answered by citing a particular part of the text. They give you an opportunity to check how thoroughly you have read and how much you have remembered of what you have read. You can mark your score by referring to the list of answers which appears immediately after the Guide to the Fifteenth Reading.

3. *Additional Readings.* These provide suggestions for those

readers who wish to pursue further their study of ethics. They include both writings in *Great Books of the Western World* and an extensive list of other works. The latter comprises histories of ethical thought and of morals, general philosophical works, and works dealing with the political and religious aspects of ethics. A special attempt has been made to include significant works by British and American moral philosophers during the past hundred years, down to the latest developments.

II

Ethics is the branch of philosophy of greatest interest to the general reader. Indeed, many people look to philosophy to provide guidance on the conduct of life, and even identify philosophy with practical wisdom. This common tendency to emphasize the practical and to neglect the purely theoretical and abstract aspects of philosophy should not be lightly regarded—it goes back at least as far as Socrates. The centrality of ethics has been stressed by some of the greatest philosophers in our tradition.

Moreover, ethics—the study of what is right and wrong in human conduct—is closely connected with other studies which we have already considered in this series of Reading Plans. It is closely linked to the study of political, social, and economic problems, to basic legal questions, and to religious and theological issues. Ethical questions have already been raised in these Reading Plans: *The Development of Political Theory and Government, Religion and Theology,* and *Philosophy of Law and Jurisprudence.* It would be difficult to think of any writings which deal with human action, including imaginative literature, in which moral questions do not arise.

In this Reading Plan, we concentrate on the problem of right and wrong, good and evil, in human behavior, attending to politics, law, and religion only as they are relevant to basic ethical concerns. Hence, our selections are taken for the most part from the great writings in moral philosophy; but we have necessarily also included selections from works in Christian theology, political and legal philosophy, epistemology, and biology. To these we have added a number of genial and provocative essays by a great master of the essay form who had a special interest in moral questions.

Of course, a series of selections which includes both Plato and Hobbes, both Aristotle and Kant, and both Aquinas and Darwin is bound to express a wide variety of approaches, attitudes, and beliefs. However, as will become evident as we read through these selections, certain basic problems tend to be stressed by these widely differing thinkers.

One of these is the question of whether ethical knowledge is possible, and if so, just what kind of knowledge it is, how it is attained, and how exact and certain it is. A somewhat similar question is the relation between knowledge and virtue; that is, whether knowing the good and doing the good necessarily go together, and if so, again, just what kind of knowledge ethical knowledge is.

Another type of question deals with the relation of pleasure to the good—whether pleasure is a good, the ultimate good, an accompaniment of good, or irrelevant or even dangerous from an ethical point of view. This raises the question whether pleasure is simply physical and psychological satisfaction or may have a purely spiritual form, and if so, what the relative ethical values of the various kinds of pleasure are. Associated with this kind of question is the question of the highest good—the ultimate aim of human life—and how it is related to subordinate goods; whether happiness, for instance, is the highest good, or part of it, or irrelevant to it, and what happiness consists in.

Still another type of question, and one closely related to the questions dealing with pleasure and happiness, concerns the relation between human nature and human good. It asks whether man has some specific central aim, which is inherent in the nature of things, and if so, how his various physical and mental functions are related to that central aim. The good for man may involve the whole of his nature, or only a specifically human or spiritual aspect, or be continuous with animal nature and fulfillment. Alternatively, the ethical may be separated from the natural, and even contrasted as "ought" against "is," and a formal ethics may be constructed which essentially transcends the natural realm.

Questions such as these necessarily involve a discussion of what the standard or criterion of the good is—what it is that makes an act right or wrong. Is it the fulfillment of natural potentialities, the attainment of certain ends or results, or conformity with a formal or moral standard? Is there an absolute, universal standard of right and wrong, or are all such standards relative to a particular time and culture, or even to individual desires and preferences?

Many other questions arise in the following readings and are discussed in the guides—for example, the relation of moral freedom to natural necessity, the morality of man in a state of nature and in civilized society, peace of mind as an ethical end, the ethical relevance of man's relation to the universe and to God, and the relation of individual ethics to social ethics. Certainly these fifteen readings offer an abundance of fundamental ethical themes and issues, and thus a gateway to the further pursuit of ethical inquiry, within and without *Great Books of the Western World*. The reader is also reminded that the basic ethical ideas are discussed in the Syntopicon in Volumes 2 and 3, with detailed references to the relevant passages in *Great Books of the Western World*, and with suggested additional readings.

CONTENTS

A NOTE ON
REFERENCE STYLE

In referring to *Great Books of the Western World,* the same style is used as in the *Syntopicon.* Pages are cited by number and section. In books that are printed in single column, "a" and "b" refer to the upper and lower halves of the page. In books that are printed in double column, "a" and "b" refer to the upper and lower halves of the left column, "c" and "d" to the upper and lower halves of the right column. For example, "Vol. 53, p. 210b" refers to the lower half of page 210, since Vol. 53, James's *Principles of Psychology,* is printed in single column. But "Vol. 7, p. 202b" refers to the lower left quarter of page 202, since Vol. 7, Plato's *Dialogues,* is printed in double column.

THE READING LIST

PLATO

Laches

Vol. 7, pp. 26-37

Most of us admire the quality of courage in our fellow men. We hail the brave man and wish to be brave ourselves in whatever trials life may bring us. There is a common recognition and acknowledgment of this human virtue. We all know what it means to experience fear and to face, or fail to face, the things we fear.

This common human experience is the basic starting point for anything we may say or think about courage. The complexities of this experience and the ambiguities of the various meanings we attach to the term "courage" are revealed in the critical examination of the subject by a philosopher such as Socrates in the *Laches*.

For example, the term "courage" usually calls to mind fortitude in the presence of physical dangers, as in battle and in dangerous sports. But most of us feel that this is far too limited a meaning, for the dangers we face in human existence are not all physical. It takes courage, for instance, to stand up against the disapproval of our neighbors when we are taking a lone stand for what we hold to be right.

Also we may doubt that fortitude and taking risks are virtues in any and all circumstances. Is the fearless or reckless man courageous, or is there something wrong with him? Must courage be connected with other virtues, such as temperance and prudence? Can an evil man be courageous?

These are the sorts of questions that are raised by the moral philosopher Socrates and discussed with two military men, Laches and Nicias, in this dialogue.

First Reading

I

The *Laches* belongs to a group of Platonic dialogues that are called "Socratic" because they center around the figure of Socrates and seem to transmit his personality and teaching rather than Plato's later, fully developed doctrines. It is generally considered to be one of the earliest of Plato's dialogues, because it is relatively simple in structure, brief, deals with a single topic, and ends inconclusively—a tentative sketch.

Other early dialogues, similar to the *Laches,* which deals with courage, are the *Charmides,* on temperance (self-control), and the *Euthyphro,* on piety. (The *Euthyphro* is discussed in the Reading Plan *Religion and Theology.*) Each of the three dialogues attempts to investigate the nature of a single virtue. In each the argument proceeds from an initial crude and vague definition to more adequate definitions, but in the end none is found satisfactory, and the participants—and usually the reader too—are left in a state of admitted bewilderment and ignorance about the nature of the virtue in question.

Many readers are annoyed with Plato's procedure in these dialogues, for they feel frustrated and cheated when a philosophical question is proposed for discussion and then left unresolved. Some readers may feel that Plato cannot really be serious and is only playing a game with them. Others, knowing that these are early dialogues, may dismiss them as crude, amateurish efforts of Plato before he had fully developed the art of the philosophical dialogue.

These negative reactions, however, do not do justice to the early Socratic dialogues. For, although they reach no definite conclusion, they do awaken our awareness of the subject discussed—courage or temperance or piety—through an indirect presentation of possible, tentative assertions. Both the partial validity and the inadequacies of the various statements about the nature of a virtue are presented dramatically, through a dialogue between individuals with varying characters and points of view. Instead of giving us a direct exposition of a single viewpoint or a summary and evaluation of various viewpoints, Plato invents an imaginary conversation centering around Socrates and, usually, other historical persons.

Plato apparently considered this kind of presentation ideally suited to the investigation of philosophical problems, particularly ethical questions. The note of inquiry, of search, is continually maintained in the early dialogues, and we end with a question, not with an answer that stills our thought. These dialogues, starting with common human experience, and presenting and criticizing typical notions and interpretations, awaken and challenge us to continue the inquiry. We are invited to think for ourselves, to pursue the problem of the nature of courage, for instance, after we have finished reading the *Laches*. The definitions of courage offered in the *Laches* are not presented as all that may be said about the nature of courage. We can go on to attempt some definitions of our own. And we need not accept Socrates' evaluation of the definitions. We are invited, almost seduced, to enter the argument ourselves. A dialogue such as the *Laches* does not build a fence around its subject; rather, it opens the gate to deeper discussion.

It is because of this method of teaching, if it can be called teaching, that these early dialogues are considered especially Socratic. Plato undoubtedly reproduces in these imaginary conversations the way Socrates actually engaged men in fifth-century-B.C. Athens in the discussion of ethical problems. The Socratic method became an essential element in most of Plato's works and is employed in the longer and richer dialogues, even in those in which Plato's own mature doctrines are being presented. Only in some of the later and highly abstract dialogues does Socrates become a mere mouthpiece for Plato, and the interlocutors mere yes-men. The spirit of dialogue and the presentation of philosophical inquiry through human conversation pervade most of Plato's works.

II

The *Laches* is a typical example of the early Socratic dialogue. Socrates and the other participants in the dialogue discuss the virtue of courage. The subject is raised by two old Athenian gentlemen, Lysimachus and Melesias, who are concerned about the education of their sons and desire to bring them up to be distinguished and worthy citizens. With this end in view, they have invited two eminent generals, Nicias and Laches, to witness a demonstration of the art of fighting in armor. The dialogue opens just after the exhibition has finished, and the two old men ask the generals whether training in the art of fighting in armor will aid in educating their sons. Laches suggests that Socrates, who is also present, should participate in the discussion, since he is particularly concerned with the education of youth. Also present, but not participating in the discussion, are the sons of Lysimachus and Melesias.

The two military men disagree about the educational merits of training in the art of fighting in armor for young men. Nicias favors such training on the grounds that it helps to develop a youth physically, prepares him for combat, and may lead to a study of other military arts, including generalship. Laches, on the contrary, dismisses such training as practically useless and to prove it, gives a ludicrous example from the career of the "expert" they have just seen.

Lysimachus now calls on Socrates to speak up and decide the issue, since the two professional soldiers have disagreed. But the philosopher points out that a decision about education should be made by one skilled in the particular subject under discussion, not by a majority vote. Hence he raises the question whether anyone present, including himself, is qualified to discuss the subject. He also presents a new view of what the subject really is.

The art of fighting in armor, the ostensible subject, says Socrates, is a mere means to the end of caring for the souls of the young, which is the actual subject. Socrates' question, then, is, "Which of us is skilful or successful in the treatment of the soul, and which of us has had good teachers [in such treatment]?" (p. 29d) In other words, Socrates demands that anyone who ventures to speak on the subject must show either that he has had a good teacher or that he has actually improved the souls of the young—has imparted virtue to them.

Nicias and Laches accept Socrates' statement of the question and agree to exchange questions and answers with him. Nicias, well aware of what it means to engage in such an interchange with Socrates, notes that

... any one who has an intellectual affinity to Socrates and enters into conversation with him is liable to be drawn into an argument; and whatever subject he may start, he will be continually carried round and round by him, until at last he finds that he has to give an account both of his present and past life; and when he is once entangled, Socrates will not let him go until he has completely and thoroughly sifted him. (p. 30d)

III

With these preliminaries over, the argument proper begins. Socrates immediately shifts the discussion from the question of who among them is qualified to improve the souls of youth to the question of "the nature of virtue." It stands to reason, he says, that anyone who can impart virtue must know what it is. He suggests, then, that instead of presenting a record of their teachers and accomplishments they discuss virtue—not "the whole of virtue," but only that part of virtue to which the art of fighting in arms is supposed to lead, namely *courage*. (See p. 32a.) Only after they have finished discussing what courage is can they discuss the question of how the youth may learn to be courageous. The subject of the dialogue—a virtue and not a technical skill—is finally out in the open.

Laches, considering the definition of courage an easy matter, says that "he is a man of courage who does not run away, but remains at his post and fights against the enemy." (p. 32a) Socrates points out to the general that such a definition is inadequate even for a soldier, who often fights by running away and then slashing back at the enemy. Moreover, the discussion is about courage *in general,* not only about the courage of those

. . . who are courageous in war, but who are courageous in perils by sea, and who in disease, or in poverty, or again in politics, are courageous; and not only who are courageous against pain or fear, but mighty to contend against desires and pleasures, either fixed in their rank or turning upon their enemy. (p. 32c)

Hence, Socrates amends the question about the nature of courage thus: "What is that *common quality,* which is the same in all these cases, and which is called courage?" (p. 32d) [italics added]

Laches answers with his second definition, "that courage is a sort of endurance of the soul" (p. 33a). Socrates recognizes that this is an honest attempt to get at "the universal nature" of courage; but he finds it unsatisfactory because it is too inclusive, making no distinction between wise and foolish endurance. Through questioning Laches, he notes that the "wisdom" or "knowledge" involved in the right kind of endurance cannot be mere technical skill or an astute calculation of probabilities; for banking on such assurances can hardly be considered courage. Yet we cannot accept the alternative position that the right kind of endurance involves ignorance or lack of skill; for this would be foolish risk-taking rather than courage.

The question of the relation of wisdom or knowledge to courage has apparently brought the discussion to an impasse, but Socrates proclaims that they who are discussing endurance must display it by persevering in the inquiry—"and then courage will not laugh at our faintheartedness in searching for courage" (p. 34a). He calls in Nicias to come to the aid of Laches and himself. Nicias, citing an old saying of Socrates that "Everyman is good in that in which he is wise, and bad in that in which he is unwise," concludes, as Socrates has put it, that the virtue of courage is "a sort of wisdom" (p. 34b). Pressed by Socrates to specify the nature and object of this wisdom or knowledge, Nicias says that "courage is the knowledge of that which inspires fear or confidence" (p. 34c). Do we call physicians courageous because they possess medical knowledge? Nicias retorts that the kind of wisdom or knowledge he is talking about is entirely different from the kind involved in the arts and sciences; for the wisdom of courage is concerned with *good and evil—the better and the worse—* not with technical skill or empirical facts. The physician may know that a man will die or recover from a disease, but only "he who is skilled in the grounds of fear and hope" can know whether death or recovery is best for the man.

Hence Socrates amends Nicias' definition thus: "courage is the knowledge of the grounds of hope and fear" (p. 35b). Since such knowledge is possible for human beings alone, we cannot ascribe courage, as thus defined, to wild beasts. Laches concludes that Nicias' definition has thereby been rendered ridiculous, since "everybody" knows that wild beasts are courageous. But Nicias replies,

> Why, Laches, I do not call animals or any other things which have no fear of dangers, because they are ignorant of them, courageous, but only fearless and senseless. Do you imagine that I should call little children courageous, which fear no dangers because they know none? There is a difference, to my way of thinking, between fearlessness and courage. I am of opinion that thoughtful courage is a quality possessed by very few, but that rashness and boldness, and fearlessness, which has no forethought, are very common qualities possessed by many men, many women, many children, many animals. And you, and men in general, call by the term "courageous" actions which I call rash;—my courageous actions are wise actions. (p. 35d)

Despite Nicias' cogent and eloquent discourse, however, Socrates is not willing to accept his revised definition that courage is knowledge of the grounds of fear and hope. Fear and hope are directed only to the future, but real knowledge in any field must refer to the past and the present as well. It follows, then, that courage cannot be the knowledge of things to be feared or hoped for, but must be the knowledge of good and evil at all times. If this is what courage is, then it is the whole of virtue, which implies the knowledge of all the good and evil there is in the world. However, we have already admitted that courage is a part, not the whole, of virtue. With this contradiction, the discussion has reached a final impasse, and "we have not discovered what courage is" (p. 37b).

The dialogue ends with all of the participants, spurred on by Socrates, admitting their ignorance and agreeing "to go to school with the boys" whom they seek to educate. Socrates advises

. . . that every one of us should seek out the best teacher whom we can find, first for ourselves, who are greatly in need of one, and then for the youth, regardless of expense or anything. But I cannot advise that we remain as we are. And if any one laughs at us for going to school at our age, I would quote to them the authority of Homer, who says, that

Modesty is not good for a needy man.

Let us, then, regardless of what may be said of us, make the education of the youths our own education. (37d)

IV

Our main interest in the *Laches* is the philosophical discussion which has been summarized in Section II and III. However, since the discussion is presented in an imaginary dialogue centered around historical characters, we should briefly note the literary qualities and historical references which give the dialogue the appearance of an actual conversation. Certainly the particular characters chosen and the events and persons they refer to must have added to the enjoyment of the dialogue by Plato's contemporaries.

The conversation takes place during the long Peloponnesian War (431-404 B.C.), sometime between the battle of Delium (424 B.C.), in which Laches witnessed Socrates' fortitude under stress (see p. 27c), and the battle of Mantinea (418 B.C.), in which Laches was killed. Most commentators assume Socrates to be under fifty at the time of the dialogue, since he defers to Laches and Nicias as his elders (see p. 27c-d), and this would date the time of the imagined conversation about 420 B.C. or earlier.

Laches and Nicias were commanders of the Athenian forces in the Peloponnesian War. For an account of their activities, see the Index to Thucydides' *The History of the Peloponnesian War*, Vol. 6, pp. 610 and 611. Nicias was the more famous of the two generals. The peace negotiated with Sparta in 421 B.C. was brought about through his influence and named after him the Peace of Nicias. He was captured in the disastrous Sicilian expedition and executed by the victors in 413 B.C. (See Thucydides' *History,* Vol. 6, pp. 562c-563a.) For more about Nicias, see the biographical portrait and the comparison with Crassus in Plutarch's *The Lives of the Noble Grecians and Romans* (Vol. 14, pp. 423-438, 455-457).

In the dialogue, Plato presents the two generals as utterly different types of characters. The bluff and simple-minded Laches is contrasted with the more intellectual and philosophical Nicias. Note the references to Nicias' intellectual sophistication on pages 36a and 37b-c. In the discussion, Laches plays the role of the "straight man" and Nicias of the alert and cogent arguer. Both of them serve as good foils for Socrates in bringing out the main theme and problems of the discussion.

There are some nice touches too in the presentation of Lysimachus and Melesias, the two old men who occasion the argument. They are the mediocre sons of famous fathers—Lysimachus of Aristides the Just, and Melesias of Thucydides, the leader of the oligarchic party and the opponent of Pericles (not the Thucydides who wrote the *History*). They are ashamed of their own lack of distinction and anxious that their sons should do better than they have. Lysimachus, from the same deme (district) as Socrates, is delighted to find that the famous Socrates whom the boys often talk about is the son of his old friend Sophroniscus, and the old man insists that Socrates must be sure to visit them. This is one more little touch that makes the dialogue seem like an actual conversation.

That Plato should select the quality of courage for a discussion of virtue is concordant with the coupling of virtue and courage in the ancient Greek habit of mind and the ancient Greek language. The Greek terms for courage and virtue both have the root meanings of "manliness" and "valor." The meaning of virtue was extended in time to take in other kinds of human excellence. The Latin word for virtue also shows these connotations. We retain something of the original sense of manly vigor and prowess in the English word "virtue," which is derived from the same Latin root as the word "virile." Indeed, if we trace the uses of the English term "virtue" back far enough, we find that it, too, once signified manly excellence and courage.

V

What kind of wisdom or knowledge is courage?

The Socratic identification of virtue with wisdom or knowledge seems strange to us. If technical skill and training are separated from courage, as they are in the dialogue, what kind of knowledge, then, is inseparable from this virtue? According to Nicias and Socrates, it is knowledge of good and evil—about things fearful and hopeful, about the pleasant and the painful. Socrates distinguishes the knowledge involved in courage from the other kinds of knowledge. It is ethical rather than factual knowledge—knowledge that acts should or should not be done rather than knowledge that things are or are not such and such. Is Socrates proposing some kind of analytical, theoretical knowledge, such as is possessed by professional students of ethics in universities? Is it this form of virtue/wisdom that he proposes to his fellows that they learn and that they teach the young? What pragmatic test does he suggest to show whether those who profess to teach such knowledge actually possess it themselves?

Does the possession of courage imply the possession of other virtues?

Courage is described as a part of virtue in the *Laches*. Does that mean that it is separable from the other virtues, or does the possession of courage imply the possession of the other virtues, which are also parts of "the whole of virtue"? Is a brave man necessarily also a just, temperate, and prudent man? Would you call a man "good" who is lacking in any of these qualities?

Is the wisdom or knowledge that is involved in courage the same as that involved in the other virtues? Is there a special wisdom for each moral virtue or a single wisdom for the whole of virtue that is present in each of its parts? Is the "wisdom" involved in courage the same as the wisdom involved in justice or temperance?

Are the definitions criticized by Socrates of any value in understanding what courage is?

Can we develop Laches' notion of courage as steadfastness or endurance to arrive at the general idea of courage? Is endurance an essential or a secondary element in your view of courage? Which is more important in the idea of courage—risk or steadfastness? Or are they bound together?

What of Nicias' notion that courage is "knowledge of the grounds of hope and fear"? Are the emotions of hope and fear always involved where courage is present? Is this a merely psychological rather than an ethical definition, dealing with feelings rather than with good and evil? Do the words "grounds of" make any difference? How much validity is there in limiting courage to what is future—things imminent or expected? If you think this limitation is not valid, how would you refute Socrates' argument disposing of Nicias' definition and his reduction of it to a contradiction?

Does the possession of technical knowledge, skill, and experience rule out the factor of courage when a man faces danger?

The *Laches* leaves us with no alternative between mere skill or art, which cannot legitimately be called courage, and rash, foolhardy action, which does not deserve the name either. How then are we to assess the courage of technically trained men in dangerous situations? Were we right or wrong to acclaim the first astronauts as brave men? If right, what is there in such a venture that leads us to ascribe courage to the men engaged in it? If wrong, does this mean that special knowledge and training always eliminate the factor of courage? Are professional boxers brave men? Did it or did it not take courage for Floyd Patterson and Ingemar Johansson to face one another?

Would a man who had little or no preparatory training be braver than the trained astronauts if he let himself be propelled into space? Did it require more courage for the amateur Pete Rademacher to fight Floyd Patterson than it did for the professionals who fought him? Or is such action rash and foolhardy rather than courageous?

Is all action undertaken without adequate preparation and knowledge in a dangerous situation necessarily rash? Is it rash or brave for weak and unarmed men to oppose an ugly mob on a moral issue? Was it rash or brave for the handful of weak and untrained resistants in the Warsaw ghetto to oppose the armed might of the German S.S. forces?

How are we to weigh the factor of preparation or skill in judging whether an action is brave, rash, cowardly, or morally indifferent?

The following questions are designed to help you test the thoroughness of your reading. Each question is to be answered by giving a page or pages of the reading assignment. Answers will be found on page 303 of this Reading Plan.

1 Who are "the only professors of moral improvement"?

2 What is the ludicrous instance in which the "expert" Stesilaus figured?

3 Who is Nicias' teacher?

4 What state do the teachers of fighting in armor bypass?

5 How are medicine for eyes and bridles for horses related to the teaching of courage?

6 What sort of man does Laches consider a "true musician"?

PLATO

Gorgias

Vol. 7, pp. 252-294

T he view that pleasure and power should be the ultimate ends of human life is not new. Nor is the scorn of the worldly-wise man for the man who insists on pursuing the way of virtue. The conflict between the way of virtue and wisdom and the way of pleasure and power was acute in Plato's day too, and he dramatized it in many of his dialogues.

The *Gorgias* is one of the most ambitious and profound of Plato's presentations of this conflict. It is marked by powerful eloquence and the vigorous affirmation of basic ethical principles. The picture of Socrates as fighting mad, bitterly ironical, and magnificently passionate in his defense of the philosopher's way of life is unforgettable. And so is the portrait of his major opponent, Callicles, the apostle of the doctrine that might makes right.

The dialogue starts from a discussion of rhetoric and continually returns to it. The *Gorgias* takes its name from one of the greatest rhetoricians of Plato's time, who figures as one of the main characters of the work. Rhetoric, as commonly taught and practiced in the fifth century B.C., was the equivalent of modern advertising and public relations, aimed at influencing people in order to gain money, fame, and power.

To this mere empirical "knack," this practical skill, this "gift of gab," unrestricted by moral considerations, Plato opposes the ethical knowledge and attitude of the philosopher, embodied in Socrates. Against all skills, pleasures, and powers, the impassioned and relentless philosopher holds up the single ideal of "justice," or "the good." And he insists that doing injustice—harming others—is always wrong and always worse for the person who does it than suffering injustice is for the one who suffers it. This is the "rare" doctrine that he alluded to in the *Apology* and to which he returns in *The Republic*. It is a truth that only the good man can understand.

Second Reading

I

With the exception of such book-length works as *The Republic* and the *Laws,* the *Gorgias* is the longest of Plato's dialogues. It contains some of the most passionate and eloquent passages in Plato's writings, which is perhaps intentional in a dialogue named after a great rhetorician and ostensibly dealing with rhetoric. Scholars disagree as to its exact order in the Platonic writings, but generally agree that it is not among the earliest ones, such as the *Laches,* and that it precedes such works as the *Phaedo* and *The Republic.* On the one hand, the *Gorgias* is directly dramatic in form, like the earlier dialogues, rather than narrated, like the later ones. On the other hand, the long speeches given to Socrates and the other characters resemble the style of some of the later dialogues. Socrates is still the central figure, using the method of cross-examination as well as making long speeches; but the concerns and emphases are probably more Plato's than Socrates'.

Of all the characters in the dialogue, beside Socrates, the most important in actual history was Gorgias, of Leontini (in Sicily), the celebrated teacher of rhetoric (about 483-375 B.C.). Originally he was a student of natural science, and is represented in an ancient bas-relief as immersed in the study of the heavenly bodies. But his study of Zeno of Elea and several other philosophers led him to doubt that we can ever know the truth or, if we did know it, that we could communicate it to others. Hence he gave up the search for objective truth to develop the art of rhetoric, or persuasion, dealing with probabilities instead of certain knowledge. He taught his students to convince their auditors through the rhythm, form, and ornament of their language, appealing to the feelings and emotions rather than, through logical argument, to the intelligence. Eduard Zeller, the noted German historian of Greek philosophy, credits Gorgias with discoveries in practical psychology and with pioneering in the science of aesthetics, especially poetics. Gorgias, according to Zeller, discovered and developed the principle of suggestion and also the idea of illusion in art. His remarks on the psychological effects of tragedy—pity and fear—and his comparison of these effects with purgation in the body resemble and precede similar doctrines in Aristotle's *Poetics*.

In 427 B.C., Gorgias, already famous as a rhetorician, came to Athens as an ambassador from Leontini requesting aid against Syracuse. He gathered students and attained great fame in Athens and other Greek cities, earning great wealth from his fees as a teacher. He preached the doctrine of a common Greek spirit in the various city-states in which he taught. He died at about the age of eighty in Thessaly, one of the most famous men of his day. Socrates' respectful treatment of him in the *Gorgias,* a dialogue otherwise marked by the moral philosopher's pugnacity and biting tongue, probably indicates Plato's own respect for the rhetorician.

Gorgias belonged to a group of educators called the Sophists. In contrast with the early, pre-Socratic Greek philosophers, they focused their attention on the study of human behavior, institutions, and society, instead of on the natural world and the ultimate principles of things. Their aim was to provide the youth with general cultural knowledge and to train them in the arts of persuasion and argument that were necessary for success in politics, as well as to cultivate in them other attainments required for practical life. (See the *Protagoras*, Vol. 7, p. 43b, where Protagoras says his pupils learn "prudence in affairs private as well as public.") The Sophists were the pioneers of systematic education in the Western world, and with their regular courses of instruction in various subjects, such as mathematics, astronomy, and grammar, they replaced the traditional Greek home education in gymnastics, the three R's, and music. With their interest centered on the forms of thought and speech, they made contributions to the foundations of grammar, rhetoric, and logic—disciplines which were further developed by Aristotle and which became the core of the educational curriculum in medieval times.

The controversy between Socrates and Plato on the one hand and the Sophists on the other arose not from differences as to the value of the formal skills taught by the Sophists but from the ethical consequences of the Sophists' teaching. The Sophists taught their students how to make cogent arguments or moving speeches rather than how to discover and test ultimate truths. They claimed to teach the virtue and wisdom required by the citizen of the Greek city-state, which meant, in effect, how to win friends and influence people, how to be smooth, adept, and successful in politics and social life.

It is on this issue that Socrates and Plato attacked the Sophists. For the philosophers, "virtue" and "wisdom" were not merely practical skills but qualities of the soul, which would be difficult to teach if they are teachable at all. Political virtue, in their view, was inextricably bound up with the good life of the whole community; it could not be reduced to individual success in gaining office or power. The mastery of any field of learning—true knowledge—was not to be attained through verbal dexterity. Knowledge was a theoretical matter, not a practical skill.

Not all of the Sophists specialized in rhetoric. Gorgias was rare among them in concentrating on the teaching of rhetoric alone. The figure of Gorgias, however, and the rhetorical skill which he exemplified are dramatically appropriate to this dialogue which deals with the nature of virtue and with the contrast between the just and the successful man.

Callicles of Acharnae, the most important figure in the dialogue next to Socrates and Gorgias, has baffled the historians who look for the actual originals of Plato's characters. Many scholars believe that he is a composite figure, based on a type of thinker well known in Plato's time. In his doctrine that might makes right, he closely resembles the Thrasymachus of Plato's *Republic*, who was a rhetorician and Sophist of Plato's time. However, Callicles' use of the idea of "natural" right is not the same as that of some historical Sophists, who concluded from it that all men are equal by nature and should be so in society. (See below, p. 33.) Nevertheless, the Callicles of the dialogue serves as a dramatic expression of the extreme might-makes-right doctrine.

Polus of Agrigentum was a student of Gorgias. Chaerephon, Socrates' companion in this dialogue, also figures in the *Apology* as the impetuous friend who had asked the oracle of Delphi if there were any man wiser than Socrates. (See Vol. 7, p. 202a.)

It is difficult to ascertain the time when the conversation is supposed to take place. The topical allusions in the dialogue would date it anywhere from 427 B.C., when Gorgias first came to Athens, to sometime after 408 B.C., when Euripides' *Antiope*, which is quoted on p. 272b, presumably appeared. Perhaps Plato had no particular year in mind and did not mind mixing up topical allusions, as long as they were relevant to the discussion and plausible as part of the setting.

II

The question raised at the beginning of the *Gorgias* and picked up again and again throughout the dialogue—"What is rhetoric?"—is not its real subject. The real subject is the good life for man—how we should live a worthwhile existence. To reveal the possible answers to this question and the conflict among them, Plato sets up Socrates, the ethical philosopher, against the great rhetorician Gorgias, his disciple Polus, and Callicles, the eloquent protagonist of might-as-right. Thus we listen to an argument on three levels, pitting the standards of justice against the standards of mere pleasure or power, an argument in which the basic conflict becomes more and more acute, ending with Socrates' victory over his most obvious and redoubtable opponent, Callicles.

After a few gracious preliminaries, which introduce the other characters of the dialogue, Socrates engages Gorgias in a discussion of the nature of rhetoric. Prodded by the Socratic method of questions and answers, Gorgias defines rhetoric as the art of persuasion in law courts or public assemblies, the art which enables a man to get whatever he desires and to rule over others. (See p. 255b.) Pushed further, to specify about what subjects rhetoric persuades, Gorgias answers, "about the just and unjust" (p. 256a). This answer turns out to be important, for it enables Socrates to lure Gorgias into a contradiction and Plato to introduce the main subject of the dialogue. Gorgias falls into contradiction because Socrates gets him to assert that the rhetorician can teach his students what is just and to be just, after he has already conceded that some rhetoricians use their skill for unjust ends. (See p. 259c.)

Here the first stage of the dialogue ends and the second begins. Polus, Gorgias' admiring disciple, intervenes to upbraid Socrates for luring Gorgias into a contradiction by slyly appealing to his pride and inducing him to claim he knows and can teach what justice is. Socrates ironically accepts the aid of the younger generation in this discussion and invites Polus to engage in the argument with him. The latter decides that this time he will ask and Socrates will answer the question, "What is rhetoric?" Socrates proceeds to develop his point that rhetoric is a sham art ("flattery"), since it is not based on rational knowledge and does not aim at the good. It is a mere "knack" or empirical skill ("experience," in our text) which produces "a sort of delight and gratification" without doing any good for the soul. It is an ignoble form of "flattery" (which also includes cookery, cosmetics, and sophistry), for "it aims at pleasure without any thought of the best"—of the good for man (pp. 260a-261d).

But Polus is unmoved by these distinctions between the pleasant and the good, for he considers it a fact that rhetoric confers great power on men; and he is certain that power is really good for the man who possesses it, since he can do whatever he wants—like the tyrants who "kill and despoil and exile any one whom they please" (p. 262a-b). This expression of the view that power is the supreme good enables Socrates to raise the main issues to be discussed in the remainder of the dialogue.

First, he asserts paradoxically that the rhetoricians and the tyrants possess no power at all, "for they do literally nothing which they will, but only what they think best" (p. 262b). He develops the view that all men will the good for themselves—wisdom, health, wealth, etc., using various means to attain this end. We harm other men in order to gain some good; hence, if killing and despoiling other men harms us, we are not doing what we will but only what we erroneously deem best—what only *seems* good but is *not really* good for us.

At this, Polus burst out scornfully:

As though you, Socrates, would not like to have the power of doing what seemed good to you in the state, rather than not; you would not be jealous when you saw any one killing or despoiling or imprisoning whom he pleased, Oh, no! (p. 263c)

To which Socrates replies quietly, "Justly or unjustly, do you mean?" introducing his main point—that doing, not suffering, injustice is the greatest evil, that the man who commits injustice is more wretched and more to be pitied than the man who suffers it.

To Polus, this is utter nonsense. He points for refutation to the contemporary example of Archelaus, who has risen to the throne of Macedonia through unspeakable crimes and yet is the envy of many Athenians. Certainly *he* is not wretched or to be pitied. And Polus is no more inclined to accept Socrates' next assertion that the wrongdoer who is not punished is more miserable than the wrongdoer who is punished, that the unsuccessful tyrant who is punished with awful torture and execution is happier than the successful tyrant who continues "all through life doing what he likes and holding the reins of government, the envy and admiration both of citizens and strangers" (p. 266a).

Socrates proceeds to demonstrate the two points at issue: (1) that doing injustice is worse than suffering injustice, and (2) that it is worse to escape just punishment than to suffer it. To demonstrate the first point, he gets Polus to admit that doing injustice is more disgraceful than suffering it; then, that the disgraceful or dishonorable is evil; and, finally, that doing injustice, since it is more disgraceful, is a greater evil than suffering injustice. (Socrates uses "evil" here in a purely ethical sense, as contrasted with "pain," for doing injustice is certainly not more painful than suffering it; "good," then, would be the useful or beneficial as contrasted with the pleasant.)

To demonstrate his second point, Socrates gets Polus to admit that "to suffer punishment is another name for being justly corrected when you do wrong," and that "all just things are honourable" (p. 267c). It is beneficial for a man to suffer punishment justly (which also means honorably), for then he is delivered from the evil in his soul; that is, his soul is "cured," for injustice is the great disease of the soul. The best thing of all is not to be "sick" in the first place, but once one is sick, the best thing is to be cured and the worst thing is to avoid the cure.

To avoid punishment simply because it is painful is to condemn oneself to having "a soul . . . which is corrupt and unrighteous and unholy" (p. 269d). Hence the rhetoricians, instead of using their powers of persuasion to escape just punishment, should run to the judge as to a physician, "in order that the disease of injustice may not be rendered chronic and become the incurable cancer of the soul" (p. 270a). Thus there is a good use of rhetoric—to accuse rather than to excuse oneself when one has done wrong.

. . . so the wrong-doer may suffer and be made whole; and he should even force himself and others not to shrink, but with closed eyes like brave men to let the physician operate with knife or searing iron, not regarding the pain, in the hope of attaining the good and the honourable; let him who has done things worthy of stripes, allow himself to be scourged, if of bonds, to be bound, if of a fine, to be fined, if of exile, to be exiled, if of death, to die, himself being the first to accuse himself and his own relations, and using rhetoric to this end, that his and their unjust actions may be made manifest, and that they themselves may be delivered from injustice, which is the greatest evil. (p. 270b)

Indeed, says Socrates, with a bold and striking paradox, if we really want to harm an enemy of ours, when he injures someone we should strive with all our powers, including rhetoric, to prevent him from being punished—that is the greatest revenge we can have. This is too much for Callicles. He has stood all he can stand from Socrates, and now he rushes in to begin the third and final stage of the discussion.

III

Callicles expresses disbelief that Socrates can really be serious, for this would be to turn everything upside down.

For if you are in earnest, and what you say is true, is not the whole of human life turned upside down; and are we not doing, as would appear, in everything the opposite of what we ought to be doing? (p. 270d)

Socrates counters by contrasting himself, the lover of philosophy, whose words are always true and unchanging, with Callicles, the lover of the Athenian "Demus" or populace, whose words continually change. Callicles, undeterred, observes how cleverly Socrates has lured Gorgias and Polus into contradiction, because they were too timid to say what they really thought about power and success, and proclaims that he, Callicles, suffers from no such shyness. He boldly affirms the rightness of striving for power and domination over others, and clearly emerges as the main opponent of Socrates, ideally fitted to set the tone of the culminating section of the dialogue.

Callicles' first point is the distinction between "natural" and "conventional" justice. Socrates, he charges, has deliberately confused the two types of justice. By nature, suffering injustice is more disgraceful and evil than doing injustice; it is only by convention, by artificial agreement, that doing injustice is more disgraceful and evil. The law of nature dictates that the strong should dominate and possess more than the weak; but the majority of men, being weaker, have banded together to make laws which establish an artificial equality and which unnaturally check the stronger, the natural elite. Natural justice is the supreme law, hailed by the poet Pindar, which *"Makes might to be right, doing violence with highest hand"* (p. 272a).

It is shameful, says Callicles, to be a man like Socrates, an unarmed philosopher unversed in the ways of the world, who is unable to defend himself adequately against injustice, a man whose ears one may box with impunity. This is utterly disgraceful, the lot of a slave.

For the suffering of injustice is not the part of a man, but of a slave, who indeed had better die than live; since when he is wronged and trampled upon, he is unable to help himself, or any other about whom he cares. (p. 271c-d)

Socrates praises Callicles' qualities of "knowledge, good-will, outspokenness" and ironically defers to his advice on what a man's character and pursuits should be (to choose the mature life of the worldling as against the childish life of the philosopher). He asks Callicles, however, to clarify what he means by natural justice.

Do you not mean that the superior should take the property of the inferior by force; that the better should rule the worse, the noble have more than the mean? (p. 274a)

With this agreed to, he then leads Callicles to distinguish between the "better" and the "stronger," for the many are stronger than the few but not therefore "superior." Callicles asserts that by "superior" he means "better," those who are "the more excellent," not just superior in brute strength. But Socrates asks why those who are better in any respect should have more possessions than their "inferiors." Callicles, annoyed with Socrates' suggested analogies with physicians, weavers, and shoemakers, says:

. . . I mean by superiors not cobblers or cooks, but wise politicians who understand the administration of a state, and who are not only wise, but also valiant and able to carry out their designs, and not the men to faint from want of soul . . . —they ought to be the rulers of their states, and justice consists in their having more than their subjects. (p. 275c)

Here Socrates raises the question of a man's relation to himself and praises temperance as the supreme virtue. Every man must be his own ruler—"a man should be temperate and master of himself, and ruler of his own pleasures and passions" (p. 275d). Callicles considers this utter nonsense,

. . . for how can a man be happy who is the servant of anything? On the contrary, I plainly assert, that he who would truly live ought to allow his desires to wax to the uttermost, and not to chastise them; but when they have grown to their greatest he should have courage and intelligence to minister to them and to satisfy all his longings. And this I affirm to be natural justice and nobility. (p. 275d)

He regards the high place commonly ascribed to temperance and justice as the result of a conspiracy by the weak and ignoble many to dominate the noble few. Temperance is an evil for the noble, strong man, preventing him from "enjoying every good," and intemperance is a virtue for him.

> . . . the truth is this:—that luxury and intemperance and licence, if they be provided with means, are virtue and happiness—all the rest is a mere bauble, agreements contrary to nature, foolish talk of men, nothing worth. (p. 276a)

Socrates praises Callicles' "noble freedom" in saying what most people really think but are too timid to say. He recognizes that he has a worthy opponent on his hands, passionately opposed to him on the most basic ethical issues. Callicles even refuses to admit the common view that men who lack nothing are happy—that is a good recipe for happiness for stones and dead men, he retorts. "But surely," says Socrates, "life according to your view is an awful thing" (p. 276b). His attempts to convince Callicles that the intemperate man must suffer constant frustration and agony, trying to fulfill insatiable desires, as against the satisfied fulfillment of the temperate man, is unsuccessful.

> *Cal.* You do not convince me, Socrates, for the one who has filled himself has no longer any pleasure left; and this, as I was just now saying, is the life of a stone: he has neither joy nor sorrow after he is once filled; but the pleasure depends on the superabundance of the influx.
> . . . .
> *Soc.* The life which you are now depicting is not that of a dead man, or of a stone, but of a cormorant; you mean that he is to be hungering and eating?
> . . . .
> *Cal.* Yes, that is what I mean; he is to have all his desires about him, and to be able to live happily in the gratification of them. (p. 277a)

Callicles refuses to give an inch. Even a life of constant itching and scratching would be a happy one, he asserts.

Socrates points out that Callicles has implicitly identified the good with pleasure and has refused to distinguish between good and bad pleasures. He proceeds first to discuss "whether pleasure, from whatever source derived, is the good" (p. 277c). Through skillful argument he shows that the good lies in the objective fulfillment of a human need, not in the feeling of pleasure that accompanies the process of desire and gratification. The good lies not in the pleasure of eating when we are hungry or drinking when we are thirsty but in the state of fulfillment that follows, when both the pain and the pleasure have ceased.

Socrates proceeds next to show Callicles that "some pleasures are good and others bad" (p. 280b). Intensity of feeling is no criterion of good. That the coward feels more pleasure than the brave man when the enemy withdraws does not mean that he is better. And there are beneficial pains as well as harmful ones. The ethical problem, then, is "to choose and use the good pleasures and pains" (p. 280c). We must conclude that pleasure is not the good, not the end of all our actions, not what we ultimately desire, but is only a means to that end.

Socrates now begins the final phase of his argument with Callicles, bringing together all the themes previously touched on in his discussion with the three main interlocutors. He raises the question of which art can teach us how to distinguish between the good and the bad pleasures and pains, and rejects rhetoric and poetry as "flattering" arts, which are concerned with delighting rather than edifying men, with giving pleasure rather than with caring for the highest interests of the soul. He points to the possibility of a "true" rhetoric and a "true" politics, directed to the establishment of a harmonious order in the soul and the state, in contrast with the rhetoric and politics of the "great" statesmen of Athens, intended to satisfy the irrational desires of the multitude. He equates the right order of the soul with temperance. It is the key virtue that entails all the others. The temperate man is the perfectly good man. Socrates affirms "the principle that the happy are made happy by the possession of justice and temperance, and the miserable miserable by the possession of vice" (p. 284d).

If this is true, then, ethically speaking, being unjustly injured without being able to defend oneself is not the worst of evils or the greatest disgrace, as Callicles has proclaimed. It is a far worse thing to commit injustice, and the worst thing of all, and the most disgraceful, is to act unjustly and escape just retribution. Then you are injured or maimed where it really counts—in your soul. Of course a bad man, an absolute tyrant, can kill a good man through greater physical or political power. Ethically speaking, however, that makes no difference. It is not mere life but the good life that matters, and the bad man "had better not live for he cannot live well" (p. 286d). Socrates appeals to Callicles:

O my friend! I want you to see that the noble and the good may possibly be something different from saving and being saved:—May not he who is truly a man cease to care about living a certain time?—he knows, as women say, that no man can escape fate, and therefore he is not fond of life; he leaves all that with God, and considers in what way he can best spend his appointed term. . . . (p. 287 a-b)

And he presents him with these alternatives: to conform to the pattern of the present Athenian state and become a popular orator and politician, or to live a life in accord with the highest good of the soul.

To influence Callicles' choice, Socrates returns to his attack on Themistocles, Pericles, and other great leaders of the Athenian democracy, characterizing them as "the serving-men of the State," mere cooks and confectioners, who have gratified rather than transformed and raised the desires of the people. Socrates puts this hypothetical question:

Am I to be the physician of the State who will strive and struggle to make the Athenians as good as possible; or am I to be the servant and flatterer of the State? (p. 291b)

Callicles advises him that it will be safer for him to be the servent and the flatterer, warning him again of the terrible fate that may befall him if he continues on his present course. Socrates brushes Callicles' warning aside in an amazing passage, proclaiming himself the one true politician in Athens.

I think that I am the only or almost the only Athenian living who practises the true art of politics; I am the only politician of my time. Now, seeing that when I speak my words are not uttered with any view of gaining favour, and that I look to what is best and not to what is most pleasant, having no mind to use those arts and graces which you recommend, I shall have nothing to say in the justice court. . . . I shall be tried just as a physician would be tried in a court of little boys at the indictment of the cook. (p. 291c-d)

Socrates does not expect the "little boys" on the jury to be swayed by his plea that he prescribed bitter potions, instead of savory meats and delicious sweets, because it was good for their health. On the contrary, they will clamor for his punishment. All that Socrates can do in such a case is to rely on his virtue, on the fact that he has never done wrong; it is his best and only defense, the only way in which a good man can save the essential part of himself—even if he loses his life.

But if I died because I have no powers of flattery or rhetoric, I am very sure that you would not find me repining at death. For no man who is not an utter fool and coward is afraid of death itself, but he is afraid of doing wrong. For to go to the world below having one's soul full of injustice is the last and worst of all evils. (p. 292a-b)

These moving words mark the end of the long and involved logical argument of the *Gorgias* and are the transition to the imaginative myth with which Socrates closes the dialogue. This "pretty tale," Socrates points out, is no mere fable, but a true tale, an expression of the truth in imaginative form.

Socrates has hinted more than once during the dialogue that the death of the body is not the final event in the journey of the soul, and that man's ultimate destiny is decided after this life, in another world. Now he picks up the ancient mythical notion that after death the good dwell in eternal bliss in the Islands of the Blessed, while the bad go to eternal punishment in Tartarus. Originally, mistakes in judgment were made, because men were judged while they were still alive and by living judges, so that external appearances and social position influenced the judgment. Those judged were "apparelled in fair bodies, or encased in wealth or rank," while the eyes and ears and the whole bodies of the judges were "interposed as a veil before their own souls" (p. 292c). But now both the judges and the judged are dead and "naked," so that there is clear vision and correct judgment of the souls of the judged. The judge "with his naked soul shall pierce into the other naked souls" (p. 292c). After death, the soul and the body are separated and "all the natural or acquired affections of the soul are laid open to view" (p. 293a), unobscured by physical characteristics or social position. No matter how "great" a man may have been, nor what pomp and power he may have possessed, if his soul is unsound it will be clearly

. . . marked with the whip, and is full of the prints and scars of perjuries and crimes with which each action has stained him, and he is all crooked with falsehood and imposture, and has no straightness, because he has lived without truth. Him Rhadamanthus beholds, full of all deformity and disproportion, which is caused by licence and luxury and insolence and incontinence, and despatches him ignominiously to his prison, and there he undergoes the punishment which he deserves. (p. 293a-b)

Punishment serves either to reform the criminal or to warn others of the penalty for sin. Reformative punishment is applied to those whose souls are curable. Exemplary punishment is applied to those whose souls are incurable. The incurable souls are usually those of unjust men of power, the tyrants, the "great men" whom Callicles admires, for they are usually the worst of all. Against these celebrities, Socrates holds up the soul of the philosopher, "who has done his own work, and not troubled himself with the doings of other men in his lifetime" (p. 293d). Men like these go to the Islands of the Blessed, for they have taken good care of their souls; they preserved themselves for the only trial and judgment that really matter.

Hence Socrates sets his course toward the final goal, renouncing all worldly advantages and honors, aiming only to know the truth and to live a good life, and calling on all other men to do the same. Any profit or power in this world which jeopardizes our destiny in the next world is a vain bauble. In that world, Socrates will be at home and the worldly-wise will be the boobies.

Follow me then, and I will lead you where you will be happy in life and after death, as the argument shows. And never mind if some one despises you as a fool, and insults you, if he has a mind; let him strike you, by Zeus, and do you be of good cheer, and do not mind the insulting blow, for you will never come to any harm in the practise of virtue, if you are a really good and true man. . . . Let us, then, take the argument as our guide, which has revealed to us that the best way of life is to practise justice and every virtue in life and death. This way let us go; and in this exhort all men to follow, not in the way to which you trust and in which you exhort me to follow you; for that way, Callicles, is nothing worth. (p. 294c-d)

IV

The *Gorgias* is distinct in many ways from the other Platonic dialogues that we roughly label "early" or "Socratic." It departs sharply from the method of short questions and answers, used in the early dialogues, for it presents long and thundering speeches by Socrates—this despite his request that his interlocutors confine themselves to the shorter method. Far from being inconclusive, the *Gorgias* includes statements that Socrates claims to believe with absolute certainty—such as that doing injustice is worse than suffering it. In addition to being an exposition of the good life for man in general, it is an eloquent—and wonderfully rhetorical—defense of the philosopher's way against various types of opposition, reminiscent of the *Apology* and repeated in passages of *The Republic*. The Socrates of the *Gorgias*, perhaps reflecting Plato's own mood, is bitterly ironical and angry, not merely a good teacher giving students a practical demonstration of sound reasoning.

The content and tone of the dialogue affect its form. Plato here is interested mainly in getting the alternative views set forth, pitting Socrates against the three levels of opposition embodied in the three interlocutors. There are arguments back and forth between Socrates and each opponent, but each stage is more or less sealed off from the other, with little or no interplay between the opponents; nor are their arguments linked together as a whole against those of Socrates. The neatness of this three-level arrangement makes the opposition between Socrates and each of his opponents clearer and simpler to understand, but it may detract from the artistic unity and dramatic subtlety that we find in Plato's best dialogues. Some critics believe that this "mechanical" form and lack of dramatic interweaving of the arguments indicates that the *Gorgias* must be an early dialogue, occurring before such a dialogue as the *Protagoras*.

Another criticism of the dialogue from a literary point of view is that its characterizations are obvious and uninspired, as compared with Plato's great dramatic characterizations. Do you think that Gorgias, Polus, and Callicles are as fully characterized as Laches and Nicias in our previous reading? Which set of interlocutors seems more like real people?

V

Is doing harm or injustice ever preferable to suffering it?

Socrates notably excepts the case of self-defense (see p. 270c) in his injunction against harming other men. In many dialogues Socrates is portrayed as a good and loyal soldier of his city-state of Athens, as a man who counts it a virtue to be a good soldier. Is there an inconsistency between this attitude and the principle that one must never do harm to another man? Is self-defense or active military service possible without doing harm to other men? What are the limits within which such action is just? If the use of force in self-defense or war is just, does that make the harm or violence done to others just? What makes an act of self-defense or of hurting enemies in war just? Does a revolution against tyranny or injustice justify killing or harming other men?

Would it have been just to have assassinated Hitler in the 1930's or '40's in order to prevent or end the injustice and harm he was doing to tens of millions of men?

Was it just for the fighters in the abortive Warsaw Ghetto revolt of 1943 to kill and wound their enemies? Would they have been better men if they had merely suffered injustice without retaliating? Or was this justifiable self-defense?

Is it just for law-enforcement officers to detect and capture criminals through illegal means? If unjust, is it always and absolutely unjust, or must the harm done be weighed against the harm done in letting the particular criminal go unapprehended and unpunished?

Are knowing good and being good the same thing?

Socrates' entrapment of Gorgias rests on the identification of knowing and being good. Is this identification of moral knowledge and moral virtue plausible? Could you conceive of a sound moral philosopher who was not a perfectly good man and whose best students were not perfectly good men?

What kind of knowledge does Socrates (or Plato) have in

mind here? Does it follow that a perfectly good man possesses clear and certain knowledge of good and evil which he can communicate to other men? Does Socrates claim that moral knowledge is teachable, and if so, how and by whom does he imply that it can be done? Is it possible for a human being to be perfectly good? Is Socrates suffering from pride or moral blindness when he claims that he has never done wrong?

Is pleasure a good?

Socrates attacks the view that pleasure is the ultimate good, and hence dismisses all the "flattering" arts and sciences that aim merely to delight and gratify. But in his argument with Callicles he distinguishes between good and bad pleasures. By "bad" pleasures he apparently means sensual gratifications. What does he mean by "good" pleasures? Are these the pleasures of the mind, such as contemplation and inner harmony? Are there any bad mental pleasures? Are there any good physical pleasures? Are all aesthetic pleasures bad, or at best indifferent to moral virtue? Is a wholly good human life possible without sensual pleasure?

Socrates points to the possibility of a good rhetoric and a good politics. Does he rule out the possibility of a good poetry or good art in general? Is there a basic conflict or irrelevance between aesthetic good and moral good? Are poetry and other arts morally bad in their effects, or at best morally indifferent and hence dispensable for the morally good life?

Does "natural" law or justice enjoin inequality and the harming of others?

The idea that might makes right and that the strong should rule the weak occurs in one of Gorgias' extant writings and was also voiced by two of his disciples, Meno and Critias. However two other disciples, Lycophron and Alcidamas, concluded—from the assumption of a natural law, existing before and apart from written law and convention—that all men are equal by nature. Alcidamas says, "God left all men free, nature has made no man a slave."

Socrates does not argue directly against Callicles' primary assumption that the law of nature is the law of the jungle, which is expressed in the will to power, domination, and profit. But would Socrates agree that this is a true account of man's nature or of the nature of things? Is Socrates' ethics antinatural? Is ethical good, for him, opposed to nature? If not, how would he argue against Callicles' view? What primary points about the nature of the world and about human nature would have to be established to warrant the assertion of a natural law which enjoins us not to harm our fellow men?

Is there any justification for Callicles' view that civilization stifles natural human powers and instincts? Are human civilization and a peaceful social order possible without such frustration? For a modern view of this problem, see Freud's *Civilization and Its Discontents*, Vol. 54.

Is the philosopher's life a self-centered life?

As against the life of the popular rhetorician and politician, Socrates holds up the life of the philosopher, wholly concerned with the good of his soul and the attainment of virtue, not with money, fame, and power. The philosopher directs his life toward real happiness, which is based on virtue, secure against all onslaughts in this life and eventuating in bliss eternal in the next. To that end, he advocates a withdrawal from all political action and an unconcern "with the doings of other men."

Is this merely a spiritual and shrewder form of the self-centered pursuit of possessions and power sought by the tyrants and the popular demagogues? Or is there an essential distinction between the nature of the self-fulfillment pursued by the philosopher and that of the politician? Does the philosopher seek virtue only for the sake of a reward here and hereafter? Is the reward something different and separable from virtue? Why does Plato end the dialogue with his myth of a transcendental realm of eternal bliss or torment? Is he trying through myth to say something special about the nature of virtue and vice, about the meaning and value of our moral life? What is he trying to say?

Does Socrates really advocate that the good life is unsocial, unpolitical, and cut off from the lives of other men? What is the nature of the "true" politics and the "good" community to which he alludes? What is the relation of the philosopher to the community, as contrasted with that of the popular orator or politician? Is the philosopher, in Socrates' view, indifferent to the welfare of other men? If not, how does he show his concern, how does he act for other men's good?

The following questions are designed to help you test the thoroughness of your reading. Each question is to be answered by giving a page or pages of the reading assignment. Answers will be found on page 303 of this Reading Plan.

1 Why does Socrates think Polus more skilled in rhetoric than in dialectic?

2 What other arts besides rhetoric work through the medium of language?

3 What is Socrates' defense for using a long speech in his conversation with Polus?

4 By what steps did Archelaus attain and keep the throne of Macedonia?

5 Why is a "community of feelings" important to mankind?

6 What is a leaky vessel?

7 What is the aim of the Muse of Tragedy?

8 Why is the art of the pilot an admirable thing?

ARISTOTLE

Nicomachean Ethics

Books I and X

Vol. 9, pp. 339-348, 426-436

Happiness has more often been identified with feeling good than with being good, with sensual enjoyment and a high standard of living than with moral and intellectual virtue. Indeed, that happiness should be the chief goal of human activity has been vigorously questioned by some moral philosophers. Aristotle, however, made happiness the central theme of ethical inquiry.

For Aristotle, happiness is man's highest good, the end to which all human activities contribute when properly performed. Happiness is attained through the satisfaction of all human needs and through the perfection of all of man's natural faculties. It is the fulfillment of human nature and also, in its ultimate, ideal stage, a sharing in the divine activity and bliss of contemplation.

What is remarkable about the *Nicomachean Ethics* is the way in which it takes account of the various powers and needs of man, its many-sided approach to the attainment of happiness. Aristotle is not concerned only with moral virtue; the directive role of reason, as well as the disciplined action of the will, are also of primary importance in his analysis. The highest pleasure, from his ethical viewpoint, is intellectual; it is achieved through the contemplation of eternal truths.

Yet this is not "pure," "spiritual" ethics. Aristotle also includes the satisfaction of man's material and emotional needs in the good life. Proper treatment of the body and the passions plays a part in his ethics. Pleasure of the right kind and love or friendship are important in his account of the good for man. Aristotle's happy man is healthy, adequately nourished, clothed and housed, and in harmony with his society, while leading a life of virtuous activity, according to right reason.

Third Reading

I

The *Nicomachean Ethics* belongs to Aristotle's "practical" writings. He divided human knowledge into three main branches: theoretical, practical, and productive. "Theoretical" sciences, in this view, are a disinterested inquiry into truth for its own sake; they include natural philosophy and metaphysics. "Practical" sciences are concerned with knowledge for the sake of action, with the ultimate purpose of achieving the good life. "Productive" sciences deal with the activities in which men make things, including the making of poems and paintings as well as the making of houses and ships. The practical and productive sciences are similar in that what they study is affected by human will and skill, while the theoretical sciences deal with what is necessarily and unchangeably so. The practical and the productive sciences are distinguished as dealing, respectively, with the doing of deeds and the making of things. For a further discussion of these distinctions, see Aristotle's *Metaphysics,* Vol. 8, p. 547d, and the *Nicomachean Ethics,* Vol. 7, pp. 388c-389d.

Three major works in moral philosophy have been ascribed to Aristotle: the *Nicomachean Ethics, the Eudemian Ethics,* and the *Magna Moralia* (the *Great Ethics*). The first two works are believed by scholars to take their names from Nicomachus, Aristotle's son, and Eudemus, a disciple of Aristotle's, and possibly to have been edited by each, respectively, from Aristotle's lectures on ethics. Scholarly opinion varies on the authenticity of the three ethical treatises. However, there is general agreement that the *Nicomachean Ethics* is from Aristotle's hand; disagreement as to whether the *Eudemian Ethics* is directly Aristotle's or a version of the

Nicomachean Ethics by another hand; and agreement that the *Magna Moralia* was done at a later time by someone else who probably had the other two works before him. (The extant manuscripts of the *Eudemian Ethics* carry the editorial notation that Books IV-VI are the same as Books V-VII of the *Nicomachean Ethics* and therefore omit them, picking up again with Book VII.) The *Nicomachean Ethics* is therefore usually the preferred text for presenting Aristotle's moral philosophy.

The term "ethics" comes from a Greek word which originally meant the "accustomed place" or "abode" of animals, then was transferred to mankind, to mean "habit," "disposition," or "character." Aristotle's choice of this term indicates his emphasis on training and habituation in the attainment of virtue and his predominant interest in the study of human character and conduct rather than in abstract, formal, ethical principles.

Virtue, for Aristotle, is both moral and intellectual, and the good life is one lived in accordance with reason. Hence, he devotes the whole of Book VI to the subject of the intellectual virtues. But, except for Book VI and the last few chapters of Book X, dealing with contemplation, the *Nicomachean Ethics* is mainly concerned with the discipline of the will, the relations between men, and the attainment of the moral virtues. (See Aristotle's discussion of the term "ethics" in connection with the moral virtues, pp. 348b-349b.) Aristotle's handling of the moral virtues is discussed in the Fourth Reading.

II

Book I introduces the basic theme of the *Nicomachean Ethics*: "The Good for Man." (See the analytical table of contents, p. 335a.) The "good" here means the "end" at which human activity aims. Health, for instance, is the good or end sought by the art of medicine. What, then, is the ultimate end or highest good to which all human activities contribute, the end for which the ends of the various "actions, arts, and sciences" are themselves means? The end of the construction industry is shelter or buildings, which serve the end of human life. What is the end of human life which is served by the subordinate end of shelter and which is not a means to any further end?

The branch of knowledge which will help us to arrive at the answer to this all-important question, says Aristotle, is "political science, in one sense of that term" (p. 339c). Politics is the master art which decides what men are to learn and what they are to do; hence, "the end of this science must include those of the others, so that this end must be the good for man" (p. 339c). Politics and ethics are intertwined in a single science which studies human nature, virtue, and institutions. Politics has an ethical end: "making the citizens to be of a certain character, viz. good and capable of noble acts" (p. 345b). In the *Nicomachean Ethics* we approach the human good insofar as it is embodied in individual life; in the *Politics*, we approach it as it is embodied in the community. The two works are complementary.

This part or aspect of "political science," then, will help us to discover the universal good at which all our activities aim, and hence it will help us to live rightly—to "hit the mark," that is, to arrive at the fulfillment of human life. Aristotle warns us, however, not to expect more precision than is possible in such an inquiry, dealing as it does with a subject matter—"fine and just actions"—which is far too variable and contingent to afford us exact knowledge.

We must be content, then, in speaking of such subjects and with such premises to indicate the truth roughly and in outline, and in speaking about things which are only for the most part true and with premises of the same kind to reach conclusions that are no better. (p. 339d)

The distinction between a science which deals with man and an abstract science like mathematics is made again in terms of method. Ethics, says Aristotle, goes from the familiar facts of common experience to first principles, unlike the sciences which start from first principles. (See also the remarks on scientific method in ethical inquiry, pp. 343c-344a, 433d-434a.)

For ethics, then, "the fact is the starting-point," and the facts are all the beginner need know at first. But this minimum prerequisite for the ethical inquirer is not mere spectatorial awareness that such and such is the case.

Hence any one who is to listen intelligently to lectures about what is noble and just, and generally, about the subjects of political science must have been brought up in good habits. For the fact is the starting-point, and if this is sufficiently plain to him, he will not at the start need the reason as well; and the man who has been well brought up has or can easily get starting-points. (p. 340c)

The moral character of the inquirer is of essential importance in the study of ethics. So are a certain amount of experience "in the actions that occur in life," emotional stability, and general maturity. Those who are either "young in years or youthful in character" are not qualified to undertake the study of ethics (p. 340a).

III

The above (dealt with mostly in Chapters 1-3) is what Aristotle calls "our preface" to the inquiry on the good for man. Starting in Chapter 4, Aristotle accepts the common opinion that happiness, that is, "living well and doing well," is the highest good. However, there is wide disagreement as to what this consists in—sensual pleasure (the good of the vulgar type of men), honor (the good of superior men of active disposition), or contemplation. Aristotle questions whether either pleasure or honor can be a final and self-sufficient end; he leaves the discussion of contemplation to Book X. (See Section IV below.) He also discusses the Platonic view of the good and rejects it as too abstract and not fitted for an inquiry into the attainable good for man. (See Ch. 6.)

Having taken due account of the common and previous philosophical views of the highest good, Aristotle proceeds to give his own view, a rough sketch or "outline." (See Ch. 7.) He lists two criteria for such a good. (1) It must be *final,* that is, desirable for itself alone, and not a means to any further end. (2) It must also be *self-sufficient,* by itself alone making "life desirable and lacking in nothing" (p. 343a). Happiness alone measures up to these criteria. It is the end of the highest virtues and by itself it makes life worthwhile. It is the fulfillment of human life.

These assertions, however, do not tell us what happiness is, and Aristotle, aware of the inadequacy of mere "platitude," proceeds to give us "a clearer account." He does this in terms of man's nature and functions; that is, he relates the nature of happiness to the specific function of the human species. Just as we call a flute-player "good" because he plays the flute well—for "the good and the 'well' is thought to reside in the function" (p. 343b)—there must be some generic human function that justifies our calling someone a "good" man. What is it?

The specific characteristic which distinguishes man from all other forms of life is his rational faculty. The specific human function, then, is "an active life of the element that has a rational principle"; and we consider a man good if he performs this function well, "in accordance with the appropriate excellence [or virtue]." Then,

. . . human good turns out to be activity of soul in accordance with virtue, and if there are more than one virtue, in accordance with the best and most complete. (p. 343c)

Aristotle notes that his version of happiness agrees with commonly held views on the final good, in stressing the goods of the soul rather than external goods or the goods of the body; in identifying "the end with certain actions and activities"; and in stipulating "that the happy man lives well and does well; for we have practically defined happiness as a sort of good life and good action" (p. 344a). There are certain differences, however, between his view and former views which identify happiness with virtue, pleasure, or external prosperity.

Aristotle agrees that virtue is an essential component of happiness, but he emphasizes the good activity to which virtue leads rather than virtue as a state of mind, a mere disposition or tendency. He also agrees that the happy man takes pleasure in his life, but he stresses the noble quality of the acts which elicit pleasure and enjoyment in the good man. As for external goods—good fortune, prosperity, a good appearance—these, says Aristotle, seem to be a necessary condition for happiness in this life: "happiness seems to need this sort of prosperity in addition" (p. 344d).

The apparent necessity for external prosperity creates a perplexing problem. (See Ch. 10.) The Greek word for happiness, *eudaimonia,* had the basic meaning of "good fortune" or "prosperity." Aristotle never allows this sense of happiness to be neglected in his account of the highest good. That is why he makes it a condition of happiness that it be an enduring thing.

For there is required . . . not only complete virtue but also a complete life, since many changes occur in life, and all manner of chances, and the most prosperous may fall into great misfortunes in old age, as is told of Priam in the Trojan Cycle; and one who has experienced such chances and has ended wretchedly no one calls happy. (p. 345b-c; see also p. 343c)

But Aristotle qualifies this doleful judgment, for happiness is based on an "activity of soul in accordance with virtue" (p. 343c). Not what happens to a man, what comes to him from the outside, but how he bears himself in the presence of catastrophe and misfortune determines whether a man is virtuous or not. Is a virtuous man, then, happy, even when he suffers the fate of Priam? Here Aristotle makes a distinction between "happiness" and "blessedness." A good and wise man, he says, can never become miserable, "for he will never do the acts that are hateful and mean," and he "bears all the chances of life becomingly and always makes the best of circumstances" (p. 346b). Such a man has an enduring happiness, which only the greatest misfortunes can upset; yet "he will not reach *blessedness,* if he meet with fortunes like those of Priam" (p. 346b). Then, we must not call a man happy until we "see the end," the whole of his life. Aristotle ends his discussion of the paradoxical double requirement of inner virtue and external prosperity with this tentative summation:

When then should we not say that he is happy who is active in accordance with complete virtue and is sufficiently equipped with external goods, not for some chance period but throughout a complete life? Or must we add 'and who is destined to live thus and die as befits his life'?

Certainly the future is obscure to us, while happiness, we claim, is an end and something in every way final. If so, we shall call happy those among living men in whom these conditions are, and are to be, fulfilled —but happy *men.* (p. 346c)

The nature and conditions of happiness having been discussed, there remains the question as to how it is to be acquired. Since happiness is based on virtue, on human power and excellence, Aristotle is sure that it is attainable by learning and training, "by a certain kind of study and care," rather than by providence and chance. (See Ch. 9.) Since virtue is an excellence of the soul, education in virtue requires some knowledge of the soul, and particularly of the relation between the "appetitive and . . . desiring element," or the will, as we would call it, and the rational element. The appetitive element may resist or obey the commands of the rational element; hence, it is to the appetitive element that we address moral advice, reproof, and exhortation. The moral virtues, discussed in Books II-III, have to do with this element of the soul. The intellectual virtues, discussed in Book VI, have to do with the rational element. (According to Aristotle, we may consider the appetitive element either as that part of the irrational element which shares in the rational principle or as that part of the rational element which is rational in a secondary and passive way.)

IV

Book X completes Aristotle's discussion of the good for man, culminating in a final discussion of happiness. The final words on happiness, however (Ch. 6-9), are preceded by a discussion of pleasure (Ch. 1-5), which was listed in Book I as one of the goods commonly associated with happiness.

Aristotle opposes ascetic or puritanical attitudes toward pleasure and rejects any implication that pleasure as such is alien to the human good. On the other hand, he also rejects the view that pleasure is the highest good, contending that pleasure is *a* good but not *the* good, or, rather, that it is an accompaniment of the good. The good life is a pleasant life, but it is not good because it is pleasant; it is pleasant—for the good man—because it is good.

And there are many things we should be keen about even if they brought no pleasure, e.g. seeing, remembering, knowing, possessing the virtues. If pleasures necessarily do accompany these, that makes no odds; we should choose these even if no pleasure resulted. It seems to be clear, then, that neither is pleasure the good nor is all pleasure desirable, and that some pleasures *are* desirable in themselves, differing in kind or in their sources from the others. (p. 428b)

Pleasure *completes* any activity, being present whenever any human faculty is functioning properly in relation to its proper objects; it accompanies or "supervenes" on perfect activity. Moreover, pleasure *intensifies* activity, leading men to pursue and grasp what they most enjoy, to "make progress in their proper function by enjoying it" (p. 429d), so that "activities are made precise and more enduring and better by their proper pleasure" (p. 430a). This brings us to a considera-tion of the kinds and comparative worth of activities and of the pleasures that complete them, for there are good, bad, and morally indifferent activities and pleasures.

It is of the utmost importance, then, to determine what the proper human pleasure is, in view of the widely varying human activities with their complementary pleasures. The proper human pleasure must be that which accompanies and completes the virtuous activity of the rational element of the soul. Now, such activity is no mere disposition but involves the doing of "good and noble deeds" and is attended with the "pure and generous pleasure" that Aristotle contrasts with the mere "pleasant amusements" that many men consider the chief end of life. It would seem, then, that the serious life of moral action and exertion is the highest activity, and its at-tendant pleasure the highest pleasure.

But here Aristotle surprises us by selecting contemplation, the forgotten good of Book I, as the highest human activity, which provides the purest and most enduring pleasure. Con-templation is a function of the highest human faculty, reason, and is directed to the highest object, eternal truth. It is the most self-sufficient of all human activities, for it needs noth-ing else—no external equipment, no further activity, no other person. In this it is contrasted with the life of moral action, which requires a certain amount of external goods and has to do essentially with other men. And in its leisureliness, it fulfills one of the requirements for the happy life and contrasts with the bustle and busy-ness of military and political action. Says Aristotle,

. . . the activity of reason, which is contemplative, seems both to be superior in serious worth and to aim at no end beyond itself, and to have its pleasure proper to itself (and this augments the activity), and the self-sufficiency, leisureliness, unweariedness (so far as this is possible for man), and all the other attributes ascribed to the supremely happy man are evidently those connected with this activity. . . . (p. 432b)

He is convinced "that perfect happiness is a contemplative activity," and is certain that this is the closest thing to the divine activity and blessedness that is available to mankind. It is through the exercise and cultivation of the rational faculty and contemplative activity that man becomes beloved of the gods. "Happiness extends, then, just so far as contemplation does," and "must be some form of contemplation" (p. 433c).

But man is not a god. He comprises human and earthly as well as divine elements in his "composite nature." Hence Aristotle recognizes that the life of pure contemplation "would be too high for man" (p. 432c). The human condition requires nourishment, external goods, and a life with other men — "our nature is not self-sufficient for the purpose of contemplation" (p. 433c). Since the contemplative man "is a man and lives with a number of people, he chooses to do virtuous acts; he will therefore need such aids [external goods] to living a human life" (p. 433b). Yet man should not be deterred by these difficulties from striving to live the life of contemplation, the highest, most pleasant, and happiest open to man—his approximation to the life of the gods.

The life of moral action is also a properly human and happy life, though "in a secondary degree." Aristotle describes this "secondary" life of moral virtue thus:

Just and brave acts, and other virtuous acts, we do in relation to each other, observing our respective duties with regard to contracts and services and all manner of actions and with regard to passions; and all of these seem to be typically human. Some of them seem even to arise from the body, and virtue of character to be in many ways bound up with the passions . . . Being connected with the passions also, the moral virtues must belong to our composite nature; and the virtues of our composite nature are human; so, therefore, are the life and the happiness which correspond to these. The excellence of the reason is a thing apart . . . (p. 432d)

In the final chapter of Book X, which is also the final chapter of the *Nicomachean Ethics* and forms the transition to the *Politics*, Aristotle discusses the role of laws in moral education. The life of virtue requires training and habituation, a molding of character so that the soul becomes responsive to moral guidance and argument. Indeed, such training is needed not only in youth but all through life. Hence the need for law and punishment to lead men to right action. Granted that noble natures are moved by the stimulation to noble conduct, still base natures—or potentially good natures—require "the stick" of pain and punishment. Training for the life according to "reason and right order" requires the sanction of force, either through state laws or family regulations, where the father is a kind of legislator. The making of good laws, then, is required for the making of good men. Hence, the study of lawmaking—of "politics" in the common meaning nowadays—is necessary "to complete . . . our philosophy of human nature" (p. 436c). Man's nature and virtue are perfected through the political community.

V

Is happiness an unethical motivation for a virtuous life?

Is it wrong to make human fulfillment and well-being the end of virtuous activity? Is this an "impure" motivation, and should virtue be its own reward? Is being virtuous and doing right an end in itself? Is it so for Aristotle in the *Nicomachean Ethics?* Is it so for Plato in the *Gorgias?* Can a virtuous man be miserable? Could he be so for Aristotle? Could he be so for Plato?

Is external prosperity necessary for happiness?

For Aristotle, external goods are less necessary for the life centered in contemplation than for the life of moral and political action, and less necessary for the latter than for the sensual and incontinent life. Yet external goods are necessary for the well-being of even the contemplative man, most removed from the strenuous life.

Is external prosperity necessary for happiness? Is it so for Plato in the *Gorgias?* Is his just man *happy* while undergoing scorn and harm from other men, or is he merely secure in his virtue, with the prospect of eternal bliss after death?

Can a man be happy while undergoing spite, persecution, and physical harm for an ideal or a conviction? Paul the Apostle, in one of his letters, tells of rejoicing in the midst of all kinds of ill treatment and catastrophes while spreading the Gospel. Was Paul a *happy* man or was he merely inspired by his mission to ignore his sufferings? What would have been an overwhelming catastrophe for a man like Paul that would undeniably make him unhappy?

Is feeling good the criterion of happiness, and feeling bad or suffering pain the criterion of unhappiness for Aristotle? In his view, does the happy man feel good?

How is the contemplative life related to the life of moral action?

Is the life of contemplative activity separate from or connected with the life of moral action, in Aristotle's view? If separate, how are the two modes of life related? Is the moral life a preparatory stage, coming before the contemplative life? Or does the man who has reached the contemplative level engage in contemplation at one time and moral action at another? Or are they bound up together for him, so that he is contemplative and morally active at the same time?

Do contemplative activity and enjoyment affect the other modes of human activity? If so, how do they affect moral activity? productive activity? Is a man better morally or artistically because of his contemplative virtue and pleasure? Does Aristotle assert or imply such a connection?

What part does productive activity play in the good life?

Aristotle divides human activity into moral action, artistic production, and theoretical contemplation. What part, if any, does excellence in making things play in Aristotle's view of the good life? Are excellence in this mode of activity and the pleasure that accompanies it essential for the good life? Is the good of such activity merely instrumental for Aristotle, serving the ends of moral action and contemplation? Are productive activities good and satisfying in themselves, or valuable merely for their products? Does "good" here mean merely technical proficiency? Or are artistic productivity and enjoyment requisite for a completely full and happy human life? Does the good of productivity conflict with the requirement of leisureliness for the highest form of happiness?

Is political activity necessary for happiness?

Ethics, for Aristotle, is an aspect of political science. The good of the state, he asserts in Book I, is higher and better than the good of the individual. Yet in Book X political activity is denigrated because it is unleisurely and aims at an end beyond itself. The life of contemplation, which is free of these defects, is described as the only truly happy life. Does this mean that the happy man, when he is happy, is withdrawn from political activity, either as a citizen or as a leader?

Aristotle says that moral action and external goods are essential to the good life in the human condition. Does this mean that the happy man must be politically concerned and must engage in political activities? Is political activity essential to happiness? If so, does it contribute by securing the common good or by fulfilling an essential requirement of the individual man's nature?

What is the relation between human nature and happiness?

Aristotle sets up his theory of happiness—of the good for man —in terms of human nature and its functions. Thus the highest good, or happiness, is the fulfillment of human nature. This fulfillment becomes problematic with regard to the influence of external events and the capacity for living a purely contemplative life.

Is happiness attainable, in Aristotle's view, for men in this life? If not, what is there in human nature or the human condition that may or must prevent it? Leaving aside contemplative felicity, is it possible, in Aristotle's view, to achieve a completely virtuous life, in the moral sense? Does Aristotle view human nature as bad or good? Or is it only the activities which are possible for human beings that can be judged good or bad?

What role does the afterlife play in Aristotle's view of happiness? How does its role in the *Nicomachean Ethics* compare with its role in the *Gorgias*?

The following questions are designed to help you test the thoroughness of your reading. Each question is to be answered by giving a page or pages of the reading assignment. Answers will be found on page 303 of this Reading Plan.

1 What subordinate arts fall under the master art of politics?

2 What type of man, according to Hesoid, is "a useless wight"?

3 What essential ethical quality does participation in the Olympic games symbolize?

4 What is the end of political science as regards the citizens of a state?

5 What is the difference between things that are "praised" and things that are "prized"?

6 What was Eudoxus' view of pleasure?

7 What sort of pleasure is highly esteemed at the courts of tyrants?

8 Which is the greater pleasure—inquiring after the truth or knowing it?

9 What state is a model in directing the life of its citizens?

ARISTOTLE

Nicomachean Ethics

Book II complete; Book III, Ch. 1-5

Vol. 9, pp. 348-361

"Be good" is the constant injunction of parents, preachers, and educators. What being good consists in and how one attains such a state, however, are often neither clear nor certain. It is to these questions that the moral philosopher directs his analysis. An excellent example of such analysis is provided by Aristotle in the present reading.

Aristotle opens his discussion with what may seem a surprisingly modern emphasis on habit and "learning by doing," stressing the view that we become virtuous by doing virtuous acts. Yet at the same time he emphasizes the inner aspects of moral goodness—the disposition, intent, and choice that he regards as essential to true virtue. Moral goodness, for Aristotle, is not possible for an automaton or for a non-human organism, but only for a being with reason, will, freedom, and moral responsibility.

It is also in this reading that Aristotle proposes his

famous theory of the mean—that each virtue is somehow intermediate between opposite vices, which are extremes. This conception of virtue as the mean appeals to common-sense notions of balance and proportion in human conduct. Our everyday judgments and expressions, such as "overindulgent" or "overcautious," convey some of the meaning of this basic assumption.

The objection is often raised, however, that Aristotle's mean is an arithmetical rather than an ethical notion and that it idealizes mediocrity or a lukewarm moral personality, whereas more intense actions and attitudes may be right for particular persons in particular situations, or even as a general rule. We must do the reading and see exactly what Aristotle says about the mean in action and feeling to see whether this objection is pertinent and just.

What is Aristotle's idea of the morally good man? Is his virtuous man a namby-pamby person, always playing it safe, taking the sure middle way—calculable as an arithmetical midpoint between two arithmetical extremes—and never getting angry or passionate, never acting violently? Or does Aristotle have another notion of what it means to be a morally virtuous man?

Fourth Reading

I

Books II-V of the *Nicomachean Ethics* are concerned with moral virtue. Book II and Chapters 1-5 of Book III, which make up this reading, deal with moral virtue in general. Aristotle discusses the particular moral virtues in Chapters 6-12 of Book III and in Books IV-V. (See the analytical table of contents, pp. 335b-336b.)

Before attempting a definition of moral virtue, Aristotle first inquires into how it is attained, the particular characteristics of morally virtuous actions, and the relation between moral virtue and pleasure or pain. (See Book II, Ch. 1-4.) In the first place, he notes, moral virtue is not a gift of nature but is acquired by repeated actions, leading to the formation of habits. We become virtuous or vicious through doing certain acts, by behaving justly or unjustly, temperately or intemperately—"states of character arise out of like activities" (p. 349b). The kind of habits we form, then, makes *all* the difference in the kind of character we have. (For other views of habit in the *Great Books of the Western World*, see William James's *Principles of Psychology*, Vol. 53, pp. 68-83, and *The Great Ideas*, Vol. 1, pp. 665-683.)

Aristotle compares moral virtue to physical strength. Just as we become strong through a certain course of exercise and diet, so we become virtuous by acting or not acting in certain ways. Abstaining from pleasures or facing dangers unflinchingly gives us the virtue—or strength of soul, the settled disposition or habit—to abstain from pleasure or to face danger. The virtues are fully "actualized" in the same kinds of acts which form them. (See pp. 349d-350a.)

This analysis implies that men who are not yet virtuous

may perform good acts, for a process of habituation is required before a man becomes virtuous and can act virtuously. Aristotle readily agrees to this implication, for he distinguishes between morally right actions and being morally virtuous. For example, a man may do seemingly just and temperate acts through chance or at another's prompting, without being a just and temperate person. Not the mere objective doing but the inner motivation and disposition decide whether such acts have been done virtuously and by a virtuous man.

> The agent also must be in a certain condition when he does them; in the first place he must have knowledge, secondly he must choose the acts, and choose them for their own sakes, and thirdly his action must proceed from a firm and unchangeable character. (pp. 350d-351a)

Of these three requirements, Aristotle notes, knowledge is the least important as a condition of moral virtue.

In this introductory section, Aristotle also observes the central role of our handling of pleasures and pains in the attainment of moral virtue—"For moral excellence is concerned with pleasures and pains" (p. 350a). It is one of the facts of life that we are attracted by what pleases us and repelled by what pains us. Hence the aim of moral education is to attain a state of character, or "disposition," in which we habitually delight in good actions and are pained by bad actions. Of the three main objects of choice—the noble, the advantageous, and the pleasant—it is the last which is most important in its effect on human conduct for good or for ill. (For the good man, the noble and the advantageous appear pleasant.) However, pleasures and pains are neither good nor bad in themselves; it is how we handle them that determines whether we become virtuous or wicked.

> . . . but it is by reason of pleasures and pains that men become bad, by pursuing and avoiding these—either the pleasures and pains they ought not or when they ought not or as they ought not. . . . (p. 350b)

II

It is only after this preliminary reconnoitering that Aristotle takes up the question of *what moral virtue is.* (See Ch. 5-7.) It must, he says, belong to one of the three types of things that are present in the soul: "passions, faculties, states of character."

By passions I mean appetite, anger, fear, confidence, envy, joy, friendly feeling, hatred, longing, emulation, pity, and in general the feelings that are accompanied by pleasure or pain; by faculties the things in virtue of which we are said to be capable of feeling these, e.g. of becoming angry or being pained or feeling pity; by states of character the things in virtue of which we stand well or badly with reference to the passions, e.g. with reference to anger we stand badly if we feel it violently or too weakly, and well if we feel it moderately; and similarly with reference to the other passions. (p. 351b; see also Aristotle's *Categories*, Vol. 8, pp. 13d-15a)

It cannot be a passion, since we judge a man morally not by his having certain feelings but by his having them in a certain way. And it cannot be a natural, inborn capacity, since, as we have seen, we attain it through habit, through the development of our natural capacities in a certain way. Hence it must be a state of character or disposition.

Now that we have located the "genus," the general category to which moral virtue belongs, says Aristotle, we must find its "species," the specific sort of state or disposition which it is (for vice, too, is a state of character). Here he harks back to a previous observation, that virtue is "destroyed by excess and defect, and preserved by the mean" (p. 349d). Moral virtue is concerned with passions and actions, which may be excessive, defective, or intermediate, that is, too much, too little, or just right.

For instance, both fear and confidence and appetite and anger and pity and in general pleasure and pain may be felt both too much and too little, and in both cases not well; but to feel them at the right times, with reference to the right objects, towards the right people, with the right motive, and in the right way, is what is both intermediate and best, and this is characteristic of virtue. (p. 352b)

But this is no merely arithmetical mean, objective and universal, the same for all men in every situation; for example, "if ten pounds are too much for a particular person to eat and two too little," it does not follow that he should eat six pounds —the arithmetical mean. It is the mean "relative to us" that must be sought, for the health of the soul as well as of the body. The choice of the mean, then, is of the utmost importance in the moral life and depends on "the right rule," which is determined through the intellectual virtue of prudence or practical wisdom.

> Virtue, then, is a state of character concerned with choice, lying in a mean, i.e. the mean relative to us, this being determined by a rational principle, and by that principle by which the man of practical wisdom would determine it. (p. 352c; see also p. 349c)

Formally speaking, then, "by substance and definition," virtue is a mean between two vices, which are extremes of excess or deficiency—as courage is the mean between recklessness and cowardice. But Aristotle qualifies this definition, for in a strictly ethical sense, "with regard to what is best and right," virtue is an extreme, for it is the contrary of vice. Moreover, there are certain acts and feelings which are unqualifiedly evil, not because they are excessive or deficient. There are acts and feelings which can never have a mean; for instance, adultery, murder, and theft or spite, shamelessness, and envy. For these, there can be no right object, time, or way. Conversely, there can be no excess or deficiency in the virtues, because they are already means and at the same time extremes; there can be no such thing as being too temperate or too just.

Aristotle's discussion of various moral virtues, and of the vices between which they are means, illustrates concretely what he means by his doctrine of the mean. (See Ch. 7.) His basic assumption is that the same psychological endowments and human characteristics are embodied in a particular virtue and its pair of correlative vices. Courage, for instance, combines the capacity to confront dangers with the capacity for a careful appraisal of a dangerous situation; when one of these capacities is developed at the expense of the other, a man may become reckless, taking foolhardy risks, or cowardly, never daring to confront danger or take a risk. Similarly with temperance, which combines the capacity for sensual enjoyment with the capacity to restrain it within reasonable bounds; a one-sided development may result either in profligacy, a weak submission to sensual desires, or insensibility, an arid withering away of sensual enjoyment.

Feeling	Action	Excess	Mean	Defect
Fear		Cowardice	Courage	Unnamed
Confidence		Rashness	Courage	Cowardice
Certain pleasures of touch (Pain arising from desire for such pleasures)		Profligacy	Temperance	Insensibility
	Giving of money	Prodigality	Liberality	Illiberality
	Taking of money	Illiberality	Liberality	Prodigality
	Giving of money on large scale	Vulgarity	Magnificence	Meanness
	Claiming of honor on large scale	Vanity	Self-respect	Humility
	Pursuit of honor on small scale	Ambitiousness	Unnamed	Unambitiousness
Anger		Irascibility	Gentleness	Unirascibility
	Telling the truth about oneself	Boastfulness	Truthfulness	Self-depreciation
	Giving of pleasure— By way of amusement	Buffoonery	Wittiness	Boorishness
Social Intercourse	In life generally	Obsequiousness	Friendliness	Sulkiness
Mean states of feeling				
Shame		Bashfulness	Modesty	Shamelessness
Pain at good or bad fortune of others		Envy	Righteous indignation	Malevolence

On the preceding page is a list of the feelings, actions, excesses, means, and defects involved in each of the moral virtues, according to Aristotle, as arranged by our translator, W. D. Ross.[1]

The last two chapters of Book II (Ch. 8-9) deal with the question of how to become good, that is, of how to attain the mean, an admittedly difficult achievement. Aristotle observes that "it is no easy task to be good" (p. 354d). His practical advice on how to be good, in Chapter 9, is based on his judgment in Chapter 8, that sometimes the excess and sometimes the deficiency is further away from the mean. For example, in attaining courage we must counter most vigorously the deficiency rather than the excess of boldness, and in attaining temperance we must struggle most to avoid self-indulgence rather than insensibility. This advice is based not only on formally defined distinctions ("from the thing itself") but also on the natural tendencies of human nature to follow the way of comfort and pleasure ("from ourselves").

Thus Aristotle's advice amounts to the doctrine of aiming at the second best or the lesser evil, in order to achieve the best, something like steering a vessel against winds and currents to keep on a certain course. Each person must decide which way his weakness lies and point in the opposite direction. There will always be a certain amount of yaw, or temporary deviation from the straight course, as "we must incline sometimes towards the excess, sometimes towards the deficiency" in our attempt to "hit the mean and what is right" (p. 355c). A slight deviation from goodness, then, is allowable and not censurable.

III

Moral virtue or vice can be ascribed to persons only when their conduct is voluntary and freely chosen. Hence, in the first five chapters of Book III, Aristotle deals with the subject of moral responsibility. He starts with an analysis of involuntary actions, of deeds done unwillingly or against one's will.

---

[1] W. D. Ross, *Aristotle, A Complete Exposition of His Works and Thought* (New York: Meridian Books, Inc., 1959), p. 198.

Involuntary action occurs either through compulsion or because of ignorance. A compulsory action originates in a force
outside the agent (the person who performs it) to which he
contributes absolutely nothing, but is impelled like a leaf in
the wind (for instance, a man being pushed off a plank into
the ocean by pirates). There are also "mixed" actions, which
combine external compulsion with inner decision: for example,
doing an evil deed at the command of a tyrant who holds one's
parents and children as hostages, or throwing goods overboard
to keep a ship from going down. In these cases we do things
which we would ordinarily be unwilling to do; but in the
extraordinary situation, which acts on us as an external force,
we choose to do them, acting from an inner decision in which
the end is "relative to the occasion." Such "mixed" actions involve difficult decisions as to "what should be chosen at what
cost, and what should be endured in return for what gain"
(p. 356a).

There are also involuntary actions which are done through
ignorance. However, not all actions done through ignorance
are involuntary, but only those which are followed by remorse
and repentance. Aristotle calls actions done through ignorance
which are not so followed simply "not voluntary," in distinction from "involuntary." Apparently Aristotle generically desig-
nates *all* actions that are done through ignorance as "not
voluntary," signifying that *none* of them is deliberately willed
and that any harm done is not done purposely. However, once
the agent realizes that such an action was wrong and regrets
it, it is designated specifically as an "involuntary" act, in which
ignorance has prevented a man from acting as he would have
acted had he known the situation, circumstances, etc.

Ignorance acts in such cases as physical compulsion does in
the other type of involuntary actions. (An example of such
action is firing on one's fellow soldiers, friendly planes, etc. in
wartime.) However, when a person who has done such an act
"feels not the least vexation," his deed remains a "not voluntary" action, and his moral disposition remains indeterminate,
too, to say the least. (An example of such an action is an unnecessary hurting of another person's feelings by some chance

remark, or a public misinterpretation of someone's motivations, or putting the blame on the wrong person in some base action.)

Aristotle also excludes from the class of involuntary actions done *through* ignorance, actions done *in* ignorance, caused by drunkenness or rage. Although such actions are done ignorantly, they are essentially voluntary, since the cause of the ignorance was controllable by the agent. On the same principle he thinks all actions caused by anger or appetite voluntary, since the irrational passions are controllable and can be directed to the proper objects in the proper way.

The ignorance that causes an involuntary action is not an ignorance of ends, not an ignorance of what we ought or ought not to do, but of "the circumstances of action," an ignorance of the particular situation. Aristotle lists the things we may be ignorant of as follows:

A man may be ignorant, then, of . . . what he is doing, what or whom he is acting on, and sometimes also what (e.g. what instrument) he is doing it with, and to what end (e.g. he may think his act will conduce to some one's safety), and how he is doing it (e.g. whether gently or violently). (p. 356d)

Hence the choice of means to accomplish good ends, and the process of deliberation by which choice is decided, are of primary importance in ethical action. Aristotle takes up these topics in Chapters 2-3 of Book III.

IV

Not all voluntary actions are deliberately chosen. Acts of animals, children, and those of mature persons done suddenly are voluntary—because the cause of action, physically and emotionally, lies in the agent—but they are not deliberately chosen. But a properly human voluntary action requires *awareness of the particular circumstances* of action and *deliberate choice.* Choice is not mere "wish," for it relates (1) to things that are in our power to control, and (2) to means, not to ends. We wish to be healthy or happy, and we choose the means to become so. Nor is choice identical with mere "opinion," for choice is ethical, concerned with good and bad, whereas opinion relates to true and false. Some people have right opinions, a true awareness of things, but choose wrongly, because of bad character.

The *voluntary* aspect, the element of will, then, is essential in choice. However, it also "involves a *rational* principle and thought," a process of "previous deliberation," since the very term for choice in Greek (*proairesis*) means a choosing of one thing before another, a selective preference. We deliberate, says Aristotle, (1) about things that are in our power, which can be affected through human will and action, not about things determined by nature, necessity, or chance; (2) about things which generally happen in the same way but in which the particular event is not clear or certain; and (3) about means, not about ends.

Thus the process of deliberation is a process of thought, in which the end—health, justice, happiness, or the good life—is assumed. We seek the best means of achieving it, and then the means of achieving that means, and so on until we come to the proper starting point in the process of action—which is also the last point in the process of deliberation. We keep the end in mind and, working backward from that to the particular situation we are in at the present moment, we arrive at some small particular act that will initiate the process of action. For example, if I want to be healthy, and I am presently overweight, short-winded, easily fatigued, I may start by cutting down on cigarettes, sweets, and fats and beginning a program of physical exercises. The achievement of my end— health—begins with the first refusal of a piece of pie or with my first push-up.

The particular deed to be done or instrument to be made or procured, then, is the definite "object of choice"—the object of a decision or act of will that is the result of rational deliberation. Thus we *desire* (prefer, choose) what we *ought to* in the particular case. Choice, then, is

. . . deliberate desire of things in our own power; for when we have *decided* as a result of deliberation, we *desire* in accordance with our deliberation. (p. 359a) [italics added]

Aristotle concludes these chapters on moral responsibility with the argument that virtue and wickedness are voluntary.

(See Ch. 4-5.) Assuming that certain acts are within our power, and that such acts are either good or bad, "it is in our power to be virtuous or vicious" (p. 359c). Where ignorance is involved in evil acts, ignorance is no excuse if it is avoidable or caused by carelessness and irresponsibility. We are responsible for the kind of men we are, for our states of character; our various acts of omission and commission have made us what we are. Unjust and self-indulgent men, says Aristotle, *want* to be that way—they have become so through their choices. But once such a man has become so, it is not possible for him to change.

. . . not now, when he has thrown away his chance, just as when you have let a stone go it is too late to recover it; but yet it was in your power to throw it, since the moving principle was in you. (p. 360b)

Moral responsibility may apply not only to the right choice of means but possibly also to the rational wish for a good end. Self-indulgence, for instance, may *appear* as the good to certain men because of the natural defects of their minds. But even if we grant this, says Aristotle, and conceive of an innate "eye" for the good, which some men have and others do not, we still judge men by their particular actions, of which they are the originating source. However, it may be that evil appears good to us because we are men of bad character; to the good man, what is absolutely and truly good is also the apparent good. (See p. 359b.)

We reply that if each man is somehow responsible for his state of mind, he will also be himself somehow responsible for the appearance . . . (. . . and it is by being persons of a certain kind that we assume the end to be so and so) . . . (p. 360c-d)

Aristotle recognizes that the whole idea of moral responsibility is undermined if we accept the notion that our view of the good is determined by natural forces or endowments beyond our control. If men's view of the good is determined by nature—and Aristotle does not say definitely that it is or is not—then we cannot ascribe virtue or vice to them, since the central aim of all their actions, on this theory, is predetermined by forces over which they have no control.

Aristotle's discussion of moral virtue in this reading is summarized thus at the end of Chapter 5:

With regard to the virtues in *general* we have stated their genus in outline, viz. that they are means and that they are states of character, and that they tend, and by their own nature, to the doing of the acts by which they are produced, and that they are in our power and voluntary, and act as the right rule prescribes. But actions and states of character are not voluntary in the same way; for we are masters of our actions from the beginning right to the end, if we know the particular facts, but though we control the beginning of our states of character the gradual progress is not obvious any more than it is in illnesses; because it was in our power, however, to act in this way or not in this way, therefore the states are voluntary. (pp. 360d-361a)

V

Certain themes recur in this reading which play an important role in Aristotle's general theory of ethics.

He reminds us again that ethics is a practical rather than a theoretical inquiry.

. . . the present inquiry does not aim at theoretical knowledge like the others (for we are inquiring not in order to know what virtue is, but in order to become good, since otherwise our inquiry would have been of no use.) . . . (p. 349b)

Hence, he ridicules those who try to become good through theory alone.

But most people do not do these [virtuous acts], but take refuge in theory and think they are being philosophers and will become good in this way, behaving somewhat like patients who listen attentively to their doctors, but do none of the things they are ordered to do. As the latter will not be made well in body by such a course of treatment, the former will not be made well in soul by such a course of philosophy. (p. 351a-b)

He reiterates the observation that ethics deals with an uncertain subject matter of which we can give only a general account. It is broadly but not precisely true. It is the particular application and judgment that is important in ethics.

The general account being of this nature, the account of particular cases is yet more lacking in exactness; for they do not fall under any art or precept but the agents themselves must in each case consider what is appropriate to the occasion, as happens also in the art of medicine or of navigation. (p. 349c)

For among statements about conduct those which are general apply more widely, but those which are particular are more genuine, since conduct has to do with individual cases, and our statements must harmonize with the facts in these cases. (pp. 352d-353a)

The judgment of the exact variation from the mean allowable in particular cases, he observes, is a matter of something like sense perception.

. . . it is not easy to determine by reasoning, any more than anything else that is perceived by the senses; such things depend on particular facts, and the decision rests with perception. (p. 355c)

Hence, Aristotle constantly insists on the importance of the intellectual virtue of practical wisdom (or "prudence") in attaining moral virtue and acting "according to the right rule" in the particular case. (See pp. 349b, 352c; see also Book VI, Ch. 5, 12-13.)

This reading also makes it plain that, for Aristotle, passion as well as action is of central concern in moral virtue—not, however, in the sense that the passions are bad and must be suppressed, but in the sense that they must be felt rightly, in the right degree, toward the right objects.

. . . to feel them at the right times, with reference to the right objects, towards the right people, with the right motive, and in the right way, is what is both intermediate and best, and this is characteristic of virtue. (p. 352b)

. . . we ought both to be angry at certain things and to have an appetite for certain things, e.g. for health and for learning. Also what is involuntary is thought to be painful, but what is in accordance with appetite is thought to be pleasant. Again, what is the difference in respect of involuntariness between errors committed upon calculation and those committed in anger? Both are to be avoided, but the irrational passions are thought not less human than reason is, and therefore also the actions which proceed from anger or appetite are the man's actions. (p. 357b)

Balancing Aristotle's stress on particularity and immediate perception in moral judgments is his borrowing of basic concepts and methods from the mathematical sciences to interpret the practical realm of human action and passion. The doctrine of the mean which plays so large a role in this reading applies to ethics the quantitative notions of more, less, and equal and the geometrical notion of a point equidistant between two extremes. (See p. 351d.) In the human sphere, this intermediate point varies with the individual person, and the awareness of deviation from the norm is a matter of immediate perception, but nevertheless the notion of the mean is formally quantitative.

Aristotle also compares the process of deliberation, which is essential for moral choice, to the method of investigation used by the mathematician in analyzing a geometrical construction, in which he goes from the figure to be drawn to the basic conditions and elementary operations required to construct the figure. (See p. 358c-d.)

VI

Do we become good solely by doing good acts?

Suppose a dour and withdrawn person tries to overcome his disposition by always greeting people with a smile and a hearty handshake. Will these acts make him friendly and outgoing to other people? Suppose an extremely self-centered person tries to change his character by always keeping in mind the other person's needs and viewpoint. Will that make him more considerate of other persons? Would a job that required a genial and outgoing demeanor change a man inwardly? Why or why not? Must a person be inwardly disposed toward such wholesome attitudes and gestures before he starts to form "good habits"? Or does his starting the process of habituation indicate the germ, at least, of an inward disposition?

Does Aristotle affirm that a good disposition can be achieved mechanically, by mere repetition of certain acts, without the will entering in? If he does not, how can he talk about virtuous acts which are done by a man who is not virtuous? If moral virtue essentially involves a certain kind of character and disposition, how can acts be described as morally virtuous if they are done by a person who is not morally virtuous? Can we distinguish meaningfully between the moral quality of the objective act—which may be the proper one in a certain situation—and the moral quality of the person who does it? Must we consider morally virtuous the mere facing or withdrawal from danger in a certain situation—apart from inner disposition, character, and intention?

What are the consequences of Aristotle's idea that some men are irreformable?

Aristotle affirms that there is a point where the moral fiber has been so impaired by repeated and longstanding vice that change is no longer possible. The will in this case is rigidly restricted and action is unchangeably oriented in one direction —toward doing evil. Is such a rigidity—or "hardening of the heart," in Biblical language—a characteristic of vice and bad habits? Are openness and variability implied in Aristotle's view of virtue and good habits, of practical wisdom and moral judgment? Or does it imply a rigid orientation toward the good?

Is any kind of ethical action possible for the man hardened in evil ways? Can such a man be conscious of his hardened state, of the irredeemable evil within him? If so, would his consciousness lift him above his state and permit him some limited ethical act? What act is open to such a man?

What action can society take toward such a man? If cure is impossible, must it either incarcerate him permanently or execute him?

Do we choose only between means, never between ends?

Do situations occur in which we have to choose between conflicting ends or "values"? In the situation cited by Aristotle (see p. 356a), where we ought to endure awful sufferings and death rather than perform a base act, are deliberation and choice involved or not? Is some weighing of alternatives involved in this as well as in the previous case cited of the man who does do a base deed in order to save his hostage family? Is moral virtue or the good life considered to be the end previously willed, and are all other decisions regarded as dealing with alternative roads to that goal? If different ends are assumed— justice, health, etc.—is it also assumed that they are essentially harmonious and never in conflict? Might a man choose a course of action which ruined his health, in order to do good—in the service of art, science, his family, or his country? Is a hierarchy of ends implied, to guide our choice and deliberation? Is it the same for all men in all situations?

What process of moral deliberation and evaluation is involved in the case of the awful alternative offered in the Nazi concentration camp where a prisoner had to decide between condemning either his mother or his wife to death? If he chose neither, they would both die. If he chose one, she died by his choice. This situation fits the category of "mixed" actions described by Aristotle, but is far more complicated and diabolical than the cases suggested by Aristotle. The responsibility for the situation was that of the Nazi officials. However, the particular choice, of the wife or the mother, or even the non-choice, was the responsibility of the prisoner.

What does a man deliberate about in such a situation—ends, or means, or neither? One alternative is to resolve not to collaborate with evil, and let both women go to their death without sharing in the moral responsibility. Another is to resolve to reduce the evil by half and save one woman, regarding oneself as practically responsible if both die and accepting the mixed responsibility—partly forced and partly chosen—for the evil done. But what particular factors must be weighed, then, to decide which of the two should live and which die?

Are men morally responsible for particular acts which follow from general moral blindness?

Aristotle says (see p. 360d) that even if we grant hypothetically that a man may have an innately distorted view of the good, yet he is responsible for the particular actions he performs, since such actions originate with him. But is an essentially ethical, fully human voluntariness involved in such actions, or only the kind of voluntariness which Aristotle ascribes to animals and children? If Aristotle is merely referring to the objective, observable motor action, apart from any real moral virtue or vice, how can a truly moral judgment be made?

What would be the possible legal judgments in such a case? Is a morally blind person—who does not know that stealing, murder, and rape are wrong—legally responsible for such particular acts?

The following questions are designed to help you test the thoroughness of your reading. Each question is to be answered by giving a page or pages of the reading assignment. Answers will be found on page 303 of this Reading Plan.

1 What is the basis for the analogy between becoming a good or a bad man and a good or a bad lyre-player?

2 Why is the desire for pleasure so hard to "rub off"?

3 Are there many ways of succeeding in attaining virtue?

4 What are the three means involved in social intercourse?

5 What is the basis for the analogy between Helen and pleasure?

6 Are the irrational passions as human as reason?

7 What are the causes of events?

8 Is all deliberation investigation?

9 Is it true that "no one is involuntarily wicked nor involuntarily happy"?

EPICTETUS

Discourses

Book I

Vol. 12, pp. 105-138

Men have long looked to philosophy for a guide to the conduct of life as well as for knowledge of the nature of things. They have sought a philosophy which would show them how to cope with evil and misfortune, how to achieve and maintain stability and calm in the face of the suffering and frustration that beset most of us during our lifetime. They have required philosophy to teach them not only what virtue and happiness are, but also and most importantly how to become virtuous and happy.

The most important philosophy offering this type of guidance that has come down to us from the ancient world is Stoicism. Its basic view of man's relation to the world and the method by which he can attain inner control and peace had an inestimable influence on the later development of religion and philosophy in our culture.

Epictetus' *Discourses* is one of the main sources

through which these teachings have come down to us. It is one of the most enjoyable pieces of writing in the history of Western philosophy, conveying the teachings and personality of a very remarkable man. For Epictetus, a man who began life as a slave and was lame and weak in body, was himself the best example of the philosophy he was trying to teach. When he asserted man's capacity to transcend external adversities and attain inner tranquillity, he spoke with the authority of personal experience. In the dialogues that are recreated for us by his pupil Flavius Arrian, he comes through to us as a friendly, direct man with pithy expressions and evocative examples chosen from the everyday events and things of life.

Fifth Reading

I

Stoicism was a philosophy which originated in Athens toward the end of the fourth century B.C., taking its name from the "stoa," or colonnade, where its founder, Zeno of Citium, delivered his lectures. Zeno was originally a follower of the Cynics, a school of philosophers that advocated a life of pure virtue, involving utter simplicity, indifference to external goods, and detachment from family and social ties. For Zeno, the aim of philosophy was the attainment of moral virtue, and he, as well as later Stoics, shared with the Cynics a reverence for Socrates, who had seen the good life as the goal of philosophical inquiry.

Unlike the Cynics, however, Zeno emphasized the value of scientific knowledge and sought a basis for ethics in the structure of the universe. He held that the *logos*, or "reason," which the Cynics saw at work within man, pervades nature; and he went back to the ancient sage Heraclitus for a physics which would provide the natural basis for ethics. He also developed a formal logic (he was perhaps the first philosopher to use the term "logic") and made it the first stage in philosophical education, followed by physics, and then by ethics. Zeno's doctrine was given systematic form by Chrysippus of Solsus, whose version of Stoicism became authoritative for future ages and is mentioned frequently by Epictetus in this reading.

Historians of philosophy divide Stoicism into three periods: Early, Middle, and Later "Stoa." The first, the Early Stoa (roughly 300-200 B.C.), ends with the death of Chrysippus. The second, the Middle Stoa (roughly the last two centuries B.C.), is the period when Stoicism was introduced to Rome and became the philosophy of such eminent Romans as Cicero.

Stoicism was suited to the practical temper of the Romans and became their predominant philosophy, exercising an important influence on Roman ethics and jurisprudence. The third period, the Later Stoa (roughly the first two centuries A.D.), was the time of the great Roman Stoic philosophers, such as Seneca, Epictetus, and Marcus Aurelius.

Stoicism, which had always been a way of life as well as a theory of the universe, offered a practical guide to happiness for men harassed by the miseries and insecurities of the early Roman empire. For many, it functioned as their religion, one far more satisfactory and far more acceptable to them than the old-time Roman religion. A glance at some of the main teachings of Stoicism may reveal some of the reasons for its widespread appeal to the Romans.

According to traditional Stoic doctrine, man is a microcosm corresponding to the macrocosm of the universe. Through reason he is able to discern the universal law and order present in nature and to live a life in accord with it. Through self-discipline and self-control he may attain virtue and happiness, which are mainly a matter of inner tranquillity. Nothing else matters—external goods, common pleasures, even social ties.

Stoicism was a strongly universalist doctrine, emphasizing the common nature of men, who are under a universal natural law governing the cosmic community. In theory, this common bond was to be expressed in ordinary social and political life, in such communities as the family and the state; but, in practice, the Stoics tended to withdraw from the community. This was true even of the Stoic emperor, Marcus Aurelius, in his essential inner attitude. Through reason men are the kinsmen or sons of God, considered as a pantheistic spirit pervading the cosmos and the human soul. The world is providentially ordered, and any apparent suffering or evil is not what it seems but is part of a cosmic plan purposing ultimate good; apparent misfortune is only a divinely imposed trial and training in the attainment of virtue and indifference to external events.

It is one of the quirks of the history of culture that the basic writings of the founders of Stoicism have come down to us only in fragments when they are available at all; whereas the writings of the later Stoics have been well preserved and have provided the main channel through which Stoicism has exercised influence on Western thought and culture. The *Discourses* of Epictetus has been one of the most influential of these later Stoic writings.

It is interesting to note how many of the basic Stoic teachings listed above appear even in the partial selection from the *Discourses* which is included here. Like the teachings of Socrates, the favorite moral hero and philosopher of the Stoics, the teachings of Epictetus have been transmitted to us through an intermediate author; for as the Biographical Note in Vol. 12 indicates, the author of this great book is not Epictetus but one of his pupils, Flavius Arrian. Of the eight books comprising the *Discourses,* four have come down to us.

Arrian's work is different in form from the Platonic dialogues and the Aristotelian treatises, which are the sources of our first four readings. The books are made up of short chapters, dealing with various topics which recur throughout a book, though not in any obvious sequence. The chapters devoted to the discussion of Providence, for instance, or to the fatherhood of God, are not grouped together. A book of the *Discourses* has a thematic rather than a structural unity. We cannot break it up into parts dealing with a specific topic, as we were able to do with Aristotle's *Ethics.*

In a sense, the *Discourse* is more Platonic than Aristotelian in form, for it includes dialogues, fancied or real, between Epictetus and various interlocutors, somewhat like those centered around Socrates in Plato's dialogues. You will rarely find a chapter in this reading which consists only of impersonal discussion. It may start out that way, but it soon changes into a dialogue. Sometimes, as in Chapter 11, discussing family affection, the whole chapter is a dialogue. Even the chapters without "parts" written in for interlocutors have the air of dialogue, as if Epictetus were addressing the reader and carrying on a discussion with him. Arrian announced it as his intention to present the *Discourses* "in the very language Epictetus used, so far as possible" and to preserve "the directness of his speech" (p. 101d), and apparently he succeeded. The reader gets the impression of a real, strongly individualized man, with a direct and salty turn of phrase ("only sleep with a good will and snore"), talking to him.

II

The main distinction upon which Epictetus' teaching rests is that between *the inner and the outer,* between what essentially belongs to a man and what is external to him. To the inner realm belong the things that are *in our power,* to the outer realm belong the things that are *not in our power.*

The inner, essential things comprise our attitudes, intentions, responses, desires, and aversions. The outer things comprise events, changes of fortune, public opinion, physical suffering, and death. The inner things are important and valuable for human virtue and happiness; the outer things are of no real import or concern. (See p. 128a.)

Epictetus' view of human nature accords with this basic distinction between inner and outer. The central human faculty is the rational one, which is the capacity not only "of judging of appearances" but also "of pursuing an object and avoiding it, and the faculty of desire and aversion" (p. 105b-c). It combines the functions of reason and of will—of discrimination and impulse. The body, on the other hand, belongs to external things. My body, in this view, is not my own; it is a temporary prison-house, mere clay, "fetters"—outside the real me.

Hence, for the wise and virtuous man, threats of physical pain, mutilation, or death carry no terror or perturbation. In the first place, such things are of no importance, affecting only the body; secondly, if they are unavoidable and out of our power to prevent, there is no point in getting perturbed about them. What is important and in our power is our attitude and response to such events.

I must die. Must I then die lamenting? I must be put in chains. Must I then also lament? I must go into exile. Does any man then hinder me from going with smiles and cheerfulness and contentment? (p. 106b)

This attitude is essential in achieving the *tranquillity,* calm, or "peace of mind" which is, for Epictetus, the main result of moral virtue and training. This mental state, which is the sign and seal of virtue, expresses man's "conformity with nature"; it is the psychic accompaniment of man's harmony with the universe. Tranquillity is accessible only to the man who accepts the necessary and natural order of things, making the best use of things in his power and assenting to whatever happens that is not in his power.

... to be instructed is this, to learn to wish that everything may happen as it does.

. . . .

Remembering, then, this disposition of things, we ought to go to be instructed, not that we may change the constitution of things—for we have not the power to do it, nor is it better that we should have the power—but in order that, as the things around us are what they are and by nature exist, we may maintain our minds in harmony with the things which happen. (p. 119b-c)

This means accepting all kinds of weather, all types of men, all situations, all conditions, all the roles, everything that life has in store for us in the world constituted as it is; that is, it means living in conformity with nature, which is the basic law of life for Epictetus. (See pp. 110a, 131b.)

With this imperturbability in the face of all kinds of events, and the willing acceptance of whatever happens, goes a *self-sufficiency* in relation to other men. For the most essential things needed to accomplish the ends of human existence, a man need not rely on anyone else.

For, in fact, what a man has from himself, it is superfluous and foolish to receive from another? Shall I, then, who am able to receive from myself greatness of soul and a generous spirit, receive from you land and money or a magisterial office? (p. 116a)

Similarly, he need not fear what other men may do to him, for "one man is not miserable through the means of another" (p. 116b). Socrates, as he is portrayed in Plato's *Apology*, is Epictetus' recurrent example of the man who possesses this knowledge and virtue.

Attaining tranquillity and self-sufficiency involves a long and arduous course of *self-discipline*. Epictetus' good man is a moral athlete who attains virtue through various trials which test and develop to the utmost his imperturbability in the

face of pain and pleasure and all the temptations which human
flesh and spirit are heir to.

> Who then is the invincible? It is he whom none of the things disturb
> which are independent of the will. Then examining one circumstance
> after another I observe, as in the case of an athlete; he has come off
> victorious in the first contest: well then, as to the second? and what if
> there should be great heat? and what, if it should be at Olympia? And
> the same I say in this case: if you should throw money in his way, he
> will despise it. Well, suppose you put a young girl in his way, what then?
> and what, if it is in the dark? what if it should be a little reputation, or
> abuse; and what, if it should be praise; and what if it should be death?
> He is able to overcome all. What then if it be in heat, and what if it is
> in the rain, and what if he be in a melancholy mood, and what if he be
> asleep? He will still conquer. This is my invincible athlete. (p. 125a; see
> also pp. 111d-112a, 129a-b, 136b-d)

III

Man is self-sufficient in relation to other men, in Epictetus'
view, but he is not alone; human will and purpose are not the
only will and purpose in the universe. There is God, and there
is Providence.

God is man's "maker and father and guardian" (pp. 114d-
115a). Man is the son and kinsman of God through the faculty
of reason; rational beings "are by their nature formed to have
communion with God, being by means of reason conjoined
with Him" (p. 114d). Man should realize that he bears something within him of supreme value and he should bear himself
accordingly in the affairs of life. Since our opinion of anything
makes a difference in how we use it, Epictetus advises us to
think of our affinity with God rather than with the animals
(through our bodies), so that we will use ourselves rightly and
nobly.

> For they say, "What am I? A poor, miserable man, with my wretched
> bit of flesh." Wretched, indeed; but you possess something better than
> your "bit of flesh." Why then do you neglect that which is better, and
> why do you attach yourself to this? (p. 108c)

(In this connection, see also the discussion in Book II, Chapter
8, of man as "a fragment of God," and the bearer of God within
him, the trustee of the divine, and hence maintaining or defil-
ing God through his thoughts and actions.)

Through inner awareness of his rational capacity, man realizes his kinship with God. Through an understanding of the universe, man realizes that the world is ordered by Divine Providence. (See Ch. 6, 14, 16.) Acknowledgment of Providence requires, first, insight into the design or purposeful order of nature, and hence of a Designer or Artificer, "who has fitted this to that and that to this" (p. 110d). It also requires a sense of gratitude to the Designer. This understanding and gratitude result in a certain attitude toward the universe, an acceptance of man's own role in it and of one's own particular endowment and situation.

"Yes, but my nose runs." For what purpose then, slave, have you hands? Is it not that you may wipe your nose? "Is it, then, consistent with reason that there should be running of noses in the world?" Nay, how much better it is to wipe your nose than to find fault. (p. 111d)

The acknowledgment of Providence brings with it also the realization that God has given us the means we need to meet whatever trials we may have to endure, the faculties "by which we shall be able to bear everything that happens without being depressed or broken by it" (p. 112a-b). For Providence includes not only the administration of the natural order but also the tutelary care for each man's welfare. Every man has a guardian angel or "Demon," placed there by God in constant watch over his thought and conduct. Hence men should swear this oath of allegiance to God.

Never to be disobedient, never to make any charges, never to find fault with anything that he has given, and never unwillingly to do or to suffer anything that is necessary. (p. 121b-c)

The recognition of Providence means not only that there is a divine order and purpose in the cosmos and that every man's "actions are under the inspection of God" but also "that all things are united in one" (p. 120d), including God, men, and all things in a great universal community. Right disposition and action, then, ensue from the recognition that one is a member or "citizen" of the community of all beings.

He then who has observed with intelligence the administration of the world, and has learned that the greatest and supreme and the most comprehensive community is that which is composed of men and God, and that from God have descended the seeds not only to my father and grandfather, but to all beings which are generated on the earth and are produced, and particularly to rational beings—for these only are by their nature formed to have communion with God, being by means of reason conjoined with Him—why should not such a man call himself a citizen of the world, why not a son of God, and why should he be afraid of anything which happens among men? (p. 114d)

Yet, in spite of this eloquent affirmation of the providential arrangement of the world, to which all men must conform, Epictetus at the same time affirms the freedom of the will, untrammeled by anything or anyone, including God Himself.

. . . like a good king and a true father, He has given us these faculties free from hindrance, subject to no compulsion, unimpeded, and has put them entirely in our own power, without even having reserved to Himself any power of hindering or impeding. (p. 112b)

". . . you have the faculty of the will free from hindrance, free from compulsion, unimpeded." . . . ". . . If you choose, you are free; if you choose, you will blame no one: you will charge no one. All will be at the same time according to your mind and the mind of God." (p. 123d)

IV

The role of the will, its freedom, and its discipline are essential in the attainment of virtue and in establishing perfect conformity with nature. But the intellectual factor in man's divine endowment—what we commonly call "reason"—is also important in Epictetus' interpretation of man's moral life. It is man's divinely appointed role to be both a "spectator" and an "interpreter" of the universe; his natural end is "contemplation and understanding" (p. 111c). Through reason man is able to distinguish among things, to state moral questions properly, and to discern the meanings of the terms used in moral statements.

For how few words it requires to say that man's end is to follow the gods, and that the nature of good is a proper use of appearances. But if you say, "What is 'God,' what is 'appearance,' and what is 'particular' and what is 'universal nature'?" then indeed many words are necessary. (p. 127a)

Moral faults are more serious than logical errors, but carelessness and rashness in reasoning and argument are certainly grave faults. (See p. 113c-d.) Epictetus mistrusts moral judgments delivered by a man who cannot understand a complex argument or see what follows from a certain hypothesis. If he goes astray "in such small matters" as a hypothetical syllogism, argues Epictetus, how can we trust his judgment about such important things as good and evil? (See p. 132a.)

Moreover, moral judgments involve the specific application of basic notions, or "precognitions," to particular cases. (See Ch. 22.) Men agree on the basic "precognition" that we should pursue justice and holiness, but they disagree whether a particular man in a particular action has done rightly or not.

What then is education? Education is the learning how to adapt the natural precognitions to the particular things conformably to nature. . . . (pp. 127d-128a)

However, Epictetus is averse to training students in the fancier kinds of argument, on the grounds that it may distract "from the study of morality"—that is, "from more necessary things"—and also make us arrogant and vain (p. 114a). All study must serve the ends of virtue and conformity to nature. Anything else is futile. Hence the constant polemic in the book against mere theory or book learning in the quest for virtue.

Moral improvement is not attained by reading the books of Chrysippus, says Epictetus, but by disciplining our desires and aversions, our impulses to pursue and to avoid, our assent or suspension of assent.

So, when you say: "Take the treatise on the active powers, and see how I have studied it." I reply, "Slave, I am not inquiring about this, but how you exercise pursuit and avoidance, desire and aversion, how you design and purpose and prepare yourself, whether conformably to nature or not. If conformably, give me evidence of it, and I will say that you are making progress: but if not conformably, be gone, and not only expound your books, but write such books yourself; and what will you gain by it? . . ." (p. 109b)

It is in the everyday things of life that the purified and disciplined will must be exercised and demonstrated. The man who makes moral progress is the man who acts out his basic principles from the time he arises in the morning—he "bathes as a man of fidelity, eats as a modest man" (p. 109c). It is in immediate, common activity, not in abstract theory, that a man learns virtue.

But if he has strained his efforts to the practice of reading books, and labours only at this, and has traveled for this, I tell him to return home immediately, and not to neglect his affairs there; for this for which he has traveled is nothing. But the other thing is something, to study how a man can rid his life of lamentation and groaning, and saying, "Woe to me," and "wretched that I am," and to rid it also of misfortune and disappointment, and to learn what death is, and exile, and prison, and poison, . . . (p. 109c-d)

The end of philosophy is to teach men how to live, "the art of living" (p. 121c). Philosophers begin their teaching, however, with theory (or speculation), because that is easier. They then proceed to teach us how to live, which is much more difficult to learn. But the knowledge provided by philosophy is necessary for leading a good life, since ignorance is the cause of evil conduct. (See p. 131d.)

V

Is calmness or "peace of mind" the highest good?

We should put this question in two ways. First, is tranquillity of spirit the highest good, *in Epictetus' teaching?* Second, *is it true* that it is man's highest good?

To answer the first question, we must look back through the reading and see whether Epictetus is interested primarily in calming men's minds, or in bringing men to right action and disposition, or in accomplishing the latter through the former. Is this teaching a form of psychotherapy or "psycho-salvationism" rather than an ethics in the classical Greek sense? Does Epictetus ever hint that, even if his view of things were an illusion, it would help men avoid unnecessary misery? Would Epictetus accept a quietness of spirit based on a view of things opposed to his own? Or must any permanent "peace of mind" be based on some notion of a providential order, in which all evil and misfortune are only apparent? What are the practical ethical consequences of such a view?

Does tranquillity have the same central role in the portrait of the virtuous man in the previous readings from Plato and Aristotle as it does in this reading? Is it the highest good for Plato and Aristotle? In what respect is the lack of perturbation advocated by Epictetus similar to or different from that preached in the Gospels? What is the difference in the way the heroes of the great Greek tragedies face misfortune and suffering and the way counseled by Epictetus? (See Epictetus' comment on tragedy, p. 109d.) Does tragedy, too, end in acceptance, even in affirmation, of whatever happens? If so, what is the difference between the acceptance of the Stoic wise man, with his indifference and self-sufficiency, and that of the tragic hero?

What does Epictetus mean by equating the "right" with the "natural"?

Obviously, he cannot mean that the right is what most men do, since his doctrine is intended to change men from their present mode of conduct and disposition, to free them from their "normal" bondage to external goods, and to alleviate their widespread misery. In the dialogues with the father who ran away from his sick child because he could not bear to see her suffer (see Ch. 11), Epictetus is unwilling to accept what most fathers do or feel as the criterion of the natural and right. The natural, then, is not something necessarily evident in common conduct, not an empirical "is" but a transcendent "ought." Where does Epictetus find "the criterion of good and bad, and of things according to nature and contrary to nature" (p. 117b)? Is a tumor natural and good? (See p. 117a.) If not, what is the proper Stoic attitude toward tumors?

Is the will the sole cause of all our actions and feelings?

Epictetus says that our actions, emotional moods, desires, and aversions are all determined by our will alone. (See p. 118a-d.) Achilles lamented Patroclus so intensely because he willed to do so. He could have done otherwise, that is, accepted it quietly and "stoically," had he willed to do so. According to

Epictetus, it is all in the mind. "If we do not think things to be what we do think them to be, we do not [do] the acts which follow from such opinions" (p. 118c)—and thinking, by definition, is within our power to control.

Could Achilles, with his particular temperament, not have lamented Patroclus? (See Homer's *Iliad*, especially Books I, IX, XVIII-XIX, Vol. 4.) Can a man will himself not to feel or think what he feels or thinks? Can he control or suppress the expression of his feelings or thoughts? Is it only the outer behavior or is it also the inner thought that Epictetus thinks can be controlled by the will? Must the will itself, then, be changed or "cured"? Can the will change itself by willing to do so?

Does a man's biological and psychological constitution limit his freedom of choice, action, and disposition? Do previous choices and conduct over a long period of time act as an obstacle to freedom of the will, as in the "hardening of the heart" sketched by Aristotle in our last reading? (See the *Discourses*, Ch. 18 and 28.) Does the social environment act broadly and generally, either to restrict or to shape the will? Could Bigger Thomas in Richard Wright's *Native Son* have willed to do otherwise—not to express himself through violence, not to become a murderer? Similarly, in Theodore Dreiser's *An American Tragedy*, could Clyde Griffiths have overcome his weakness of will and attraction to the "plush" life, so that he would not have been tempted to murder his sweetheart?

Is Providence a limiting factor on the freedom of the will? Are Epictetus' assertions of a providential government of events and also of complete freedom of the will a contradiction? Read again the passages on free will cited on pages 112b and 123c-d. God has placed no restrictions on your will, says Epictetus; your choice is perfectly free; and yet, "All will be at the same time according to your mind and the mind of God." Are murders, then, willed by God? If not, what does Epictetus mean by "according to the mind of God"?

Is it possible for a human being to be immune from influence by physical or mental pain?

A large part of Epictetus' teaching depends on the assumption that the body is an excrescence, not an essential part of the self. Hence beating, mutilation, fetters, or external pains or misfortunes do not affect the self—the inner citadel of the virtuous and self-controlled man. Leaving aside the important philosophical question of the role of the body in the make-up of the self, we must raise the question of whether it is physically and psychologically possible for men to remain immovable and unchanged by physical and mental torture.

Epictetus' examples are mostly of pains which are over in a short time—such as having a hand or a head cut off, or undergoing a death that has been chosen before dishonor. Would his counsel have been useful, however, to the men in our own time who had to spend thousands of days in concentration camps, under continual torture, deprivation, humiliation, and conditions of corruption and degeneration; who found themselves in a situation where getting a scrap of food became more important than anything else in the world and where even cannibalism occurred? Could these men have drawn the line between things in their power and not in their power?

What would Epictetus say to men in such a situation? Would his teaching about Providence be helpful? Could a man in such a situation find some small area, an inner sanctuary, where his spirit could be free? Or would the will to find and maintain it be destroyed?

What is the role of social and political life in Epictetus' ethics?

On the one hand, Epictetus tentatively lists "parents, brothers, children, country, and, generally, all with whom we live in society" among things not in our power (p. 128a); and he inveighs against those who seek to advance themselves in public place and power, who busy themselves with "business." (See Ch. 10.) On the other hand, he argues against Epicurus in favor of bringing up children (see Ch. 23), and elsewhere for family affection (see Ch. 11). It is not clear, however, whether or not he accepts Epicurus' view that "we are by nature social," and yet that "a man who has any sense . . . does not engage in political matters" (p. 128c-d).

What part do society and the state play in Epictetus' ethics? Compare his views in this respect with those of Plato and Aristotle in the previous readings. How does the condition of man's will and desires affect his social conduct and political action? (See p. 128a-b.) Which is more important in Epictetus' ethics—our relation to other men or our relation to ourselves? What are the main principles of the conduct which Epictetus enjoins in our relations to other men? How would he counsel us to act with regard to social injustice?

Is Epictetus' emphasis on individual character destructive of the universality of his ethical principles?

Epictetus constantly emphasizes that all men may attain virtue, that is, self-control, self-sufficiency, and imperturbability. Yet in Chapter 2 he stresses the factors of individual character and temperament in determining what we consider good and bad, appropriate and inappropriate, and hence in determining our conduct. In deciding what is rational and right, we consider not only external things but "also what is appropriate to each person" (p. 106d). For some men it is right to hold the chamber pot for another, for others it is not; some men put honor and worth above comfort and security, while others do not—"for men sell themselves at various prices" (p. 107a).

Epictetus places a high value on individuality, on acting according to one's unique character. He counsels us not to sell our individual character cheaply, and also not to despair if we are not moral heroes like Socrates. A man is to take the best care of the character that he has, just as of his mind, body, and goods. We should not withdraw from the strenuous effort of the moral life just because it is not in our character to be Socrateses. (See p. 108a-b.)

But what of the man who holds the chamber pot, preferring that to going hungry or being whipped? What of the man for whom it is appropriate to act in the spectacle because he considers himself "like the rest of men," just one of the ordinary threads in the pattern of existence? Are such men below the level of virtue or do they embody any of the principles taught by Epictetus? Are they and their characters and appropriate actions providentially ordered too? Or is it required of all men to attain virtue and wisdom in order to cooperate with the divine will?

The following questions are designed to help you test the thoroughness of your reading. Each question is to be answered by giving a page or pages of the reading assignment. Answers will be found on page 303 of this Reading Plan.

1 What human traits are symbolized by the wolf, the lion, and the fox?

2 What are the "two kinds of hardening"?

3 What are the respective functions of men and animals in the divine plan?

4 Why was "burning the Capitol" irrelevant in Epictetus' discussion with Rufus?

5 Where does Epictetus refer to his lameness?

6 Why should we not be angry at the moral faults of men?

7 What are the four types of appearances?

AQUINAS

Summa Theologica

"Treatise on the Last End"

Part I-II, QQ. I-V

Vol. 19, pp. 609-643

Our readings in Plato, Aristotle, and Epictetus should have prepared us for Aquinas' view of the good for man. We have encountered Plato's vision of the eternal blessedness that is the reward of the righteous; Aristotle's view of contemplation as the divine activity through which man attains as perfect a happiness as is possible in the human condition; and Epictetus' belief in a perfect contentment resulting from a willing conformity with nature and Divine Providence, based on an inner detachment from the body and the outside world.

Yet Aquinas' assertion of a transcendental end of human activity seems quite radical and revolutionary when we first hear it. Man's ultimate good, the final end of all human activity, says Aquinas, is the God of the Bible, who was revealed to man in the history of the Jewish people and in the life and deeds of Jesus of Nazareth. Universal ethical questions are answered in terms of a particular religious faith, Christianity—a faith based not on the poetic myths or rational speculation of men but on truths believed to be handed down by God Himself through a special revelation.

Like Aristotle, Aquinas asserts that contemplation is man's highest activity, but whereas Aristotle leaves it open as to what that act concretely consists in, Aquinas describes it specifically as the vision of the Essence of God—seeing God as He is, "face to face." However, this supreme experience cannot be had here and now, but only in a realm beyond this life and this world.

Thus viewed, the ultimate end of man is of a staggering grandeur, in both its content and its location. Ethics, the specifically human, is joined to the superhuman and the supernatural, to a realm beyond all finite goods, including finite moral and intellectual goods. Action and knowledge, hope, faith, and love are joined together in man's central urge toward his last end, his final good. In the grand view of Thomas Aquinas, the good for man is God.

Sixth Reading

I

The *Summa Theologica* is a systematic presentation of theology, written, according to Aquinas, for "beginners" in theological studies. (See "Prologue," p. 1.) Intended to summarize methodically all theological knowledge, it includes discussions of God, man, and the world. The First Part of the *Summa* includes a treatise on man, as well as treatises on God, the Trinity, the Creation, etc. The Second Part contains the basic ethical teachings of the *Summa*—including treatises on man's last end, human acts, habits (virtues and vices), law, the theological virtues (faith, hope, and charity), and the cardinal virtues (prudence, justice, fortitude, and temperance).

Readers who desire a full understanding of Aquinas' ethical thought should read the "Treatise on Man" in the First Part (pp. 378-527) and the treatises mentioned above in the Second Part (of the latter, only the treatise on the cardinal virtues is lacking in *Great Books of the Western World*). Aquinas also discusses ethical matters in Book III of the *Summa contra Gentiles,* an earlier work which treats philosophical questions in the light of Christian doctrine. The reader may compare the discussion of the last end there (in Book III, Ch. 1-63), presented in direct, expository style, with that given in this reading, where Aquinas follows the medieval scholastic form of questions and answers.

In this form, each treatise is divided into "questions," which are numbered consecutively (with Roman numerals) and entitled according to the topic discussed—as in this reading Question I is entitled "Of man's last end." Each question is itself divided into "articles," also numbered consecutively (with Arabic numerals) and dealing with various questions concerning the title topic. Each article has a title, which begins with "Whether" and puts the question affirmatively—as in Question I, Article 1, *"Whether It Is Proper to Man To Act for an End?"* Next come the words *"We proceed thus to the First Article:"*—or whatever number the article may be—followed by a general negative statement, as here: "It seems unfitting for man to act for an end." Then come the specific "objections" to the affirmative view, also numbered sequentially (with Arabic numerals).

After the various objections have been expressed, Aquinas, beginning with the words *"On the contrary,"* succinctly states the affirmative position, usually citing some authority—the Bible, a Church Father, or a philosopher. Then follow the words *"I answer that,"* and a full presentation of Aquinas' own view on the question. Finally come the "replies," numbered consecutively to correspond to the particular "objections" with which they deal. Thus a complete circle is made, starting with the "objections" and ending with the "replies."

Readers who are new to this style of writing are advised to read each article just as it is written, from the first objection to the last reply. The objections, whether cogent or trivial, start the process of thought about the topic under discussion and prepare the way for Aquinas' main statement. The replies to the objections often contain some of his main insights and most incisive observations on the subject. Proceeding in this methodical manner, the reader will get the full picture of what Aquinas has to say on the topic and will make certain that he does not miss anything.

To avoid confusion, it should be noted that the Second Part of the *Summa Theologica* is, in turn, divided into two parts. The "Treatise on the Last End" begins what is called "Part I of the Second Part" (Part I-II), which is continued in Volume 20 and is there followed by "Part II of the Second Part" (Part II-II).

I I

This work differs significantly from the writings we have considered in the first five readings. It is the work of a Christian theologian, who derives the basic premises of his thought from a special historical revelation, not from the intuitions or ideas arrived at by universal human reason. However, Aquinas accepts in general the analysis of human nature and the methods of thought handed down by the ancient Greek philosophers, particularly Aristotle. Believing in the divine creation of man and the natural order, and accepting in large part the Greek analysis of human nature and the universe, Aquinas was bound in his ethics (as in other aspects of his thought) to arrive at a view that would harmonize reason and revelation, the natural and supernatural orders. He therefore devised an ethics that took account both of Aristotle's teaching about the good for man and also of the message and promise proclaimed by the Christian faith.

For Aquinas, as for Aristotle, man is a unity of body and soul (not a soul imprisoned in a body), dependent even in his intellectual operations on sense experience, and affected in temperament and disposition by his bodily make-up. His action is directed to the attainment of natural ends or goods, ranging from the physical and biological to the contemplative, and culminating in the ultimate end of human activity—happiness. Through reason, man is able to discern his natural ends or goods. Through habit he acquires virtue or vice; indeed, the virtues and vices are settled habits of acting. As with Aristotle, virtue lies in "the mean." Moral actions are deliberate, conscious, intentional. A process of deliberation precedes rational human activity.

So far Aquinas is a good Aristotelian, but he departs from his philosophic master in very important respects. For him, man has a supernatural end, and is naturally constituted for fulfillment in a supernatural realm, since his soul is separable from his body. This means that the individual soul of the particular human person can participate in the fulfillment that lies in a state beyond life, in the natural, biological sense. Here Aquinas goes far beyond anything suggested by Aristotle, even in his obscure references to a kind of impersonal immortality of the intellectual part of the soul. Furthermore, man, for Aquinas, is under the ultimate governance of a personal God

Who is man's Creator and Redeemer—not the impersonal First Cause and Prime Mover of Aristotle's theology. Man, however, is not only created and commanded, but he is created free (as he is created rational), with the capacity to act willingly one way or the other in the vital choices that lead to happiness or misery.

If we turn now to a careful reading and consideration of the "Treatise on the Last End," we may see more concretely what Aquinas' basic ethical thought is.

III

The "Treatise on the Last End" consists of five questions. Question I discusses whether there is a last end of human life. Question II discusses what the last end, namely, happiness, consists in, by showing what it does *not* consist in. Question III discusses the specific human activity that constitutes happiness. Question IV discusses the things required for happiness— mental and physical qualities, as well as external goods and friends. Question V discusses whether man can attain happiness.

In Question I, Aquinas reasons along lines already familiar to us from our readings in Aristotle. Since all properly human or moral activity is deliberately directed to specific ends or goods (such as health, wealth, or knowledge), there must be "one last end of human life," an absolute, universal good to which all lesser ends or goods are directed as man's final goal and fulfillment. This "first good is the last end," which orders all human desires in unity and harmony. It is the object of the whole of human desire and action, just as the lesser ends or goods are the "principles"—the motivating forces—of particular desires. Thus Aquinas' view, like Aristotle's, is teleological (from the Greek term *Telos*, meaning "end"). There can be only one final, universal end of human activity—"the First Good," in which all the lesser goods participate—and this supreme, perfect good must be the same for all men.

Toward the end of the discussion in Question I, Aquinas calls this last end "happiness" (pp. 614d, 615b) and links it concretely, in its objective content, with the God of Biblical faith, who is "man's beginning" as well as his last end, and the beginning and end of all things. It is open to man, as distinct from the irrational creatures, to attain his last end "by knowing and loving God." (p. 615c)

After the definite, positive statement at the close of Question I that God is the last end, Aquinas proceeds in Question II to consider what happiness, the last end, is *not*. It is as if the reader had said to Aquinas, "What do you mean by saying that God is the last end?" Question II—and indeed Questions III-V also—may be regarded as an answer to this question.

Aquinas argues in Question II that whatever happiness may be, it certainly cannot consist in such imperfect, finite, or merely instrumental things as material wealth, public honor and acclaim, political or social power, bodily health, sensual pleasure, or even the goods of the soul, such as the limited knowledge and wisdom that man can attain in this life. Man cannot find his final fulfillment in any created, finite good— neither in things outside him, in material things or social status, nor in things inside him, in qualities of his own mind and body.

I answer that, It is impossible for any created good to constitute man's happiness. For happiness is the perfect good, which, quiets the appetite altogether since it would not be the last end if something yet remained to be desired. Now the object of the will, that is, of man's appetite, is the universal good, just as the object of the intellect is the universal true. Hence it is evident that nothing can quiet man's will except the universal good. This is to be found not in any creature, but in God alone, because every creature has goodness by participation. Therefore God alone can satisfy the will of man, according to the words of Ps. 102. 5 [King James 103. 5]: *Who satisfieth thy desire with good things.* Therefore God alone constitutes man's happiness. (p. 622a)

Here again is as positive a statement of the objective content of happiness as one could ask for, and it would seem that the answer to Question III, "What is Happiness?", might be found in the "Treatise on God" (pp. 3-152) or indeed in the whole of the First Part, which precedes this discussion of the last end. However, it is human happiness that we are concerned with here, and with the properly human or moral activities ("for moral acts are the same as human acts" [p. 611d]) which are directed to the last end. Hence Aquinas distinguishes in Article 1 of Question III between the *uncreated* good (God), which is the objective content of happiness—"the thing itself," outside man and the world—and "the attainment or possession, the use or enjoyment of the thing desired," which is something *created*, existing in man, and related to his natural powers. (See pp. 622d-623a.)

Since Aquinas accepts Aristotle's view that happiness is an "operation," or activity (in Article 2 of Question III), the question then becomes what kind of activity, what specific human function, is *essentially* involved in actualizing happiness—for perfection must be actual, not merely potential. Is it an act of the senses, the will, or the intellect?

Aquinas eliminates activities of the senses and the will by saying that they do not pertain *essentially* to happiness. Clearly, man "cannot be united" to God, the Uncreated Good, "by an operation of the senses," although sense activities may contribute to or be affected by happiness. (See p. 624c-d.) As for activities of the will, a distinction must be made between the *essence* of happiness and its proper *accident*. Man desires happiness and delights in it when he attains it, but the desire precedes the attainment while the delight follows it. Hence "the attainment of the end does not consist in the act of the will itself," which only leads to it. (See p. 625c.) Happiness, then, must be an intelligible end, which can become *present* to us, that is, be actually attained, only by an act of the intellect. "So, therefore, the essence of happiness consists in an act of the intellect" (p. 625d).

But this is still not specific enough, for, in the Aristotelian view which Aquinas accepts, the intellect is either practical (moral) or speculative (theoretical). Is the last end, then, attained through an activity of the practical or of the speculative intellect? In his answer to this question, Aquinas agrees again with Aristotle that perfect happiness lies in the activity of contemplation, since it is man's highest activity, is sought for its own sake, and shares in a divine activity.

Now man's highest operation is that of his highest power in respect of its highest object, and his highest power is the intellect, whose highest object is the Divine Good, which is the object not of the practical, but of the speculative intellect. Consequently happiness consists principally in such an operation, namely, in the contemplation of Divine things. (p. 626c)

This conclusion fits in with the Biblical text chosen by Aquinas to precede his answer: *"This is eternal life: that they may know Thee, the only true God"* (John 17:3). He is quick to point out that the particular speculative activity he has in mind is not the kind that goes on in the philosophical sciences, since it depends on knowledge that comes from a source above human intellect. (See p. 627c-d.) The vision of God, that is, man's "seeing" God in the act of contemplation, is a vision of God as He is, in His Essence; that is, seeing *what* He is (as First Cause of all that is), not merely, as is possible in philosophical speculation, knowing *that* He is (by inference from His effects). And this can occur only when the intellect is actually united with God. Again the conclusion of Aquinas' answer leads back to a Biblical text, this time from the First Epistle of John: *"When He shall appear, we shall be like to Him; and* (Vulg., *because) we shall see Him as He is"* (I John 3:2).

IV

Now that we have reached the apex of Aquinas' argument, in the beatific vision of God in His Essence, we return in Question IV to a consideration of somewhat the same finite goods and qualities that were discussed in Question II. In what sense, if any, are these things in the natural order required for the happiness which has been located in the supernatural order? How, if at all, do pleasure ("delight"), comprehension, rectitude of the will, the body and its perfection, external goods, and the fellowship of friends contribute to the attainment of the last end? Aquinas' answer to this question rests basically on a distinction between the perfect (supernatural) and the imperfect (natural) levels of reality, as well as on the distinction between what is *essential* and what merely contributes to, follows from, or accompanies the essential.

For instance, Aquinas is quite sure that delight is a necessary "concomitant," or accompaniment, of happiness; *but it is the latter that is essential and the cause of the delight*, "the appetite being at rest in the good attained" (p. 630a). That is why it is not delight in this sense, not peace of mind, that is the end, but the beatific vision, *an activity which is good in itself*. It is *the good* that is essential, not delight, which is an accompaniment or consequence.

For delight consists in a certain repose of the will. Now that the will finds rest in anything can only be on account of the goodness of that thing in which it reposes. If therefore the will reposes in an operation, the will's repose is caused by the goodness of the operation. Nor does the will seek good for the sake of repose, for thus the very act of the will would be the end, which has been disproved above (Q. I, A. 1, Reply 2; Q. III, A. 4), but it seeks to be at rest in the operation, because that operation is its good. Consequently it is evident that the operation in which the will reposes ranks before the resting of the will therein.

. . . .

But the intellect apprehends the universal notion of good, the attainment of which results in delight; hence its purpose is directed to good rather than to delight. (pp. 630c-631a)

Similarly, granted that the beatific vision has been attained, comprehension and rectitude of will are necessarily involved; not in the sense that we attain the ultimate good through these things, but that these things necessarily follow from this attainment. "Comprehension" is involved, not in the sense that the finite mind can encompass the infinite but in the sense that *the ultimate good is present to the mind* (Aquinas refers to the original meaning of "comprehension" as "catching," "grasping," or "laying hold of"). Rectitude of the will is required in two senses: (1) *antecedently,* in the sense that a proper disposition, "being duly ordered to the last end," which is what rectitude of the will consists in, is a prior requirement to the attainment of the last end; and (2) *concomitantly,* because the will is made right through the beatific vision of God, "the very essence of goodness," and once the vision is attained, all loving and willing is done in subordination to the Divine Goodness that has been envisioned. (See Art. 3 of Q. IV.)

When it comes to the body and its perfections, as requirements for happiness, Aquinas has to take into consideration the Christian view that the soul will be reunited to a resurrected body after death, as well as his constant distinction between imperfect, earthly happiness and perfect, supernatural happiness. He is certain that the body is necessary for earthly happiness, since man's highest faculty, his intellect, depends on the images contributed by the senses; but since the beatific vision of the Divine Essence does not depend on such things, he concludes that happiness in this sense does not essentially require the body. He grants, though, that the body in some sense ("a spiritual body") is required for the well-being and proper operation of the soul—for its "natural perfection." Hence bodily perfections do contribute to perfect happiness, antecedently and consequently—*antecedently*, in the sense that a body in a good and pure state is required for the attainment of happiness; *consequently*, in the sense that happiness of the soul "overflows" into the body. Hence, although perfect happiness does not consist in bodily good, perfection of the body adds "a certain grace and perfection to Happiness" (p. 635a).

For since it is natural to the soul to be united to the body, it is not possible for the perfection of the soul to exclude its natural perfection. (p. 634d)

Although Aquinas admits that bodily perfection (an internal good) is in some sense necessary to perfect happiness, he remains certain that external goods (wealth, status, fame, etc.) "are incompatible with that spiritual life in which perfect Happiness consists," although instrumental to imperfect, earthly happiness, that is, "ordered to the animal life" (p. 635d).

Again, at the end of the discussion in Question IV, Aquinas asserts flatly that "nothing else is necessary for Happiness," that is, the "perfect Happiness which will be" in Heaven besides the beatific vision of God. In this sense, then, friendship, the love of one's neighbor, is external to perfect happiness and plays no part in it; although it is essential to the earthly life of virtue and "conduces to the well-being of Happiness"—just as bodily beauty and a keen wit add something to human perfection, though they are not essential to it. (See

p. 633c.) Although, in this view, man's ultimate happiness *essentially* has to do only with God and nothing to do with other men, love of neighbor is a *consequence and accompaniment* of love of God. God is all in all; from intimacy with Him follows all that is good in human life and the world.

In Question V, Aquinas returns to some of the same points he has made in the previous discussions, but he does so in a consideration of whether happiness is attainable. He deals with this subject quickly at the outset, holding simply that its attainability is proved by man's capacity to apprehend and desire perfect good, and also by a previous demonstration, in the First Part, that man has the capacity to see God. Man's "natural desire" for the abiding and perfect good indicates that it must be attained beyond this life, with its unavoidable evils and transitoriness. Aquinas appeals to man's natural exigence and hunger for the happiness which satisfies all desires as pointing to the transcendental locus of its fulfillment, and, in a sense, proving its transcendence. This appeal is made in terms of what he calls the "general" abstract notion of happiness. It is also made in terms of the "special" concrete notion of happiness, that is, that it consists specifically in the vision of the Divine Essence, and hence must be attained beyond this life, since by definition it is perfect, eternal, and never lost.

But although man has the intellectual capacity to apprehend perfect good, and a natural desire for perfect happiness (the will "is ordered of natural necessity to the last end"), it does not follow that he attains happiness by his own natural powers. The actual immediate apprehension of the Divine Essence is beyond man's natural powers, indeed beyond the power of any creature. Rational creatures need God's help to attain the beatific vision—the grace which is added to their natural powers. Man does, however, have "free choice," whereby he may turn to God and pray for happiness. Aquinas drives his point home by pointing out, in Article 6, that not even angels, who are also creatures and participate imperfectly in happiness, can make man happy. God alone has that power.

V

How does Aquinas' view on happiness compare with Epictetus'?

How, if at all, does the role of peace of mind differ in the ethical views presented in Epictetus' *Discourses* and Aquinas' "Treatise on the Last End"? What are the similarities and the differences between the ancient Stoic and the medieval Christian in their conceptions of God, the relation between man and God, and the role of that relation in ethical life? Do Providence and free will have the same meaning and are they related in the same way for Epictetus and Aquinas? Are both thinkers agreed in their evaluation of the body, its goods and its ills in their relation to ultimate happiness?

How does the beatific vision function concretely as a guide to conduct?

In most cases it is easy to see how such a principle as "Render to each his due" or "Love your neighbor as yourself" is relevant to everyday life. But how does the idea of the beatific vision serve in guiding human conduct? Is it necessary for our performance of acts of love and justice in this life that we be inspired by the knowledge that such acts serve a final good and blessedness beyond this life? If so, how does such knowledge guide us in particular cases?

Is this a "happiness ethic" in the invidious sense that it counsels us to be good and act rightly in order to attain absolute joy and good—as a means to a self-serving end? Or is Aquinas simply saying that, as a matter of fact, this is the ultimate end which all our good acts intend—consciously or not— and which gives them their essential meaning and value?

Is the beatific vision too "subjective" to be considered man's final goal? Why or why not? Is it too "intellectual," being concerned with thought rather than action? Why or why not?

Is Aquinas' evaluation of contemplation in conformity with Biblical faith?

In the prophetic tradition, knowledge of God is connected or even identified with the doing of acts of justice and loving-kindness. (See, for instance, Hosea 2:19-20, and Jeremiah 22:15-16.) Is Aquinas' emphasis on the contemplative knowledge of God completely at variance with the prophetic emphasis on the practical knowledge of God? Can the prophetic and the Thomistic views be harmonized? Are the New Testament passages cited by Aquinas, such as those from the Gospel of John and the First Epistle of John, more concordant with his emphasis on "seeing" rather than on "doing"? Are loving and knowing distinguished in the Bible, as they are in Aquinas?

What is the mode of apprehension of the beatific vision?

Would you say that, in Aquinas' view, the beatific vision is like the apprehension that follows a step-by-step rational demonstration of truth—as in mathematics? Is it like the satisfaction that follows a completely adequate conceptual analysis? Is the Divine Essence that is apprehended in the beatific vision "seen" in the same way as the concepts of rational knowledge? Or is the beatific vision more like immediate experience or intuitive apprehension than rational knowledge in the common sense? If so, is such immediate vision possible in this life? Is it possible for men, as contrasted with Angels, in the next life? Are there any accounts of the beatific vision of God experienced by living men in the Bible?

Is love of neighbor prior or consequential to the love of God?

Aquinas says that love of neighbor "results from perfect love of God" (p. 636c). Is this the actual process in human experience, or do men come to know and love God through knowing and loving their fellow men? Does Aquinas assert the priority of man's love of God in a literal, temporal sense, requiring a conscious prior direction of man's heart to God? Or is he simply saying that a loving, responsive God is the ultimate origin and end of all man's acts of love toward his fellows? Or is a third interpretation possible?

Can love of God and love of neighbor be separated in the Christian faith? Is the mystical union of the (human) alone with the (divine) Alone conceivable in traditional, normative Christianity—an at-oneness of the individual soul and God apart from the created world and other men? Is the attainment of the last end a solitary state, or does it occur in a community with other spirits? If there is personal, individual survival, does that imply love of others in the next life?

In what respects would Aquinas agree or disagree with the First Epistle of John, which makes man's love of neighbor as well as man's love of God a consequence of God's love of man: "Beloved, if God so loved us, we ought also to love one another" (4:11). "We love him, because he first loved us" (4:19). "And this commandment have we from him, That he who loveth God love his brother also" (4:21).

Can love be "commanded"?

Is man necessitated, or free, to choose happiness, according to Aquinas?

In the Prologue to this reading, Aquinas says that man has free choice and controls his own actions. (See p. 609a-c.) However, throughout the reading he speaks of a "natural desire" for happiness, and at one point he says that the will "is ordered of natural necessity to the last end" (p. 640a-b). Is Aquinas guilty of contradiction here, or may both moral freedom and natural necessity be present at the same time?

In Aquinas' view is a man free to reject any concrete good, even the ultimate good of God Himself? Is this a matter of deliberate free choice? Or is man *free* only in the choice of acts leading to the ultimate good, and *naturally necessitated* to will the latter? If Aquinas accepts the view that man is free to turn *toward or away from* God, what exactly does he mean by saying that man is also naturally necessitated toward the last end? How does he harmonize freedom and necessity?

Philo of Alexandria, a Jewish thinker of the first century and probably the first philosopher to argue for freedom of the will on the basis of the Scriptures, asserted that such freedom is a "miraculous" power, working wonders against refractory natural necessity within man, just like God's power to act against the necessary laws of nature. Would Aquinas agree or disagree with this view of freedom of the will?

Would he, on the other hand, agree with the view of Augustine, the great Christian theologian of the fourth century, that man has lost his natural capacity for free choice through the original sin of Adam, and is doomed to follow natural necessity unless he is saved by a special, selective, unearned act of divine grace?

Does Aquinas' introduction of the idea of divine grace detract from his assertion of human freedom?

The following questions are designed to help you test the thoroughness of your reading. Each question is to be answered by giving a page or pages of the reading assignment. Answers will be found on page 303 of this Reading Plan.

1 What actions are properly called "human"?

2 What is Aristotle's argument against an infinity of ends?

3 The will of what sort of man is the best indication of the last end for all men?

4 What are the four general reasons why happiness cannot consist in external goods?

5 Why cannot the soul be its own last end?

6 Why is the contemplative life more perfect than the active life?

7 Which is higher, the love of God or the intellectual knowledge of God?

8 What are the four ways in which one thing may be necessary for another?

9 How is man ordered to an intelligible end through his will?

10 Why does the happy man need friends in this life?

HOBBES

Leviathan

Part I, Ch. 6, 8, 10-11, 13-15

Vol. 23, pp. 61-65, 66-71, 71-79, 84-96

Hobbes's version of the good for man contrasts sharply with that of Aquinas. Where the latter sets up God as man's final good, to be attained in a beatific vision after this life, Hobbes is concerned with the well-being of man as a living body in the material world revealed by the new physical sciences. For him, there can be no soul apart from the body, and thought or vision is a form of material motion. Human felicity is to be found on earth, in bodily existence, not in an other-worldly realm.

Hobbes's ethical thought is of special interest to the present-day reader, because it attempts to interpret human behavior in terms of physical bodies and their movements—inner emotion in terms of outer motion. Hobbes's materialistic account of human psychology and conduct, based on the mechanico-mathematical world picture of his day, provides us with a first look at a type of interpretation that became more prominent in the nineteenth and twentieth centuries. This view is presented with systematic consistency and with the force and vigor of Hobbes's magnificent and idiosyncratic prose style.

Hobbes's interpretation is more complex and much richer than that of modern "behaviorism," because it rests on political philosophy as well as on physical philosophy. Physical motions do not indicate the meaning of such ethical terms as "justice" and "right." Such terms are meaningful for Hobbes only in civil society, in the political commonwealth, where men are mutually pledged to certain rights and duties. Ethical man, strictly speaking, is social man.

Seventh Reading

I

The first thing to notice about these selections is that they are taken from a work on the state. Ethics for Hobbes, as for Aristotle, seems to be a part of political philosophy. It has to do with the individual living in a political community, or in society, as we would say nowadays. Hobbes asserts that there is no distinction between right and wrong outside organized society.

The next thing to notice, however, is that this consideration of ethical questions rests on a certain view of the physical universe, on a theory of the properties and motions of material bodies. Philosophy for Hobbes is basically physics; that is, the causal explanation of physical events. Man is a natural body; hence his behavior may be understood in terms of physical properties and motions (with due attention, though, to human reason and foresight). Man is also a part of the state, which is an artificial body—"the body politic"—and has its own special kind of motions.

Hobbes was convinced that the study of human affairs could be reduced to "the rules and infallibility of reason," on the model of mathematics and the physical sciences. A contemporary of Kepler and Galileo, he lived in the great age of the flowering of modern science, when the mechanico-mathematical explanation of the universe was being accepted and applied fruitfully. The central role of motion in this new world view was to be duplicated in Hobbes's explanation of human nature and conduct. It was motion and not rest—as in the old Aristotelian physics—that was the central fact about the world. (See the opening remarks on motion in the chapter on imagination in the *Leviathan*, p. 50a.)

Inspired by the new physics, Hobbes conceived the grand plan of dealing systematically with various aspects of the world in terms of bodies and their motions. He once stated that philosophy consists of three main branches: geometry, physics, and morals, comprising, respectively, the study of the motions of points and lines, of the motions of bodies and their parts, and of the motions of the mind (desires and passions).

In the chart on page 72 we have Hobbes's detailed breakdown of philosophy—or "knowledge of consequences"—into its various specialized sciences. The major division is between "natural" philosophy, dealing with natural bodies, and "civil" philosophy, dealing with political bodies. Natural philosophy takes up almost the whole chart, and includes ethics, which deals with human passions, as well as the science of the just and unjust, which deals with contracts. As a part of nature, man is animal as well as human; and ethics must take account of all three aspects. As a part of the artificial body politic, man possesses special rights and duties.

Hobbes originally planned to write three works, dealing, respectively, with material bodies and their motions, with the bodily motions involved in human sensation and knowledge, and with the political community. He did complete these works, written in Latin (*De Corpore, De Homine,* and *De Cive*); but he developed his basic ideas on man and the state more fully in *The Elementes of Law, Naturall and Politique,* which was divided into two parts—*Human Nature* (psychology) and *De Corpore Politico* (law and government). These works laid the groundwork for his master work, the *Leviathan,* of which the first two parts, "Of Man" and "Of Commonwealth," correspond roughly to *De Homine* and *De Cive* and to the two parts of *The Elementes of Law.* The work on the body (*De Corpore*) is implied in the discussion—"I have elsewhere written of the same at large," Hobbes remarks (p. 49a).

At the beginning of the *Leviathan,* Hobbes deals with human psychology in terms of bodily motions. (See Part I, Ch. 1-3.) Man's thoughts are derived from sensation ("sense"), which is caused by the motions of external bodies upon our sense organs, setting up counter motions within us. Imagination and memory are the residues of these basic motions, and experience consists of many memories. "All fancies are motions within us, relics of those made in the sense . . ." (p. 52c).

Man moves as well as is moved; he acts as well as thinks and imagines. Indeed the images based on sense are systematically ordered by the desire to attain some end. Although, in Hobbes's view, man shares these mental activities with the beasts, he is inclined to consider "prudence"—the prevision or presensing of future consequences—as a specifically human capacity. (For an exception see p. 53d; see also p. 267b.)

In any case, all man's thoughts are derived from sense experience. The motion of his mind—consisting of sense, thoughts, and the ordered train of thought—originates in the motions of external objects upon his body. Since "whatsoever . . . we conceive has been perceived first by sense . . . a man can have no thought representing anything not subject to sense" (p. 54b). And since whatever is sensed or imagined must be finite, man cannot conceive anything infinite (even God).

This, in brief summary, is the basic psychological analysis that precedes Hobbes's discussion of the motivating forces of human behavior and his consideration of good and evil. A full treatment of his psychological theory will be presented in the Reading Plan *Biology, Psychology and Medicine*.

II

At the beginning of this selection, Hobbes discusses "voluntary motions" or "passions." The role of imagination distinguishes voluntary from "vital," or spontaneous, motions (such as blood circulation, breathing, and excretion), for an image of the voluntary action precedes its performance. Even more important and distinctive in voluntary motions is "endeavor"—a specific drive toward or a pulling away from an imagined object or event.

This endeavour, when it is toward something which causes it, is called *appetite*, or *desire*. . . . And when the endeavour is fromward something, it is generally called *aversion*. These words *appetite* and *aversion* . . . signify the motions, one of approaching, the other of retiring. (p. 61b-c)

Hobbes adds "contempt" as a third type of endeavor, an attitude of indifference, "immobility or contumacy."

All individual judgments of "good" and "evil"—that is, the moral judgments of the natural man apart from society—are based on these three types of endeavor. They are relative to the state of a particular man and his body at a particular time. They are particular, not universal, judgments of good and evil.

> But whatsoever is the object of any man's appetite or desire, that is it which he for his part calleth *good;* and the object of his hate and aversion, *evil;* and of his contempt, *vile* and *inconsiderable.* For these words of *good, evil,* and *contemptible* are ever used with relation to the person that useth them: there being nothing simply and absolutely so; nor any common rule of good and evil to be taken from the nature of the objects themselves; but from the person of the man, where there is no Commonwealth. . . . (pp. 61d-62a)

The terms "fair" and "foul"—what appears promising or unpromising, pleasant or unpleasant, useful or hurtful—remarks Hobbes, may convey more effectively this sense of good and evil. Since pleasure is intimately connected with our appetites, it is an important factor in our estimation of good and evil.

> Pleasure therefore, or delight, is the appearance or sense of good; and molestation or displeasure, the appearance or sense of evil. And consequently all appetite, desire, and love is accompanied with some delight more or less; and all hatred and aversion with more or less displeasure and offence. (p. 62b-c)

The elementary human emotions or "passions" are forms of appetite and aversion. Love and hate are directed toward objects actually present, whereas appetite and aversion, strictly speaking, are directed toward the same objects when they are absent. Joy and grief are emotions expressed in anticipation of foreseen events, corresponding to the pleasure and pain of immediate sense experience.

Hobbes lists the basic passions loosely as *"appetite, desire, love, aversion, hate, joy,* and *grief"* (p. 62c). Actually there are six and not seven basic passions, for appetite and desire, broadly speaking, are the same things. (See p. 61b.) In terms of these "simple passions" Hobbes interprets all of man's emotional life—hope and despair, fear and courage, confidence and diffidence, benevolence and covetousness, etc. (See pp. 62d-64a.)

He also interprets *deliberation* in terms of the passions. Deliberation, in this view, is a process of alternative appetites and aversions toward imagined events and their results—"the whole sum of desires, aversions, hopes and fears, continued till the thing be either done, or thought impossible, is that we call *deliberation*" (p. 64a). Deliberation ends with the action (or non-action) with which the whole process has been concerned. *Will* is "the last appetite, or aversion," immediately preceding the overt action (or avoidance).

By "will," Hobbes means the concrete act, not the power, of willing. He does not mean any mere "inclination" which is not acted upon, a mere velleity. Nor does he limit the will to the specifically human or "rational," for the brute beasts deliberate too. Their action also is preceded by the "alternate succession of appetites, aversions, hopes and fears. . . . And beasts that have deliberation must necessarily also have will" (p. 64b).

The process of deliberation is always concerned with the *apparent* good or evil, involving a weighing of prospective good and evil consequences against one another, so far as human foresight stretches. The right choice is no certain matter. "Felicity" consists in continual success and prosperity in this uncertain process, in obtaining what one wants out of life. This, by definition, is something impermanent and imperfect. Hence the "beatific vision" of the Schoolmen (the medieval scholastics, such as Aquinas) is incomprehensible.

. . . I mean the felicity of this life. For there is no such thing as perpetual tranquillity of mind, while we live here; because life itself is but motion, and can never be without desire, nor without fear, no more than without sense. What kind of felicity God hath ordained to them that devoutly honour him, a man shall no sooner know than enjoy; being joys that now are as incomprehensible as the word of Schoolmen *beatifical vision,* is unintelligible. (p. 65a-b)

As for the intellectual virtues, those specifically human qualities of mind which men praise and prize, these too depend on the basic impulses and passions. Natural wit, developed through use and experience, consists of two basic elements: "*celerity of imagining* (that is, swift succession of one thought to another); and *steady direction* to some approved end"

(p. 66d). Differences in quickness and directedness of judgment originate in differences in passion. A man deficient in the passion for power—the basic object of human desire, under which riches, knowledge, and honor may be subsumed—is also deficient in fancy and judgment.

> For the thoughts are to the desires as scouts and spies to range abroad and find the way to the things desired, all steadiness of the mind's motion, and all quickness of the same, proceeding from thence. For as to have no desire is to be dead; so to have weak passions is dullness; and to have passions indifferently for everything, giddiness and distraction; and to have stronger and more vehement passions for anything than is ordinarily seen in others is that which men call *madness*. (p. 68c)

III

The passion for power develops a man's wit. The possession of power determines a man's worth. Hence, in Chapter 10, Hobbes discusses power and its relation to worth, dignity, honor, and worthiness.

A man's *power* is simply his capacity to obtain what appears to be good. It consists in certain "natural" mental or physical capacities and in the "instrumental" or secondary powers (such as "riches, reputation, friends") acquired by the original power. A man's *worth* is simply the market value of his power, what other men are willing to pay for the use of his capacities in terms of dignity and honor. *Dignity* is the public worth of a man, "the value set on him by the Commonwealth" (p. 73c), and is shown in the offices, titles, etc., bestowed on him. *Honor* may be demonstrated in various ways—by requesting aid, obeying, bestowing great gifts, flattery, love or fear, high praise, deference, etc. It is bestowed on the powerful and the fortunate. Success and strength are honorable, failure and weakness are dishonorable.

> *Honourable* is whatsoever possession, action, or quality is an argument and sign of power.
> And therefore to be honoured, loved, or feared of many is honourable, as arguments of power. To be honoured of few or none, *dishonourable*.
> Dominion and victory is honourable, because acquired by power; and servitude, for need or fear, is dishonourable.
> Good fortune, if lasting, honourable; as a sign of the favour of God. Ill fortune and losses, dishonourable. Riches are honourable, for they

are power. Poverty, dishonourable. Magnanimity, liberality, hope, courage, confidence, are honourable; for they proceed from the conscience of power. Pusillanimity, parsimony, fear, diffidence, are dishonourable. (p. 74c)

Conspicuousness is honorable; obscurity, dishonorable. Covetousness and ambition for great things are honorable; for small things, dishonorable. Honor depends only on power, and has nothing to do with right or justice.

Nor does it alter the case of honour whether an action (so it be great and difficult, and consequently a sign of much power) be just or unjust: for honour consisteth only in the opinion of power. (p. 75a)

Yet previously Hobbes has labeled as pusillanimity "the use of unjust or dishonest means . . . prompted to men by fear or want, . . . that crooked wisdom which is called *craft*" (p. 68a). And here he specifically says that "craft, shifting, neglect of equity, is dishonourable," as compared with the "actions proceeding from equity, joined with loss," springing from magnanimity, which is "a sign of power" (p. 75a). Here the equitable and the just are linked with the powerful and hence are regarded as honorable.

Worthiness is simply a man's specific fitness or aptitude for a certain office or honor, apart from his right to it from the worth set on him by his fellow men.

IV

With the central role of power in human life established, Hobbes goes on to deal with happiness, or "felicity." (See Ch. 11 and 13.) As we have seen, in discussing deliberation he has emphasized the uncertain quality of human happiness. Now he connects the will to attain and retain power with felicity as a continually unfinished and ongoing process.

Human life consists in a perpetual drive toward satisfaction and power which ends only with death.

. . . I put for a general inclination of all mankind a perpetual and restless desire of power after power, that ceaseth only in death. (p. 76d)

The reason for this is that a man must always attain more power merely to keep the power he already has—he cannot stand still. Besides, once he has attained what he wants, "there succeedeth a new desire," in the unresting quest for ever new forms of satisfaction and power. The king who has assured his power at home may turn to foreign conquests, or sensual pleasures, or cultural endeavors—all, for Hobbes, new forms of power.

Hobbes asserts that this unceasing and restless quest is what human felicity consists in, for it corresponds with human nature and the human condition.

> . . . the felicity of this life consisteth not in the repose of a mind satisfied. For there is no such *finis ultimus* (utmost aim) nor *summum bonum* (greatest good) as is spoken of in the books of the old moral philosophers. Nor can a man any more live whose desires are at an end than he whose senses and imaginations are at a stand. Felicity is a continual progress of the desire from one object to another, the attaining of the former being still but the way to the latter. (p. 76c)

However, it seems that if everyone is inspired by the "perpetual and restless desire of power after power" (p. 76d), there is bound to be conflict, preventing men "living together in peace and unity"—the central theme of the *Leviathan*. Whether there is contention or amity among men is determined, says Hobbes, by the object of their desires, by the type of satisfaction they seek. Competition for the possession of riches, honor, or similar power leads to conflict, whereas the desire for "ease, and sensual delight" or for "knowledge, and arts of peace" makes men willing "to obey a common power"—to live in peace and unity (pp. 76d-77a).

Various types of desires, fears, and ignorance lead to conflict or amity among men. But more fundamental than these is man's natural condition as contrasted with his life in civil society. The state of nature is a state of war, a war of each man against every other man, in which all men strive for life, security, and power—"without a common power to keep them all in awe" (p. 85b).

The reason for this, says Hobbes, is that all men are by nature equal. Physical differences are easily overcome—by craft or banding together with others—and mental differences are more apparent than real. "From this equality of ability ariseth equality of hope in the attaining of our ends" (p. 84d).

Hence, there is conflict when two men want the same thing. From this equality there also arises fear of what other men may do, and the necessity to conquer everyone within range, in order to assure one's own security. Also operative is the basic human desire to be valued highly, so that when a man thinks his fellows are not valuing him highly enough he harms them just to show them his true worth.

So that in the nature of man, we find three principal causes of quarrel. First, competition; secondly, diffidence [apprehension]; thirdly, glory. (p. 85b)

This is the condition of man in a state of nature, where the individual can rely only on his own prowess and his wits for security and the necessities of life. There is no common industry, commerce, culture, or knowledge, but only "continual fear, and danger of violent death; and the life of man, solitary, poor, nasty, brutish, and short" (p. 85c). What we think of the nature of our fellow men, even in a state of civil society, is evident in the measures we take to secure our houses, possessions, and persons—locking our doors and chests and carrying arms.

But none of this, insists Hobbes, may be taken to mean that human nature is bad. The distinctions of good and bad apply only in a state of civil society. That man has certain passions which inspire his actions, unless restrained by law, is just a fact of life without any moral implications.

The desires, and other passions of man, are in themselves no sin. No more are the actions that proceed from those passions till they know a law that forbids them; which till laws be made they cannot know, nor can any law be made till they have agreed upon the person that shall make it. (p. 85d)

Hobbes points also to the state of anarchy and war—overt or potential—which prevails among sovereign national states. Obviously the old saying that all is fair in love and war is applicable here, for killing, stealing, and lying are accepted normal acts in war—hot or cold—among nations. The state of war among civilized countries is a perfect concrete example of the state of nature. In the war of each against all, all is fair—or rather, the concepts of fair and unfair do not apply.

To this war of every man against every man, this also is consequent; that nothing can be unjust. The notions of right and wrong, justice and injustice, have there no place. Where there is no common power, there is no law; where no law, no injustice. Force and fraud are in war the two cardinal virtues. Justice and injustice are none of the faculties neither of the body nor mind. If they were, they might be in a man that were alone in the world, as well as his senses and passions. They are qualities that relate to men in society, not in solitude. It is consequent also to the same condition that there be no propriety, no dominion, no *mine* and *thine* distinct; but only that to be every man's that he can get, and for so long as he can keep it. And thus much for the ill condition which man by mere nature is actually placed in; though with a possibility to come out of it, consisting partly in the passions, partly in his reason. (p. 86a-b)

Thus in man's nature lies the remedy as well as the cause of war and anarchy. There are passions that foster peace—fear of death, love of ease, and hope to obtain ease by industry—as well as passions that foster war. And through reason man can discern the natural laws which provide the basis of civil society, and hence truly ethical judgment.

V

Hobbes deals with these basic laws of nature in Chapters 14-15. First he distinguishes between a natural *right* and a natural *law*. A man has a natural right to preserve his life and take whatever steps are necessary to do so; that is, he is naturally *free* to do so. This is the "right" that prevails in a state of nature, where "every man has a right to every thing, even to one another's body" (p. 86d).

A natural law, on the other hand, is "a precept, or general rule, found out by reason, by which a man is forbidden to do that which is destructive of his life" (p. 86c). It is obligatory, rather than permissive; it *binds* men absolutely to take whatever steps are necessary to the preservation of life. It is a dictum of objective reason rather than a matter of private judgment or need.

Hence the general rule, discerned by reason, is *"that every man ought to endeavour peace"* (that he *should* or *must* do so), but when that becomes impossible *"he may seek and use all helps and advantages of war"* (he is *free* to make war, kill, steal, etc.). This precept includes the basic natural law, "*to seek peace and follow it*," and the basic natural right, "*by all means we can to defend ourselves*" (pp. 86d-87a). Hence follows the second law of nature, requiring a man to give up his natural right or liberty (to do anything necessary for self-preservation) in order to obtain peace, as commanded by the first law of nature—provided that other men do the same.

It is only when such a voluntary renunciation or transference (e.g., to a sovereign authority) of natural right has occurred that we can talk of "obligation" and "duty" or "injustice" and "injury." A man is guilty of a violation of faith—he is wrong—if he breaks the mutual agreement whereby he gave up his natural right. The renunciation, however, is solely for the sake of self-preservation and security of the individual, for his own good. Hence, a man cannot be required to give up the right to defend his person, life, and liberty when he is attacked by other men. This would contradict the general rule of reason on which the first and second laws of nature are based.

In any case, the only sure guarantee that men will abide by their mutual agreement not to harm one another is the coercive power of some authority set above them, since human passions outweigh promises unless men are forced to keep them. Once such a power prevails over men, the third law of nature, "*that men perform their covenants made*" (p. 91a), becomes operative, and so does the distinction between "just" and "unjust."

> And in this law of nature consisteth the fountain and original of *justice*. For where no covenant hath preceded, there hath no right been transferred, and every man has right to everything; and consequently, no action can be unjust. But when a covenant is made, then to break it is *unjust:* and the definition of *injustice* is no other than *the not performance of covenant*. And whatsoever is not unjust is just. (p. 91a)

But the fear that even if we keep covenants, others may not, can be removed only by a common coercive power, which guarantees to each man what properly belongs to him, fulfilling the traditional principle of justice—"to each his own."

. . . justice is the constant will of giving to every man his own. And therefore where there is no *own,* that is, no propriety, there is no injustice; and where there is no coercive power erected, that is, where there is no Commonwealth, there is no propriety, all men having right to all things: therefore where there is no Commonwealth, there nothing is unjust. So that the nature of justice consisteth in keeping of valid covenants, but the validity of covenants begins not but with the constitution of a civil power sufficient to compel men to keep them: and then it is also that propriety begins. (p. 91b)

Hobbes makes an interesting distinction between the injustice of manners and of actions. By "manners" Hobbes means what Aristotle meant by "habit"—it is the whole ethical build or stance of a man, whereby he is called just or unjust. Specific actions are also called just or unjust. A just man does not become unjust because of a few unjust actions, proceeding from impulse or mistaken judgment; nor does an unjust man become just because of a few just actions done from fear or covetousness. This distinction, as Hobbes spells it out, is between ethical and legal merit and fault.

This justice of the manners is that which is meant where justice is called a *virtue;* and injustice, a *vice.*

But the justice of actions denominates men, not just, but *guiltless:* and the injustice of the same (which is also called injury) gives them but the name of *guilty.*

Again, the injustice of manners is the disposition or aptitude to do injury, and is injustice before it proceed to act, and without supposing any individual person injured. (pp. 92d-93a)

The many laws of nature set down in Chapter 15 command gratitude for favors, sociability or adjustment to living with other men, pardon of repentant offenders, punishment only to correct the offender or to guide others, prohibit overt hatred or contempt for others, and enjoin acknowledgment of others as equal by nature, not claiming rights for oneself not granted to others, and the Golden Rule: *"Do not that to another which thou wouldest not have done to thyself"* (p. 95c).

The laws of nature are absolute so far as *intention* is concerned—"they bind to a desire they should take place"—but not so far as *action* is concerned—"to the putting them in act, not always" (p. 95d). In the first place, overt observance of the laws requires that other men should keep them too; and, secondly, action apparently in conformity with the laws may be intended against them. Nevertheless, what the natural laws forbid is absolutely unjust and unlawful; and knowledge of them comprises moral philosophy.

The laws of nature are immutable and eternal; for injustice, ingratitude, arrogance, pride, iniquity, acception of persons, and the rest can never be made lawful. For it can never be that war shall preserve life, and peace destroy it.

The same laws, because they oblige only to a desire and endeavour, I mean an unfeigned and constant endeavour, are easy to be observed. For in that they require nothing but endeavour, he that endeavoureth their performance fulfilleth them; and he that fulfilleth the law is just.

And the science of them is the true and only moral philosophy. For moral philosophy is nothing else but the science of what is good and evil in the conversation and society of mankind. (pp. 95d-96a)

In the state of nature or war, "good" and "evil" are merely names for private appetites and aversions. But in the state of civil society there is a common agreement upon what actions are rational and good.

. . . and consequently all men agree on this, that peace is good, and therefore also the way or means of peace, which (as I have shown before) are *justice, gratitude, modesty, equity, mercy,* and the rest of the laws of nature, are good; that is to say, moral virtues; and their contrary vices, evil. Now the science of virtue and vice is moral philosophy; and therefore the true doctrine of the laws of nature is the true moral philosophy. (p. 96b)

The moral philosophers of the past, says Hobbes, have been mistaken in their interpretation of virtue as the mean, "a mediocrity of passions." The goodness of the virtues consists in their being "the means of peaceable, sociable, and comfortable living" (p. 96b).

VI

Does Hobbes's description of human nature provide any ethical norms?

Hobbes has provided us with an account of human motivations, of the basic emotions and "drives" that underlie human conduct. Does he also thereby provide us with standards of good and evil, of right and wrong in human behavior? If so, just how are these norms connected with his description of man's psychological make-up?

Aristotle (and Aquinas too, so far as he follows Aristotle) also finds a basis for ethics in man's nature. How does Aristotle's "nature" differ from Hobbes's as regards ethical implications? What norms for human conduct, what idea of the good for man, does Aristotle derive from his analysis of human nature?

Are *pleasure* and *power* Hobbes's naturally based norms of good and evil? Any kind of pleasure? Any kind of power?

Are *peace* and *order* ethical norms for Hobbes? If so, are they derived from Hobbes's study of human nature? Are they the chief ends of Hobbes's natural man? How does Hobbes arrive at the conclusion that they should be man's chief aims?

Why "ought" men "to endeavour peace"? Why is peace good? For the practical reason that otherwise there would be continual rapine and warfare? But why, then, are rapine and warfare evil? Because they are harmful to human life and its full development? Is the harmful to human life, then, what is evil, and the beneficial what is good?

Can psychological analysis provide the basis for ethics?

Hobbes, as we have seen, has based his inquiry into judgments of good and evil on a description of the "inner motions" of men. Is such psychological analysis a necessary basis for ethical inquiry? Must any relevant ethics take full notice of man's mind and nature? Is an ethics conceivable which is completely abstracted from human impulses, inclinations, feelings, emotions, etc.? If not, just how do we go from the "is" of psychological description (that "this is the way men react to certain stimuli or events") to the "ought" of ethical judgments (that "this is the way men should or must act")?

Are the terms "fair" and "foul," as used by Hobbes, really ethical terms, the correlatives of "good" and "evil"? Hobbes's terms suggest external appearances (such as good-looking and bad-looking), or odors and tastes (good smells and bad smells). The reactions of "fair" or "foul" toward the same object, in Hobbes's view, differ among individuals or even for the same person at different times. Is the fair/foul distinction, therefore, merely subjective?

It would seem so from Hobbes's remark that "good" and "evil" are "used with relation to the person that useth them," not absolutely nor with reference to "any common rule of good and evil to be taken from the nature of the objects themselves" (pp. 61d-62a). But does not the external object or motion play an essential role in eliciting the particular response of the particular person? The terms "good" and "evil" apply only where there is a relation between a person and an object (material or imaginary). Is there not, then, an objective as well as a subjective factor involved in ethical judgments for Hobbes, even though he denies that they can be universalized?

We might inquire whether the judgments of foul and fair tastes, smells, and sights do not have a fairly wide basis of agreement among men. We might find through empirical research that normal persons generally desire to attain health, prosperity, and nourishment, and want to avoid wounds, poison, starvation, poverty, etc. But whatever the results, would we still be proceeding within Hobbes's basic framework of deciding good and evil by human appetites and aversions? Would we still be making ethical judgments a matter of psychological predisposition and preferences—although generalizing them and allowing for the action of the object?

Is peace good because we desire it, or do we desire it because it is good? Or is it a psychological fact that all men do not desire peace and order, while it remains an ethical requirement that all men should desire them? Is there any moral *obligation* for men to pursue peace, whether they want to or not? *Must* they pursue peace? It is possible to arrive at such a moral obligation, such a "must," through an empirical description of how men are moved to act the way they do?

Or would Hobbes reply that this line of questioning is irrelevant, since "should" and "must" do not become operative until man reaches a state of civil society? What, then, is the relevance of Hobbes's physio-psychological analysis to ethics in the social sense?

How are the ethical and the social related in Hobbes?

On the one hand, ethics has to do only with the "consequences from the passions of men" (according to the chart on page 72). It is the study of the natural man with his basic drives toward pleasure and power. It deals with the activities of the egocentric, discrete, "atomistic" individual, concerned only with what he deems beneficial or injurious to himself.

On the other hand, the very concepts of right and wrong, of just and unjust, are meaningful for Hobbes only in a state of organized society, in a political commonwealth or "body politic," whose members have definite rights and duties. Hobbes remarks in Part II that "the laws of nature, as *justice, equity, modesty, mercy,* and, in sum, *doing to others as we would be done to* . . . are contrary to our natural passions, that carry us to partiality, pride, revenge, and the like" (p. 99b).

How, then, does man get from the natural/private ethical to the political/social ethical? Not by a complete jump, according to Hobbes. His natural fears and desires (to avoid death, make a living, etc.), as well as his rational apprehension of "the laws of nature," change man into a social/ethical human being. Man is moved by his natural passions to seek peace and order, in his own self-interest; and through his natural reason he discerns the basic principles and dispositions of social/ethical life.

At one place (see p. 95c), Hobbes grants that a man may violate the laws of nature in the way he treats himself, as in drunkenness or other forms of intemperance, but since Hobbes's interest here is social peace and order he pursues this point no further. Does ethics have to do with a man's action toward himself as well as toward other men? Can a man be unjust to himself? Does Hobbes's frequent reference to the Golden Rule as a summary of the natural law imply a basic good attitude toward oneself as the criterion for one's disposition toward others, setting up our responses to self-benefit and self-injury as a model for our actions toward others?

Of course, even the Golden Rule, from Hobbes's viewpoint, might be interpreted as an expression of enlightened self-interest and expediency: "Do good to others so that they will do good to you." The virtues themselves are but "the means of peaceable, sociable, and comfortable living" (p. 96b). Could we say, then, that Hobbes's ethics, like Aristotle's and Aquinas', is teleological, with social order as the end?

Yet he scorns mere self-serving, the apparently just action of the man whose "will is not framed by the justice but by the apparent benefit of what he is to do"; and he contrasts with this the nobility of the man who "scorns to be beholding for the contentment of his life to fraud, or breach of promise" (p. 92d). He also castigates the "specious reasoning" which calls "successful wickedness" virtue (p. 91c-d). It seems clear, then, that virtue for Hobbes is not mere expediency or conformity. Does it, however, exist only in civil society, without any connection with the state of nature?

Outside the question whether man has ever existed as man outside society, whether man has not always been a social animal and is so by nature, the question does arise whether the various virtuous dispositions which Hobbes finds commanded by the laws of nature—justice, equity, mercy, sociability—are not operative in the natural man as well as in the political man. Is there a complete discontinuity between nature and society? Are these virtuous dispositions alien to the natural man? Are there any natural cooperative and societal impulses in man?

In his discussion of *power*, the dominant passion of the natural man, is Hobbes actually talking about the natural man or about man in a state of society? Are not *worth*, *dignity*, and *honor* meaningful terms only in the context of society, and do not all Hobbes's examples refer to organized political society? Is he explaining man in a state of nature in terms of man in civil society, with all the latter's jockeying for status, recognition, etc.?

Is it possible to see the ethical state of the natural man in a different way than Hobbes did?

Imagination and speculation, since the ancient Greeks, have looked back to the natural man, before civilization, as a perfectly good and happy being—the model for civilized man to emulate. The Greek and Latin poets, as well as the utopian writers of the Renaissance—Hobbes's own time—saw the state of nature as a Golden Age of glorious human existence—exactly the opposite of the state of war, in which life is "nasty, brutish, and short." Explorers, such as Christopher Columbus, hoped to find an earthly paradise somewhere among the aborigines of the new lands, untouched by civilization. Later, Rousseau founded his social theory on the idea of the good or noble savage, in contrast to the corrupted man of civil society. Anthropological research indicates that men in primitive societies too have believed in a primal age when man lived a perfect, happy existence.

What are the consequences for ethical theory if man's perfection is to be found in a state of nature rather than in a state of civil society? Would an ethics which assumes this be more "perfectionist" than Hobbes's ethics? Would it be more or less revolutionary as regards existing forms of social organization? Which view of natural man is more concordant with reality? Are they both "myths" (imaginative constructs)? Are they both, therefore, untrue, as regards man's nature and the good for man? Why or why not?

SELF-TESTING QUESTIONS

The following questions are designed to help you test the
thoroughness of your reading. Each question is to be answered
by giving a page or pages of the reading assignment. Answers
will be found on page 303 of this Reading Plan.

1 Why do a man's appetites and aversions continually change?

2 What is "covetousness"?

3 What is Hobbes's interpretation of laughter?

4 What is "acquired wit"?

5 What is the rank of the sciences in the scale of power,
   and why?

6 What is man's natural response toward receiving great
   benefits from an equal?

7 What impels men to follow custom and precedent?

8 Why are covenants with brute beasts impossible?

9 Are covenants entered into through fear obligatory?

10 What are the natural rights retained by man in civil
   society?

MONTAIGNE

The Essays

"That to study philosophy is to learn to die," "Of moderation," "Of cannibals," "That we are to avoid pleasures, even at the expense of life," "That the relish of good and evil depends in a great measure upon the opinion we have of them," "Of drunkenness," "Of cruelty," "Of glory," "Of virtue," "Of anger," "Of repentance"

Vol. 25, pp. 28-36, 89-98, 99-100, 115-125, 162-167, 200-208, 300-307, 340-343, 344-347, 388-395

Montaigne is one of the most widely read of French authors. Writing in an easy, conversational style about his thoughts and experiences, and reflecting on his particular personality and the events and manners of his own time, he became a universally read writer. There is an appeal in these genial, honest, unpretentious essays that is hard to equal in world literature. And his peculiar matter and manner bring us to an appreciation of man's moral existence which is often more impressive than what we obtain through more sober and systematic works.

Montaigne's general description of how men feel, decide, and act in certain situations, and the intimate details he summons up from his own experience, give us an impression of verisimilitude. We feel that here is a man something like us, describing authentically experiences such as we have had and problems we have had to face. What we get from his writings is the taste of an actual man in the actual world. Montaigne addresses our ordinary condition, our everyday existence.

His affinity with the ancient moralists is indicated by his more or less Stoic doctrine on how to endure the painful aspects of human existence, as well as by his emphasis on reason and will. But his thought is also in the modern temper; indeed, we might label him as the first of the "moderns" in moral philosophy. For one thing, he is keenly aware of the varieties of human manners and morals, which the great age of exploration had revealed. For another, his emphasis on his own personal experience and idiosyncrasies is alien to the ancient mind and congenial to the modern. Also his compassionate horror of cruelty toward fellow men, which was accepted in his time, as well as his belief in the goodness of primitive man—the theme of the "noble savage"—link him with modern trends of thought.

Montaigne emphasizes these moral and intellectual attitudes: moderation, tolerance, compassion, love of peace, gentle irony, an inquiring spirit, and skepticism with regard to absolute judgments.

Eighth Reading

I

Montaigne invented the essay form. "The essay as he gave it," said George Saintsbury, "had no forerunner in modern literature and no direct ancestor in the literature of ancient times." The essay is an open, rambling form, in the mode of personal conversation rather than of traditional formal litcrature. It permits an easy, genial camaraderie between author and reader, as the writer pursues a subject in an unconstrained, desultory, even haphazard fashion, without any set plan of what he is going to say, and often with no definite conclusions. The reader is able to participate in the author's tentative gropings, his personal meditations, his "table talk."

Montaigne's writings are notable as the products of a master, as well as the originator, of the essay form. His personal temperament, manner of thinking, and supple literary style fitted him for his creative mastery. He was intensely interested in whatever he read, experienced, and thought, and wanted to set it all down in writing. He was avidly curious about all the varieties and details of human behavior at all times and places. If he had a single subject, it was man—the types and varieties of human motivations, passions, and actions. His tendency to engage in concrete psychological analysis, to discern and describe what actually goes on when we deliberate, decide, are tempted, etc., has been emulated by many other French writers since his time. He was a pioneer in the description of moral consciousness.

Montaigne gets a large part of his material for this analysis from himself, as he confesses in his note to the reader—"it is myself I paint" (p. 1). There are few, if any, writers in *Great Books of the Western World* who use themselves so persistently as their subject matter, or who give us so many details about their own lives in their writings on other subjects. In his note to the reader, Montaigne refers deprecatingly to "so frivolous and vain a subject" (p. 1), but that he actually takes what Saintsbury calls his "meditative egoism" seriously, even and especially for the purposes of moral philosophy, is indicated at the beginning of his essay "Of repentance." His defense there is that Michael de Montaigne embodies the human condition.

Others form man; I only report him: and represent a particular one, ill fashioned enough, and whom, if I had to model him anew, I should certainly make something else than what he is: but that's past recalling.
. . . .

I propose a life ordinary and without lustre: 'tis all one; all moral philosophy may as well be applied to a common and private life, as to one of richer composition: every man carries the entire form of human condition. Authors communicate themselves to the people by some especial and extrinsic mark; I, the first of any, by my universal being; as Michael de Montaigne, not as a grammarian, a poet, or a lawyer . . . I have this, at least, according to discipline, that never any man treated of a subject he better understood and knew, than I what I have undertaken, and that in this I am the most understanding man alive: secondly, that never any man penetrated farther into his matter, nor better and more distinctly sifted the parts and sequences of it, nor ever more exactly and fully arrived at the end he proposed to himself. (pp. 388c-389b)

Another characteristic of Montaigne's thought which is revealed in this significant passage is his sense of the changeability of things and the difficulty, if not impossibility, of making absolutely certain statements about anything, particularly about human character and conduct. He wrote a whole book-length piece, "Apology for Raimon de Sebonde" (Book II, Essay 12), dealing with the uncertainty of human reason. In the essay "Of repentance" he accepts this changeability as a condition of his own self-portrait.

Now, though the features of my picture alter and change, 'tis not, however, unlike: the world eternally turns round; all things therein are incessantly moving . . . I cannot fix my object; 'tis always tottering and reeling by a natural giddiness: I take it as it is at the instant I consider it; I do not paint its being, I paint its passage . . . from minute to minute. I must accommodate my history to the hour: I may presently change, not only by fortune, but also by intention . . . so it is, that I may per-adventure contradict myself, but, as Demades said, I never contradict the truth. Could my soul once take footing, I would not essay but re-solve: but it is always learning and making trial. (p. 388c-d)

Montaigne lived in an unsettled and troubled time, and he reflects contemporary disturbances in his essays, sometimes commenting on them directly and using them as examples for the points he is making. His fellow Frenchmen were slaughtering one another in a civil war between Catholics and Protestants, which was marked by horrible massacres and tortures. The succession to the throne of France was uncertain and led to a dynastic dispute. The discovery of America had opened up new sources of conflict among the European na-tions, as well as new vistas in the minds of Europeans as they became aware of new peoples and new lands. Montaigne lived in a transitional era, at the end of the Renaissance and before the advent of the "modern" revolutionary age.

Montaigne's essays have certain characteristics that may prove distracting or irritating if one is looking for a definite doctrine, for instance, a moral philosophy. In the first place, he quotes copiously from the writings of the past, mostly from Greek and Latin authors, to serve as examples of various points of view or as particular instances of some general point he is making. In the second place, he indulges in various digressions from the subject he is dealing with, often without any particular purpose, as he confesses when he recalls him-self to the main topic. In the third place, it is often hard to tell just what the main topic of an essay is, since he may start with one subject and end up with another, and even the title may have little if anything to do with the content of an essay. (The essays in Book III are much more unified than those in Books I-II. See, for instance, the essay "Of repentance.")

If the reader, forewarned, will be patient and accept Montaigne's rambling, unconstrained method, he will be re-warded. He will share in the musings of a richly perceptive and keenly intelligent man, who expresses himself with a rare honesty and geniality in some of the most enjoyable writings in the Western tradition. Montaigne himself was intimately immersed in the works and thoughts of the writers of the past, as even a cursory reading of his essays will indicate. Most of the works we have discussed in this reading plan were well known to him and were an essential element in his mental nourishment. It is especially fortunate for an understanding of his moral philosophy that we have already considered Epictetus' *Discourses,* since Montaigne has a close affinity with the Stoic (and also Epicurean) philosophers. An awareness of this link, for instance, may help us better to understand what Montaigne meant by saying that our judgments of good and bad are influenced by our opinions of things.

The essays that comprise this reading have been selected to bring out the basic principles and themes of Montaigne's ethical thought and to indicate his agreement or disagreement with the thinkers whom we have previously considered in this reading plan. However, they comprise only a portion of the essays that deal with moral themes. The reader is invited, after finishing these selections, to browse through Volume 25 to discover for himself all that Montaigne has to say about human character and moral action.

II

Some of the essential principles of Montaigne's moral philosophy, as well as his closeness to the ancient Stoics, are to be found in the first essay in our reading: "That to study philosophy is to learn to die." The sole end of human reason, says Montaigne, is human contentment, living well, tranquillity of spirit. Virtue enables us "to despise pain, poverty, and the other accidents to which human life is subject" (p. 28d). Above all, it rids us of the worst affliction of all, the fear of death, which is a "perpetual torment" for the unphilosophic and the unvirtuous.

Philosophy paradoxically teaches us to live well by teaching us how to die well, that is, to face death well. Here it differs from common opinion, which advises us to ignore death, not to think about it. Montaigne confesses that he would prefer to follow this course, but recognizes that it is futile, since death comes inevitably and unpredictably and is most painful for the man who is not prepared for it. The way to overcome and disarm death is to confront it boldly, to become familiar with it, to have it always in one's thoughts. Montaigne advises us to view every accident or mishap, even a pin prick, as a possible death.

Where death waits for us is uncertain; let us look for him everywhere. The premeditation of death is the premeditation of liberty; he who has learned to die, has unlearned to serve. There is nothing of evil in life, for him who rightly comprehends that the privation of life is no evil: to know how to die, delivers us from all subjection and constraint. (p. 31a-b)

He tells how he has methodically disciplined himself to meditate on death, so that what at first brought a twinge of horror and dread has gradually become a familiar idea and image. He is ready to die, without regret, at any moment; this readiness involves a detachment from all relations with others. "Always . . . be booted and spurred, and ready to go," he advises, and above all, take care at that time "to have no business with any one but one's self" (pp. 31d-32a).

The main moral aim is to rid the soul of "disquiet, anxiety, or fear, or any other disturbance" (p. 33c). When this is accomplished, the soul becomes

. . . sovereign of all her lusts and passions, mistress of necessity, shame, poverty, and all the other injuries of fortune. Let us, therefore, as many of us as can, get this advantage; 'tis the true and sovereign liberty here on earth, that fortifies us wherewithal to defy violence and injustice, and to contemn prisons and chains. (p. 33c)

Montaigne's main argument against the fear of death, man's greatest fear, is that death is a natural necessity; hence, wisdom lies in accepting it willingly.

". . . Your death is a part of the order of the universe, 'tis a part of the life of the world . . . 'Tis the condition of your creation; death is a part of you, and whilst you endeavour to evade it, you evade yourselves . . ." (p. 34b)

Above all, we must recognize that it is not death which is evil, but not having lived well. It is within our power to make life good or evil. And the goodness and sufficiency of life do not depend on its length.

"Wherever your life ends, it is all there. The utility of living consists not in the length of days, but in the use of time; a man may have lived long, and yet lived but a little. Make use of time while it is present with you. It depends upon your will, and not upon the number of days, to have a sufficient length of life . . ." (p. 35c)

See also this comment in a latter essay: " 'tis the happy living, and not . . . the happy dying, in which human felicity consists" (p. 394c).

This concern with death and the proper way to face it is a theme that runs throughout Montaigne's *Essays*. (For his view of suicide, see "A custom of the Isle of Cea," Book II, Essay 3.)

The basic attitude of soul that he espouses in regard to death is more fully developed in the famous essay "That the relish of good and evil depends in a great measure upon the opinion we have of them," a title-theme which Shakespeare rephrased in *Hamlet* as "There is nothing either good or bad, but thinking makes it so" (Vol. 27, p. 43b). This essay indicates perhaps better than any other, Montaigne's close affinity with the Stoic moral doctrine, as we have seen it expressed in Epictetus' *Discourses*.

The main point in this essay is that we can disregard things that we usually regard as utterly evil—for instance, death, poverty, and pain—through directing our thought, imagination, and will in a proper manner. Our evaluation of things, Montaigne argues, is in the mind, not in the things.

Men (says an ancient Greek sentence) are tormented with the opinions they have of things and not by the things themselves. It were a great victory obtained for the relief of our miserable human condition, could this proposition be established for certain and true throughout. For if evils have no admission into us but by the judgment we ourselves make of them, it should seem that it is, then, in our own power to despise them or to turn them to good. If things surrender themselves to our mercy, why do we not convert and accommodate them to our advantage? If what we call evil and torment is neither evil nor torment of itself, but only that our fancy gives it that quality, it is in us to change it, and, it being in our own choice, if there be no constraint upon us we must certainly be very strange fools to take arms for that side which is most offensive to us, and to give sickness, want, and contempt a bitter and nauseous taste, if it be in our power to give them a pleasant relish, and if, fortune simply providing the matter, 'tis for us to give it the form. Now, that what we call evil is not so of itself, or at least to that degree that we make it, and that it depends upon us to give it another taste and complexion (for all comes to one), let us examine how that can be maintained. (p. 115b-c)

In this essay Montaigne considers pain, rather than death, as "the worst incident of our being," since it confronts us with something far more immediate than the mental anticipation of death. Our very physical-sensitive nature makes us shrink from pain. But our powers of reason and will enable us, "if not to annihilate, at least to lessen" the pain. The withstanding of pain is one of the chief elements of virtue.

It is the contentment of the soul that matters, and not the suffering of the body. The soul is "the sole and sovereign mistress of our condition" and can be changed in the direction we desire, while the body is unalterably set by natural necessity. Since the soul has

. . . many thousands of biasses . . . at her disposal, let us give her one proper to our repose and conservation, and then we shall not only be sheltered and secured from all manner of injury and offence, but moreover gratified and obliged, if she will, with evils and offences . . . 'Tis plain enough to be seen that 'tis the sharpness of our mind that gives the edge to our pains and pleasures . . . (p. 119c)

Reason has been given to us to render us virtuous and happy, not to make us live in fear and anxiety about what may happen to us. We should not use our great gift of understanding to "lose the tranquillity and repose we should enjoy without it," and to set ourselves "against the design of nature and the universal order of things" (p. 118a). Hence, in dealing with our "fancies" about pleasures and pains, "let us at least help to incline them to the most agreeable side," for, given a disciplined and controlled will, pain "has no more room in us than we are pleased to allow it" (p. 119d).

Montaigne testifies from his personal experience that plenty and poverty are a matter of opinion: he never felt so anxious financially as when he was hoarding a good deal of money, nor so well off as when he was living on borrowed money. He concludes,

Plenty, then, and indigence depend upon the opinion every one has of them; and riches no more than glory or health have other beauty or pleasure than he lends them by whom they are possessed. Every one is well or ill at ease, according as he so finds himself: not he whom the world believes, but he who believes himself to be so, is content; and in this alone belief gives itself being and reality. Fortune does us neither good nor hurt; she only presents us the matter and the seed, which our soul, more powerful than she, turns and applies as she best pleases; the sole cause and sovereign mistress of her own happy or unhappy condition. All external accessions receive taste and colour from the internal constitution . . . The things are not so painful and difficult of themselves, but our weakness or cowardice makes them so. To judge of great and high matters requires a suitable soul; otherwise we attribute the vice to them which is really our own. A straight oar seems crooked in the water: it does not only import that we see the thing, but how and after what manner we see it. (p. 124c-d)

Also in line with this Stoic emphasis is the essay "Of glory," in which Montaigne argues against the view that glory, reputation, or public approbation is a good to be prized and sought by virtuous men. He agrees explicitly with the ancient Stoics and Epicureans that the inner awareness of one's virtue should be prized, to the exclusion of public recognition and acclaim. We may divide his argument into a theoretical and a practical part.

He argues theoretically that virtue is essentially an inward thing, a matter of the proper "operation of the soul" which is to be pursued for itself alone. Virtue is its own reward. He argues practically that reputation is a matter of chance, a will-o'-the-wisp, which it is ridiculous to chase at all costs. Besides, public opinion, "the voice of the people," of the ignorant rabble, is not the proper judge of virtue. Reason should be our sole judge and our guide, not "this windy confusion of the noise of vulgar reports and opinions" (p. 303d). Montaigne offers a very practical argument for following this course —that it usually leads to happiness.

Even though I would not follow the right way because it is right, I should, however, follow it as having experimentally found that, at the end of the reckoning, 'tis commonly the most happy and of greatest utility . . . (pp. 303d-304a)

Montaigne also admits that reputation has certain good

side effects, practically speaking, since it brings us good will and protects us from insults; and he is aware of the pragmatic value of glory and honor in stirring men to pursue virtue and to do their duty.

> If this false opinion, nevertheless, be of such use to the public as to keep men in their duty; if the people are thereby stirred up to virtue ... let it by all means increase, and be as much as possible nursed up and cherished amongst us ... (p. 306a-b)

However, strictly speaking, there is something ridiculous in putting such great store in external judgments, which are necessarily uncertain and erroneous, in preference to the "certain testimony" of our own self-knowledge. Yet men are so pleased at hearing their names on other men's lips that they are even willing to be talked about in a derogatory way; they do not care what is said about them so long as something is said.

> This is very common; we are more solicitous that men speak of us, than how they speak: and it is enough for us that our names are often mentioned, be it after what manner it will. It should seem that to be known, is in some sort to have a man's life and its duration in others' keeping. I, for my part, hold that I am not, but in myself; and of that other life of mine which lies in the knowledge of my friends, to consider it naked and simply in itself, I know very well that I am sensible of no fruit nor enjoyment from it but by the vanity of a fantastic opinion ... (pp. 304d-305a)

III

Montaigne's insistence on the virtue of being able to withstand or disregard pain is not coupled with any espousal of the virtue of asceticism—quite the contrary. "The main thing at which we all aim, even in virtue itself, is pleasure," he says in the first essay we considered. (See p. 28b.) The main virtue for him is moderation, which he discusses in the essay "Of moderation."

Any kind of excess is wrong for him, and he holds, as opposed to Aristotle, that there can be an excess of virtue. "A man may both be too much in love with virtue, and be excessive in a just action" (p. 89b). He is shocked at any case of immoderate zeal, or "savage virtue," as he calls it, such as in the ancient tales of parents who executed their sons for minor failings. He agrees with Callicles, in Plato's *Gorgias*, that philosophy, if it is followed too far, brutalizes a man and uproots him from his natural way of life. Anything good can become bad if it is pursued immoderately.

Conjugal love provides him with a good example of this reversal. Instead of the "sober and serious delight" which is proper, couples may seek to fulfill "indecent and inordinate desires" in marital intercourse. But while cautioning against the "intemperance and excess" which is possible even in "just and lawful" pleasures, Montaigne also inveighs against ascetic disciplines which try to deprive man of his good and natural pleasures. There is a more wholesome and a more natural way to cure intemperance than through "watchings, fastings, hairshirts, remote and solitary banishments, perpetual imprisonments, whips and other afflictions" (p. 91a). Such macerations and mutilations of natural desires are comparable to the human sacrifices offered to the gods in ancient religions.

We can find contrary advice in other essays, as in the one entitled "That we are to avoid pleasures, even at the expense of life" (Book I, Essay 32). There Montaigne seems to approve of Seneca's advice that we should withdraw from all worldly ambitions and pleasures, and that if this proves impossible, we should commit suicide. And he claims to find corroboration for this "Stoical roughness," though "with Christian moderation," in such famous churchmen as St. Hilary, who, according to legend, persuaded God through his prayers to take his wife and daughter out of this life, so they might share in the "eternal and heavenly beatitude." However, it is difficult to tell whether or not Montaigne is writing this essay with his tongue in his cheek.

More to the point, as regards Montaigne's views on temperance, is the essay "Of drunkenness, "in which he points out that all vices are not of the same level. Murder and treason are certainly much worse than idleness and lasciviousness. Some vices have more human qualities in them than others—"more soul," more generosity, or even "a mixture of knowledge, diligence, valour, prudence, dexterity, and address"

(p. 162d). However, drunkenness, the vice considered here, is not of these. It is "a gross and brutish vice . . . totally corporeal and earthly" (p. 162d), overthrowing the understanding and dulling the body.

Because it puts man in the worst state of all, "that wherein he loses the knowledge and government of himself" (p. 163a), Montaigne considers it a deplorable vice. However, in comparison with some other vices, it is not so bad; for although "unmanly and stupid," it is not "malicious and hurtful" to other men. Indeed the ancients considered such overindulgence as providing a wholesome relaxation and recreation for the soul. But Montaigne cautions against following this line of thought too far, for even a wise man may be disordered by too much wine, since he is a mere man with the same psychophysical constitution and weaknesses as everyone else.

He must shut his eyes against the blow that threatens him; he must tremble upon the margin of a precipice, like a child; nature having reserved these light marks of her authority, not to be forced by our reason and the stoic virtue, to teach man his mortality and our weakness; he turns pale with fear, red with shame, and groans with the cholic, if not with desperate outcry, at least with hoarse and broken voice:

> *Humani a se nihil alienum putet.*
> [Nothing human is alien to me.] (p. 166a; see also p. 118b-c)

Here Montaigne contradicts the Stoic doctrine that thinking controls our reactions to things. He goes on to express his suspicion of any extraordinary act of asceticism or bearing of pain. In such acts a man is beside himself, entirely out of his natural place; he is mad, in an ectasy which contrasts with sober wisdom, with the "regular government of the soul, which is carried on with measure and proportion" (p. 166d). Against all such "wild sallies" Montaigne holds up the middle way of moderation, between asceticism and overindulgence.

All actions exceeding the ordinary bounds are liable to sinister interpretation, forasmuch as our liking no more holds with what is above than with what is below it. (p. 166a)

See also this statement in a later essay:

The virtue of the soul does not consist in flying high, but in walking

orderly; its grandeur does not exercise itself in grandeur, but in mediocrity. (p. 391b)

Montaigne's advice on how to handle anger is typical of his
attitude toward the passions. In the essay "Of anger," he finds
it to be one of the most dangerous and irrational of passions,
since it deprives men entirely of rational judgment, turning
them against even evident truth and goodness. The naturally
choleric man requires tremendous will power to restrain his
anger. However, Montaigne points out, anger, if it is held back,
only increases and irritates a man still more beneath the sur-
face. "A man incorporates anger by concealing it" (p. 346c).
Montaigne offers the practical advice to make good use of our
anger, not to waste it but to direct it to some purpose. In
order to have any effect—in the family or other realm where
a man has authority—it must be managed judiciously, or otherwise people will not take it seriously.

In another essay, however, Montaigne appeals to his personal experience for evidence that an urgent passion, such as
intense sexual desire, may be successfully curbed, even in the
ultimate moment of "ecstasy and rapture."

I know very well it may be otherwise, and that a man may sometimes,
if he will, gain this point over himself to sway his soul, even in the critical moment, to think of something else; but then he must ply it to that
bent. I know that a man may triumph over the utmost effort of this
pleasure: I have experienced it in myself, and have not found Venus so
imperious a goddess, as many, and much more virtuous men than I,
declare. (p. 205a)

IV

Montaigne's general discussion of the nature of virtue is
to be found in the essay "Of cruelty." He makes a basic distinction between mere good nature and the virtue that is won
through hard self-discipline. True virtue does not come naturally; it is fostered and tested by difficulty and struggle. Was
Socrates, who was apparently without vicious inclinations
and completely ruled by reason, therefore not virtuous? Were
the Stoics, who were utterly unperturbed by evil and unaffected by pleasure, hence devoid of virtue?

Such questions lead Montaigne to distinguish three types

or levels of virtue. The highest type is the state in which virtue has become man's second nature, a fixed and settled habit of soul. The second type is the state in which a man struggles successfully with very urgent and powerful natural impulses. The third is a state of natural innocence and goodness, which can hardly be called virtue since it is effortless and which is sometimes difficult to distinguish from cowardice and unmanliness.

(See also the essay "Of virtue," where Montaigne distinguishes between "the starts and sallies of the soul, and a resolute and constant habit" [p. 340a]. The latter is the true virtue, since it is something lastingly imbedded in the soul. But the sudden, "miraculous" sallies of the heroes of ancient legend are so far beyond our natural power that it is hard to see how they can become "ordinary and natural" in a man.)

Montaigne confesses that he himself has been credited with a prudence, courage, and patience which he does not possess, and that he belongs on the lowest level of virtue. "My virtue is a virtue, or rather an innocence, casual and accidental" (p. 203c-d). He is fortunate to have been born with a good disposition, though without the strength, he avows, to resist vehement passions if he had them. The fact that he, like Epicurus, is more virtuous in his actions than in his opinions leads him to ask the odd question, "Must it be true, that to be a perfect good man, we must be so by an occult, natural, and universal propriety, without law, reason, or example?" (p. 204b).

As for those vices he does have, Montaigne proceeds in the prudent practical way we have become familiar with. His policy is to restrain the vices he has and to keep them from combining with other vices. "I follow some vices, but I fly others as much as a saint would do" (p. 204c). He disagrees that there must be a unity of vice or virtue, appealing to Aristotle for corroboration that "a prudent and just man may be intemperate and inconsistent" (p. 204c). (However, Aristotle does not agree with him, if we are to judge by the discussion of prudence [practical wisdom] in Book VI of the *Nicomachean Ethics*.)

The vice that upsets Montaigne most is cruelty (and here we finally get to the title-theme), for it goes against his innate tenderness, which makes him recoil from the sight of a chicken being killed or a hare being caught by a dog. He is extremely sensitive to seeing pain inflicted on others; hence the executions of criminals, in the form current in his day, fill him with horror. The tortures of the condemned man—drawing, quartering, and slow burning while still alive—seem barbarous and inhuman to him, far worse than the cannibals' roasting and eating of men who are already dead. "All that exceeds a simple death appears to me pure cruelty" (p. 205c). If desecrations of the body are intended to strike fear into would-be criminals, doing it to dead bodies of the executed would be dreadful enough, he argues. "Those inhuman excesses ought to be exercised upon the bark, and not upon the quick" (p. 206a). Referring to the barbarous cruelty of his own time, engendered by the wars of religion, he says:

I live in a time wherein we abound in incredible examples of this vice, through the licence of our civil wars; and we see nothing in ancient histories more extreme than what we have proof of every day, but I cannot, any the more, get used to it. I could hardly persuade myself, before I saw it with my eyes, that there could be found souls so cruel and fell, who, for the sole pleasure of murder, would commit it; would hack and lop off the limbs of others, sharpen their wits to invent unusual torments and new kinds of death, without hatred, without profit, and for no other end but only to enjoy the pleasant spectacle of the gestures and motions, the lamentable groans and cries of a man dying in anguish. For this is the utmost point to which cruelty can arrive . . . (p. 206b-c)

Montaigne's sensitive compassion, his intense fellow feeling for the pain suffered by others, extends to animals as well as men. He sees in the cruelty men inflict on beasts, as in hunting, the natural root of the cruelty they inflict on their fellows. "Those natures that are sanguinary towards beasts discover a natural propension to cruelty" (p. 206c). He describes vividly his own pain at seeing beasts pursued and killed, and argues that his sympathy is well grounded in the fact that they are fellow creatures of God. He is inclined to admit that there is a close resemblance between men and beasts, but even if this were not true, he argues,

. . . there is, nevertheless, a certain respect, a general duty of humanity, not only to beasts that have life and sense, but even to trees and plants. We owe justice to men, and graciousness and benignity to other creatures that are capable of it; there is a certain commerce and mutual obligation betwixt them and us. (p. 207c)

(See also the essay "Cowardice, the mother of cruelty," Book II, Essay 27.)

The unfavorable comparison between civilized and primitive society made in the essay on cruelty is developed fully in the famous essay "Of cannibals." Montaigne's opinion of the ethical quality of man in a state of nature contrasts sharply with that of Hobbes. In this time, fascinating accounts of the peoples in the newly discovered lands were being brought back by explorers and travelers. He bases his opinion on information he has received from a man who had lived in the New World for many years.

Montaigne's interpretation of this information rests on certain basic assumptions. One of these is that it is the natural or primitive that embodies right order and the artificial or civilized that is degenerate, corrupt, and disordered. The so-called savages, says he, are still governed by the laws of nature, and still live in that Golden Age, that "happy state of man," envisioned by poets and philosophers of antiquity. (See also in his note to the reader the remark about the nations that still "dwell under the sweet liberty of nature's primitive laws" [p. 1].) The purity of life in this natural state, free from the inequities that exist in civilized society, far surpasses Plato's dream of an ideal republic. Indeed, "the very words that signify lying, treachery, dissimulation, avarice, envy, detraction, pardon, [are] never heard of" (p. 94a).

Montaigne discerns two main virtues in the ethics of these "savages": valor in war and love of their wives. As for cannibalism, it is merely the ultimate revenge against enemies captured in battle. Though admitting "the barbarous horror of so cruel an action," Montaigne argues that it is far less inhumane than the horrible executions of living men—often merely for disagreement in religious matters—by his fellow countrymen in "civilized" France. He also argues that, though there may be some excuse for cannibalism in certain situations, the familiar vices of civilized society—"treachery, disloyalty, tyranny, and cruelty"—can never be excused.

He also compares the savages favorably with civilized men in their wars, which are "throughout noble and generous," impelled solely by the desire to demonstrate valor, never by the desire to take other men's lands and goods. In their primitive felicity, they "only covet so much as their natural necessities require," and possess "this greatest of all goods, to know happily how to enjoy their condition and to be content" (p. 96a).

In this essay Montaigne discusses courage, a virtue which plays a central role in primitive ethics. He insists that courage is to be judged purely by what belongs to a man himself, to his soul, not by physical or mechanical powers and equipment. Moreover, it is to be judged by motivation, not results.

We have sufficient advantages over our enemies that are borrowed and not truly our own; it is the quality of a porter, and no effect of virtue, to have stronger arms and legs; it is a dead and corporeal quality to set in array: 'tis a turn of fortune to make our enemy stumble, or to dazzle him with the light of the sun; 'tis a trick of science and art, and that may happen in a mean base fellow, to be a good fencer. The estimate and value of a man consist in the heart and in the will: there his true honour lies. Valour is stability, not of legs and arms, but of the courage and the soul; it does not lie in the goodness of our horse or our arms: but in our own. He that falls obstinate in his courage—*Si succiderit, de genu pugnat* —he who, for any danger of imminent death, abates nothing of his assurance; who, dying, yet darts at his enemy a fierce and disdainful look, is overcome not by us, but by fortune; he is killed, not conquered; the most valiant are sometimes the most unfortunate. There are defeats more triumphant than victories . . . The part that true conquering is to play, lies in the encounter, not in the coming off; and the honour of valour consists in fighting, not in subduing. (pp. 96c-97a)

V

Montaigne's essay "Of repentance" is one of the most direct, congenial, and lucid presentations of his moral philosophy. It opens with the acknowledgment that he himself is the main subject matter of his essays. (See the citations above in Section I.) As regards the title-theme, he feels bound to tell us, "I very rarely repent . . . my conscience is satisfied with itself" (p. 389c), and then launches into a discussion of repentance on the basis of his own experience, in the context of his time.

Vice (and in this Montaigne includes what is condemned by law and custom as well as by reason and nature) always offends the guilty man and "leaves repentance in the soul, like an ulcer in the flesh, which is always scratching and lacerating itself" (p. 389c). He contrasts this with the inner glow of satisfaction that accompanies virtue. The opinion of others, as we have seen, is no substitute for this authentic satisfaction, and especially, remarks Montaigne, in "so depraved . . . so corrupt and ignorant an age" as the one in which he is living. A good conscience is far more precious than the good opinion of other men when "the licence of the time permits and teaches every one" to engage in all kinds of reprehensible vices. (See p. 389d.) We must rely on a settled pattern in ourselves to judge our actions rightly. With this, and with the intimate self-knowledge which no one else can have, we know when we are guilty of wrong acts or attitudes. This is where repentance comes in.

Repentance, however, which Montaigne defines as "a recanting of the will and an opposition to our fancies" (p. 390c), cannot follow immediately after sin when it is a matter of long habituation. Repentance involves the redirection of natural inclinations, which is no easy task. Education and external reforms have little or no effect on our inclinations, merely concealing them for the time being. Each of us has "a particular and governing form of his own, that jostles his education, and wrestles with the tempest of passions that are contrary to it" (p. 392a).

Our natural propensities, longstanding practice, and the desire for pleasure are among the many obstacles to true repentance. Where such factors are involved (Montaigne gives "the enjoyment of women" as an example), it is hard for us to recognize that what we are doing is wrong or to stop it. Nevertheless, where vices are "often repeated, deliberated, and contrived," Montaigne is convinced that they are performed with the assent of a man's reason and conscience. Hence, he is skeptical about the authenticity of "sudden" repentance, with its supposed inner grief and remorse, especially if it is not accompanied by any correction or interruption of the acts the person claims to repent of. Repentance is a matter of action, not of mere thoughts or wishes; it involves the whole man. "I know no repentance, superficial, half-way, and ceremonious; it must sting me all over before I can call it so" (p. 393b).

Montaigne is scornful of the so-called repentance that comes with the slackening of the natural faculties in old age, when reason has to contend only with temptations "so broken and mortified, that they are not worth its opposition."

Miserable kind of remedy, to owe one's health to one's disease! 'Tis not that our misfortune should perform this office, but the good fortune of our judgment. I am not to be made to do anything by persecutions and afflictions, but to curse them; that is for people who cannot be roused but by a whip.

. . . .

I repudiate, then, these casual and painful reformations. God must touch our hearts; our consciences must amend of themselves, by the aid of our reason, and not by the decay of our appetites; pleasure is, in itself, neither pale nor discoloured, to be discerned by dim and decayed eyes.

We ought to love temperance for itself, and because God has commanded that and chastity; but that which we are reduced to by catarrhs, and for which I am indebted to the stone, is neither chastity nor temperance; a man cannot boast that he despises and resists pleasure, if he cannot see it, if he knows not what it is, and cannot discern its graces, its force, and most alluring beauties; I know both the one and the other, and may therefore the better say it. (pp. 394b-395a)

Thus reason and will are central in Montaigne's interpretation of repentance. We can repent only for what is in our power and initiated by us. We may *regret* that we are not better endowed by nature than we are, but it is ridiculous to *repent* our nature. Nor can we repent bad turns of fortune in the uncertain affairs of human life. We may curse our luck, but it would be foolish to blame ourselves. Repentance has to do only with the small private sphere of personal responsibility and freedom.

Repentance should be directed to the future, to what can be changed, not to the past, which Montaigne regards for all practical purposes as determined. He regards repentance as prospective, not retrospective.

In all affairs that are past, be it how it will, I have very little regret; for this imagination puts me out of my pain, that they were so to fall out: they are in the great revolution of the world, and in the chain of stoical causes: your fancy cannot, by wish and imagination, move one tittle, but that the great current of things will not reverse both the past and the future. (p. 394a)

Montaigne looks back on his own life with satisfaction, not regret.

Were I to live my life over again, I should live it just as I have lived it; I neither complain of the past, nor do I fear the future; and if I am not much deceived, I am the same within that I am without. (p. 394c-d)

VI

Does Montaigne think that good and evil are merely a matter of opinion?

To answer this question judiciously requires a careful reading of the essay on learning to die and most of the other essays that we have considered, as well as the essay on the "relish" of good and evil. In the first essay mentioned, Montaigne states that reason has been given us to secure happiness, welfare, and tranquillity, and that virtue enables us to disregard such "accidents" as pain and poverty and, above all, death. May we assume, then, that in his mind happiness, etc. are really good, and such things as the fear of death are really evil?

If so, what is the criterion by which we distinguish good and evil? Is it peace of mind on the one hand, and disturbance and anxiety on the other, as it seems to be in Epictetus' *Discourses?* Is what makes for the one "good" and what makes for the other "evil"? If so, where does "opinion" come in?

Montaigne obviously includes in the term "opinion" our ideas, images, anticipations, and attitudes. If these are properly directed and controlled, he argues, we may face all the negative aspects of human existence, including death, courageously and tranquilly, and lead a good life. Since external and physical ills are unavoidable, he advocates that we should discipline our minds and attain the only kind of contentment and pleasure that matters—an inward state of soul.

How do "opinions" accomplish this? In the case of pain, we "incline them to the most agreeable side"; in the case of death, we simply become familiar with it and come to view it as natural. At times, it seems that Montaigne is making our estimation of good and evil in things merely a matter of subjective feeling, as in the case of his tranquillity while living in debt and his anxiety while possessed of great sums. Would it be fair, though, to say that Montaigne does consider pain an objective evil, since he purposes by controlling opinions to lessen if not to annihilate it?

What would be the difference between Montaigne's position and that of a man who affirmed that death, pain, and other ills were real evils, that it is awful to die and suffer physical pain, and the like; but who also affirmed that, since these evils are unavoidable, we must face them courageously, disciplining ourselves to live nobly and virtuously, nevertheless? Would Montaigne agree with this? Does his remark that "one person, peradventure, admits them [things] in their true being" (p. 115d) amount to an admission that we may see things as they are? See also, on page 124d, the comparison between the moral judgment of a man of weak character and the distorted appearance of the oar in the water.

Does Montaigne believe that our conduct should be governed by the moral standards of our place and time?

We have referred in Section I to the times in which Montaigne lived and the impression they made on him. But it is rash to go on from there to the easy judgment that Montaigne was simply reflecting the temper of his time. He was able to find support for his skepticism about human reason in many minds of the past; his study was decorated with carefully selected inscriptions from Ecclesiastes, Horace, Lucretius, Sextus, Empiricus, and other ancient skeptics. As for the morals and manners of his time, when he refers to them in the selections we have read, does he set them up as a model to be emulated?

We have seen in the essay "Of glory" how little he values public opinion and approbation, the temporary and unsubstantial acclaim of the present hour. In the essay "Of repentance" we have seen how he despised the morals and manners of his time and appealed against this to a settled pattern of right and wrong in our hearts. And in the essay "Of cruelty" we have seen how horrified he was by the cruel modes of execution prevalent in his time ("I cannot . . . get used to it" [p. 206b]), and how he proposes reforming them to conform with a standard of human decency.

Does such an austerely ethical position contradict his avid interest in the varieties of human behavior and customs? See, for instance, his essay "Of custom" (Book I, Essay 22), where he describes all kinds of customs, including cannibalism, without invidious moral comment, and points out the strong influence of custom in social life. How are Montaigne's anthropological and ethical concerns balanced in his essay "Of cannibals"? Is he merely providing a simple anthropological description and interpretation of the savages, or does he also give us an ethical judgment about whether their life is good or bad? Does he consider civilized society as only one variation among others in human history, or does he make a moral judgment about it? Montaigne explains the socio-cultural reasons why the savages eat their fellow men. Does he advance any ethical judgment about cannibalism?

In the instance where he makes an analogy between asceticism and the live sacrifices of archaic religions, is he making an ethical judgment on the ancient practice? Do ethical judgments transcend religious sanctions? Scholars in the archaic and primitive religions are convinced that human sacrifices and cannibal feasts were religious rites aimed at keeping up the vital economy of the universe. Would the fact that cannibalism was the fulfillment of a religious responsibility make it immune from ethical judgment?

Assuming that there are universal ethical norms, just how are they related to the variations in custom which Montaigne so avidly noted? Is the type of dress (or undress) regulable by universal ethical norms? What about marriage customs, such as monogamy, polygamy, and polyandry? What about sexual mores, dietary customs, and economic practices? What about theft, murder, and lying? What about cruelty?

Are the cruel modes of execution that Montaigne discusses a matter of permissible variation? Are they merely the understandable expressions of particular cultures? In medieval Europe such forms of punishment were accepted by the Church and applied to religious dissidents. Does this indicate that even the official repositories of moral judgments are deeply influenced by the customs of their time? If so, does this mean that cruelty is not evil—a matter of taste in a particular time and place?

Is man good in a state of nature?

On the basis of what his informant has told him, Montaigne paints a glowing picture of primitive society as a serene "heaven." On the basis of what Montaigne says, we may question just how "natural" his cannibals are and just how good they are, by his own standards. His savages are not isolated individuals like Hobbes's, but members of a social group, living according to a social code and sharing common beliefs. Their very cannibalism is the fulfillment of the social code, not of animal hunger. And the same may be said of their supreme virtue—courage.

As for the pristine goodness which the civilized reader is called upon to envy, the details in the essay on cannibals seem to contradict the laudatory reference to them in the essay on cruelty. Psychological tortures in an attempt to break the prisoners' spirits are described, which apparently include graphic descriptions not only of eating the prisoners, but also "the torments they are to suffer" before dying. Apparently the psychological and physical tortures are all part of the game of making the prisoner beg for his life, a game in which the victim accepts the rules and plays it out to the end. But how does this socio-cultural explanation absolve the savages from what Montaigne considers one of the most vicious vices of all— cruelty? (For Montaigne's own awareness of the horrible cruelties perpetrated in the new "pure and virgin" lands, see p. 91b.) And we might note that the hunting of animals has been an accepted activity in most primitive societies. Would the natural man shrink, like Montaigne, from the sight of a stag at bay?

Just how good does Montaigne really think man is by nature? He speaks of "a natural propension to cruelty," and adds: "Nature has herself, I fear, imprinted in man a kind of instinct to inhumanity" (p. 206c), that is, to cruelty. Is compassion, then, an artificial development opposed to natural instinct? Is man naturally cruel or naturally compassionate? Or is he by nature able to be either?

Is the Stoic attitude which Montaigne advocates a natural or artificial development? Do men naturally shrink from pain and other ills, and then discipline themselves, through their reason and will, not to recoil? Are reason and will—on which Montaigne places so much emphasis in his account of moral virtue—then opposed to the natural? Or are they a specific human development of the natural? What function do reason and will serve, in Montaigne's view, in relating man to the natural universe?

Is a man's treatment of animals subject to ethical judgment?

Many traditional moralists have limited ethics to a man's relations with his fellow men; others have also included his treatment of himself. Montaigne, in addition, emphasizes man's treatment of beasts. Is this acceptable? If a man treated his fellow men justly and lived a personally virtuous life, would his cruelty toward animals be a matter of indifference, from an ethical viewpoint? Is cruelty—the deliberate and unnecessary infliction of pain—evil? If so, is it evil when inflicted on animals? If so, on what grounds? Montaigne's grounds are that animals are our fellow creatures and even very near our kin. Do you agree that these are sound grounds for compassion toward them? Could you accept the maxim that we should not harm any living thing? Would you include plants in this interdiction?

Practically speaking, what would cruelty toward animals do to a man's character? Is it plausible that a man might be just and virtuous, and at the same time be cruel to animals, as in our hypothetical case?

Does Montaigne have a social ethics?

Certainly, in the essays we have read, Montaigne opposes vigorously doing harm or injustice to other men. Does he go beyond this to what our positive concerns and acts toward others should be? Or is his ethics basically an individualistic ethics, centered on the fulfillment and contentment of the self? What would be Montaigne's attitude toward political action or social reform? Why does he advise us not to get involved with other men and their problems?

The following questions are designed to help you test the thoroughness of your reading. Each question is to be answered by giving a page or pages of the reading assignment. Answers will be found on page 303 of this Reading Plan.

1 What were the hour and day of Montaigne's birth?

2 What was the Egyptian manner of reminding men of death?

3 Why does Thomas Aquinas forbid marriages between close relatives?

4 What did Chrysippus and Zeno think about eating dead men?

5 What was it about civilized society that amazed the visiting savages?

6 To what tortures do women submit themselves for the sake of beauty?

7 In what sense are vices all alike?

8 At what age, according to Plato, is it all right to get drunk?

9 Whose good opinion does Montaigne seek?

10 Why is it wrong to use the term "honor" for a lady's virtue?

SPINOZA

Ethics

Part V

Vol. 31, pp. 451-463

Imagine, if you can, a work like Aquinas' "Treatise on the Last End" written by a thinker who combined the mental dispositions of an Epictetus, an Aquinas, and a Hobbes, and who was deeply influenced by Aristotle's ethics and Descartes's metaphysics. Add to all this a geometrical form of presentation, like Euclid's, and you will have some idea of what Part V of Spinoza's *Ethics*—"Of the Power of the Intellect, or of Human Liberty"—comprises.

Like Epictetus, Spinoza sought a way to free man from suffering and frustration and to provide an abiding peace of mind. Like Aquinas, he saw God as the ultimate source and goal of man's way. Like Hobbes, he found a bodily basis for human emotions and thoughts.

But this very combination of similarities indicates his difference from each of these thinkers, who differed significantly among themselves. Man is not essentially mind for him, as for Epictetus, but is also essentially body. The movements of the mind and the body parallel one another. Hence any improvement or right ordering of human life must involve a physical as well as a mental change. But this is a parallelism of mind and body, not a reduction of mental to material activities, as in Hobbes, with whom Spinoza has so many apparent points of resemblance.

Similarly, although there is an identity of philosophical language between Spinoza and Aquinas, and although both thinkers begin and end with God, they mean something different by this term. For Spinoza, God, viewed in one aspect, is the same as the natural world. All things are part of God including man himself who through his mind and body shares in the divine attributes of thought and extension. Here Spinoza is closer to Epictetus (though without the latter's anthropomorphic language) than to Aquinas, and perhaps closer to Eastern than to Western modes of thought.

In his guide to human happiness, Spinoza combines in a unique way the mystical and the rational, the spiritual and the physical, the ethical and the natural. Opposition from religious leaders of his own day prevented the publication of the *Ethics* while Spinoza was alive, and his writings were considered damnable for a century after his death. Gradually, however, the man who was castigated in his own time as an "unclean and foul atheist" acquired widespread respect, and even veneration, as a kind of secular saint. (Novalis called him "a God-intoxicated man.") Eventually, he became honored in his own country with a monument to his memory and a plaque marking his home.

Ninth Reading

I

The most obvious thing about Spinoza's *Ethics* is its geometrical form of presentation. The book starts with a series of definitions and axioms and then proceeds to propositions that are based on the definitions and axioms. (See p. 355.) The selection we have chosen, after a preface in the customary expository style, begins with two axioms and goes on to a series of propositions. (See p. 452.) The use of the geometrical style in all its details is most unusual in philosophical writing; indeed, Spinoza's *Ethics* is the only important philosophical work in the Western tradition written in this style. (He also wrote his exposition of Descartes's philosophy in geometrical style.)

Harry A. Wolfson, who has made a careful and monumental study of Spinoza's thought, tells us that the geometrical method of demonstration, based on Euclid's geometry, consists of the following elements:

First, the primary truths which form the premises in the demonstrations are grouped together and placed apart from the demonstrations as the first principles upon which the demonstrations rest, and are divided into definitions, postulates, and axioms or common notions, second, that which is sought to be demonstrated, that is, the conclusion which is to be established by the demonstration, is summarized apart from the demonstration in the form of a proposition. Third, the demonstration itself reasons from the known, that is, the first principles, to the unknown, that is, the conclusion. Fourth, supplementary deductions, explanations, and propositions are given in the form of corollaries, scholia, and lemmas.[1]

One of the customary explanations for Spinoza's use of this

[1] Harry A. Wolfson, *The Philosophy of Spinoza* (Cambridge, Mass.: Harvard University Press, 1948), Vol. I, p. 40.

method has been that he had a "geometrical mind," and that the style came naturally to him, perfectly fitting his thought. But Wolfson says that we should hesitate to come to such a conclusion before considering the following points. (1) There is a distinction between the geometrical *method of demonstration* and the geometrical *style of exposition*. (2) One of the types of geometrical demonstration is simply syllogistic reasoning (from premises to conclusions), familiar to philosophers since early times. (3) A geometrical demonstration need not be presented in geometrical style and, conversely, the latter is not determined by a particular subject matter. (4) "Spinoza's mathematical way of looking at things means only the denial of design in nature and freedom in man, and this need not necessarily be written in the geometrical literary form."[2]

Wolfson produces much cogent evidence from the history of philosophy to prove his points, and also notes the interesting and relevant fact that Spinoza had already presented his mathematical way of looking at the world in ordinary expository style in his *Short Treatise on God, Man and His Well-Being*. Moreover, he planned to do a work on Hebrew grammar (certainly not a mathematical subject) in the geometrical manner. We might conveniently say that he chose to write the *Ethics* in the geometrical style to express the absolute necessity which rules events and human actions ("I shall consider human actions and appetites just as if I were considering lines, planes, or bodies" [p. 395c]) and to bring out clearly the essential properties of things. (See p. 370c.) But the history of philosophy and Spinoza's own works demonstrate that this kind of thought does not have to be couched in the style in which Euclid wrote his geometry. Why, then, did Spinoza write the *Ethics* in geometrical style?

Wolfson suggests some of the reasons which may have motivated Spinoza's choice. The first and most important may have been pedagogical—to present his thought as clearly and distinctly as possible, for the convenience of the reader and also to make him go through the process of thought himself.

---

[2] *Ibid.*, p. 45.

Secondly, it is also possible, judging from certain remarks which Spinoza himself made, that he wrote in this way as a reaction against the figurative literary style fashionable in the Renaissance, which made for a fuzziness of presentation if not of thought. The geometrical style may have been a way of regaining the precision of the formal scholastic method of presentation. Thirdly, it provided a convenient method of presenting one's own argument without having to argue against all the opposing views, as was customary in the rabbinical and scholastic methods. (Recall the time spent on objections and replies in the selection from Aquinas.) Finally, Wolfson suggests, Spinoza "had something new to say, and he wished to say it in a new way."[3]

In any case, whatever reasons Spinoza may have had for choosing this style, it is the style in which the book is written and, however unusual it may be, there is no reason to feel repelled by it. We are interested in getting at the thought that is presented through this form, and the thought is a good deal more difficult than the form. It is not necessary fully to understand and accept each one of Spinoza's axioms, definitions, and propositions before going on to the next. They hang together in the whole that Spinoza is constructing as he goes along, and we cannot really understand any one of them fully until we have seen the whole picture. Actually, the method he uses makes it convenient to refer to any statement made earlier in the work, somewhat as in the scholastic method used by Aquinas.

Besides, there are "breathers" from time to time in the form of prefaces, appendices, and scholia, where Spinoza writes direct expository statements and explanations of his thought. That he saw the necessity for such "breathers" is indicated by the remark in the Scholium to Prop. 18 in Part IV, where he states that before proceeding by the geometrical method he will directly set forth his thought, "in order that what I have in my mind . . . may be easily comprehended by all" (p. 429a).

Another indication that we should take the geometrical style in an easy manner, not too literally and not seeking

---

[3] *Ibid.*, p. 59.

absolute logical rigor, is that Spinoza himself seems to have ridden the geometrical method with an easy rein. Wolfson notes that

. . . his axioms, properly understood, are not necessarily self-evident truths, any more than his propositions are necessarily new truths discovered by demonstration. Most often they are merely restatements of generally accepted mediaeval brocards. It will be noticed that the "Axioms" mentioned in a letter from Oldenburg and also in the geometrical appendix to the *Short Treatise* are called "Propositions" in the *Ethics*, for the terms "definitions," "axioms," "propositions," and their like are used by Spinoza more or less indiscriminately as conventional labels to be pasted on here and there in order to give to his work the external appearance of a work of geometry.[4]

II

Spinoza's *Ethics* includes considerably more than what is included ordinarily under the term "ethics." The work is nothing less than a presentation of the basic principles of all reality, including God, nature, and man. To understand Spinoza's view of ethics, we must have some acquaintance with his view of the whole of reality, of the ways of knowing, and of human nature.

Reality is an organic whole, for Spinoza. It is not split into natural and supernatural realms, as with Aquinas, nor into separate physical and mental substances, as with Descartes. There is only one basic substance or reality, which we may call either "God" or "Nature." This absolutely infinite and primary being comprises infinite "attributes" (aspects or qualities). Only two of these attributes are known to us—thought and extension (space or matter). The finite things which make up the world are "modes" of the one basic substance; hence, they all contain thought and extension, that is, they are finite "modifications" of infinite thought and extension. Man, then, is a finite mode of God or Nature and, like Him or It, is both a physical and a mental being. So too is a fly or a stone, each in its own way.

Knowledge and understanding of the basic structure of

4 *Ibid.*, p. 58.

reality are necessary for human happiness, to fit man conformably and willingly into his place in the universe. Knowledge for Spinoza is of three kinds or levels. First comes "opinion," which comprises sense experience, imagination, and memory; through opinion, things are perceived discretely, apart from their connections in the whole. Second comes "reason," reached via intellect and abstract logic, in which things are perceived in their connections and under general laws, but not as a concrete whole. Third comes "intuition," in which the mind attains an immediate vision of the whole of reality.

Closely connected with this theory of knowledge are Spinoza's distinction between "adequate" and "inadequate" ideas, and his stress on the "coherence" of ideas as the test of truth. Only ideas that can be clearly conceived and distinguished, such as general notions, can be fitted coherently into a systematic apprehension of the whole of reality. Such ideas are "adequate." Sense perception, impressions, and images, however, are fuzzy and disjointed, each for itself and, in its raw state, unable to be fitted into a coherent apprehension of the whole. Such ideas are "inadequate." Scientific knowledge is possible only through "adequate" ideas.

Such knowledge is important from an ethical viewpoint because it plays an essential role in fitting man into the scheme of reality, enabling him to avoid suffering and frustration and to attain happiness and peace of mind. This practical goal is the end of speculative philosophy, as Spinoza noted in his work *On the Improvement of the Understanding,* where he tells us how he "resolved to inquire whether there might be some real good having power to communicate itself, which would affect the mind singly, to the exclusion of all else; whether, in fact, there might be anything of which the discovery and attainment would enable me to enjoy continuous, supreme, and unending happiness."

Spinoza's view of human nature is basic for his view of human character and conduct and for his program for the attainment of happiness. Indeed, to be good is to be what one is, to act in accordance with one's nature. Man is by nature body and mind. He does not *have* a body and a mind, but he *is* both at once. Whatever affects one, affects the other. They work in parallel. A physical change is always matched by a mental change. Such parallelism, which is obvious in pleasure and pain, occurs in all human "affects" (emotions).

The immanent principle that rules man's activity, as it rules all other things and events, is this: *"Each thing, in so far as it is in itself, endeavours to persevere in its being"* (p. 398d). (We may recall Hobbe's use of the term "endeavour.") This basic impulse or drive is identical with the *"actual essence of the thing itself"* (p. 399a). Human perfection lies in being fully what one is by nature, and the whole of man's will is directed to that end. Indeed, human *desire* is nothing but this basic drive, or "conatus," plus consciousness of it. *Pleasure* marks the transition to a higher stage of perfection; *pain,* the transition to a lower stage.

All human emotions are based on desire, pleasure, and pain. They are divided into "active" and "passive" emotions. Active emotions originate inside the person, and follow necessarily from his own nature; passive emotions originate outside the person and are "accidental" to his nature. The latter are the "passions" in the technical sense of "undergoing," and are associated with human suffering or "bondage," as Spinoza calls it. The former belong to the sphere of "action" in the proper sense, and are associated with self-realization and happiness.

The road to human freedom and happiness is marked by the transition from the passive to the active emotions. This is also a transition from the level of "opinion" and inadequate ideas to the level of "reason" and adequate ideas, and then to the level of intuitive insight, where the mind is at one with the basic eternal reality—God or Nature. A kind of psychotherapy is involved, as with the Stoics, but since body and mind are at one, we might call this a physiotherapy too, with a feeling of well-being of the entire organism as the mark of "cure."

The discussion of the emotions in Book III is followed by a discussion of human bondage, the virtues, and happiness in Book IV. Spinoza rejects the customary distinction between the emotions and the virtues, that is, between the psychological and the ethical. A man does whatever he does because he is moved to do so by some cause or combination of causes. Deliberate choice is not the originating cause of his action, for his choice and deliberation are also caused by something else. He cannot choose not to have the particular emotion he has. Only a stronger emotion can remove an emotion—not knowledge or will power. Knowledge, however, can become an emotion and can then affect action.

In any case, leaving aside customary moralistic connotations, "good" is simply what is useful or pleasant. *"Knowledge of good or evil is nothing but an affect of joy or sorrow in so far as we are conscious of it"* (p. 426b). Spinoza had some distinguished precedents in the philosophical tradition for this linking of the good with the useful and pleasant; note, for instance, Aristotle's linking of the good and the useful in the *Nicomachean Ethics* and in the *Politics*. (See Vol. 9, pp. 350b, 407a-c.)

The conflict between emotions results in "human impotence and want of stability" (p. 429a)—in human bondage to the emotions. But man can be freed from this bondage through reason, which is also a part of his nature. In the very significant Scholium to Prop. 18 in Part IV, Spinoza enumerates the "dictates of reason." In the first place, reason demands "that every person should love himself, should seek his own profit,—what is truly profitable to him" (p. 429a), that is, what leads to the perfection and preservation of his being. Virtue means "acting according to the laws of our own nature"; hence, the endeavor to preserve our own being is the basis of virtue. Happiness consists in the ability to preserve our own being. Hence virtue is to be desired for itself alone. So much for individual ethics and happiness.

But man is not alone in the world and cannot attain perfection without the aid of other beings. We depend on things outside us for our self-preservation and for the perfection of our intellect. Those things that are the most like us are the most salutary for us. "Nothing, therefore, is more useful to man than man" (p. 429c). The best thing for man would be the formation of a common body and mind, made up of all men, for the common good—that is, for the profit of each and all of them. Men governed by reason, and hence seeking their own profit, "desire nothing for themselves which they do not desire for other men," and hence are "just, faithful, and honourable" (p. 429c). Thus, contrary to common opinion, seeking one's own profit is the basis of virtue and piety.

The propositions that follow bring out the implications and applications of this significant scholium. Notable is the emphasis on the development or the understanding and the power of reason. Understanding is itself an expression of the endeavor to preserve one's being; hence, whatever conduces to understanding is adjudged good, and vice versa. Acting virtuously, in accordance with reason, and for one's own benefit (the preservation of one's being) are all the same thing. The height of this activity and of the development of the understanding is the knowledge of God—the absolutely infinite Being. *"The highest good of the mind is the knowledge of God, and the highest virtue of the mind is to know God"* (p. 431c). Reason is also stressed in the discussion of the social nature of man in Props. 29-40, for men agree through their mutual conformity with reason, and disagree through bondage to the passions.

Spinoza disagrees with Hobbes that man is by nature an egotistic anarchist. For Spinoza, man is by nature intended to live in a state of mutual aid and benefit. However, the power of emotions is too strong in a state of nature; men deviate from the dictates of reason and come into conflict with one another. Civil society, then, though an artificial construction, is a necessary means for man to achieve his natural perfection. Spinoza agrees with Hobbes, however, that there is no such thing as crime or justice and injustice until certain acts are prescribed or prohibited by civil authority. He ends the discussion with this resounding statement:

> *Whatever conduces to the universal fellowship of men, that is to say, whatever causes men to live in harmony with one another, is profitable, and, on the contrary, whatever brings discord into the State is evil.* (p. 437a)

The rest of Part IV (Props. 41-73) discusses the various virtues and vices. The main, indeed the sole, criterion of virtue is living in accordance with reason. This, according to Spinoza, rules out melancholy, hatred, hope and fear, pity, humility, repentance, and pride. The discussion ends with a eulogy of "the free man," the ideal human being. (See Props. 67-73.) He is the man of perfect virtue, who always acts rationally, gratefully, and honorably, and is most free in a state of civil society.

III

At various places in the earlier parts, Spinoza has promised that in Part V he will show the fruition of his program in human happiness. In his preface to this final section of the work, Spinoza says it concerns "the method or way which leads to liberty," that is, to freedom from the bondage of the passions—the harmful emotions. It will include two main topics: (1) the power of reason to control the emotions, and (2) what "freedom of mind or blessedness" consists in.

As regards his first point, he makes it clear that he does not hold that reason has absolute control over the emotions. Here he explicitly opposes the Stoics and Descartes, and denies that there is such a thing as freedom of the will. Through intelligence, apart from any so-called "will," we may clearly discern "the remedies against the affects," that is, against the disordered emotions. From this basic "knowledge of the mind," we may deduce "everything which relates to its [the mind's] blessedness" (p. 452c).

Spinoza's argument in Part V is based on two axioms and the famous Prop. 7 of Part III.

AXIOMS

1. If two contrary actions be excited in the same subject, a change must necessarily take place in both, or in one alone, until they cease to be contrary.

2. The power of an affect is limited by the power of its cause, in so far as the essence of the affect is manifested or limited by the essence of the cause itself. (p. 452c)

Prop. 7. [Part III] *The effort by which each thing endeavours to persevere in its own being is nothing but the actual essence of the thing itself.* (p. 399a)

Prop. 1 of Part V establishes the power of the mind over the affects, on the principle that the order in which ideas are arranged in the mind exactly parallels the order of "the affections of the body." A change in one of the orders, then, means a change in the other. Hence the mind, through ordering its ideas, can bring about a right order or transformation of the emotions which are connected with the body. This is the theoretical basis for the practical "remedies" prescribed in Props. 2-20.

Spinoza summarizes these remedies in the Scholium to Prop. 20, putting them in a slightly different order from the one in which they have been presented. First, he says, is "knowledge itself of the affects." (See Props. 3-4.) Since a "passion," in the technical sense, is a confused idea, it ceases to be a passion as soon as we form a clear and distinct idea of it. The clearer our knowledge of an emotion, the more we can control it and the less we suffer from it. Indeed, by proper knowledge and direction of an emotion, we can transform it from a "passion" to an "action" or virtue. For instance, the impulse to compel other men to believe as we do—mere bullying or bigotry—may be transformed by clear thinking into the desire to share with others the good and joy that we know and have; hence, consistent with this generous impulse, the appeal is to reason and the action is one of "humanity and kindness" rather than of compulsion. Bigotry is a perversion (stemming from a confused idea) of the desire to share the good.

The second remedy is to detach a disturbing emotion from the thought of the particular external thing that caused it and attach it to other thoughts; thereby our disturbing emotions (love or hate) directed toward the external cause will be eliminated. (See Prop. 2.) Or, as he puts this counsel a little later, the remedy is "to strive also that the affect may be separated from the thought of an external cause and connected with true thoughts" (p. 453b).

What such "true thoughts" may consist in, and another remedy, are indicated in Props. 5-6, which point out that the more we understand that all things are necessarily caused, the more control we have over emotions and the less we suffer from them. If instead of assigning to some particular external cause (person, event, etc.) the reason for some loss or disappointment, we realize that whatever happens is "determined by an infinite chain of causes," our mental suffering will certainly be lessened. "For we see that sorrow for the loss of anything good is diminished if the person who has lost it considers that it could not by any possibility have been preserved" (p. 454a). We are inclined to accept uncomplainingly what we know to be natural and necessary.

A good deal of our mental suffering arises from our attachment to things that are not present, to things that we want and have failed to obtain or keep, or to things that we do not want and that have affected us (failures, disappointments, etc.). On the principle that what is present has more emotional power than what is absent, Spinoza advises us to concentrate on "the common properties of things . . . which we always contemplate as present" (p. 454b). The emotion which arises from such contemplation ("the affect which arises from reason") is more powerful than that attached to absent things, and hence removes anxiety. This remedy is presented in Prop. 7.

There is safety in numbers—in the number of external things to which the mind is directed. The more the mind is concentrated on a few things or on one alone, the more it is hindered from thinking of other things, and the more it suffers (that is, the more its power of thought is impaired) from the emotion that arises from such thought. The remedy, then, is not to attach the mind to one or a few finite things, but to open it up "to many and different" external objects. (See Props. 8-9.)

In order to prevent our minds from being "agitated by affects which are contrary to our nature," that is, the disordered emotions, we must plan ahead and forestall this by adhering to "a right rule of life, or sure maxims (*dogmata*) of life" (p. 455a). But this requires some special exercises. For instance, taking as a maxim that hate is conquered by love, we should constantly meditate on the injuries that men inflict on one another and on how to use generosity to prevent them. It also helps to recognize the necessity behind acts of injury and hate and thus take them for granted. To attain fortitude and conquer fear, it is good to think ahead to various possible dangers and about how to face them courageously. Also, we should look on the positive side of things and be determined by joy, not rage. For instance, in redirecting our passion for glory to its proper end, we should not indulge in abusive thoughts of men's low motivations in seeking it. We should be moved by "a love of liberty alone" and filled with the joy that comes from the knowledge of virtue and its causes, not by the negative meditation on men's vices. He who follows these recipes diligently will in a short time "be able for the most part to direct his actions in accordance with the command of reason" (p. 456a). (See Prop. 10.)

After presenting the above remedies in Props. 2-10, Spinoza comes to the master remedy which comprises all of them— "the intellectual love of God." But first he deals with the factors that make one image or affect strong enough to supplant another—in this case, the factors that make rightly ordered emotions supplant wrongly ordered ones (the "passions"). These factors are (a) a greater number of objects to which the image or affect is related, and (b) "things which we clearly and distinctly understand." The affect then may be related to a greater number of causes, or the things understood may be easily contemplated along with other things. (See Props. 11-13.)

But since God includes all things (see p. 360a), the direction of the mind to the idea of God and being filled with the love of God are the best remedies of all, both intellectually and emotionally. (See Props. 14-20.) Since a clear and distinct understanding of oneself and one's emotions brings joy (see p. 413a); since love is by definition joy accompanied by the idea of an external cause (see p. 417b); and since all affections may be related to the idea of God (see p. 456b), it follows that

He who clearly and distinctly understands himself and his affects loves God, and loves Him better the better he understands himself and his affects. (p. 456c)

Man's love of God is absolutely perfect and necessarily unaffected by any contrary emotions in man or any question of whether God is good to man and loves him in return. For God is a completely impassive being, free from all passions, un-affected by joy, sorrow, or any other emotion. "God loves no one and hates no one" (p. 456d). He is just Himself, complete and perfect and self-sufficient (since He includes everything). "Love to God cannot be turned into hatred" (p. 456d), for it is impossible for anyone to hate God; only joy can accompany the idea of perfect being. It is absurd to hate God as the cause of one's sorrow, for it is inconceivable that God should hate or hurt anyone, and besides, when the causes of sorrow are properly understood (as necessary), sorrow ceases to exist. The conclusion then, is this:

He who loves God cannot strive that God should love him in return.
(p. 457a)

In the Scholium to Prop. 49 in Part II, Spinoza has already argued that this kind of relation to God as he conceives Him is the best for human amity. (See p. 394c.) Here he reiterates that envy or jealousy cannot arise with regard to the love of God, man's highest good, which is open to all men to share, and which is the more enjoyable as we think of all men sharing in it.

The Scholium to Prop. 20 of Part V summarizes what Spinoza has done in the first twenty propositions.

I have, in what has preceded, included all the remedies for the affects, that is to say, everything which the mind, considered in itself alone, can do against them. (p. 457b)

He goes on to point out the essential distinction between in-adequate ideas (linked with passions or impotence) and adequate ideas (linked with action or virtue), and warns of the sorrow that follows from the love of objects that are change-able and unpossessable. Then he states the main point of Part V: "clear and distinct knowledge, and especially that third kind of knowledge," that is, intuitive knowledge, has the power to control the passions, "to make them constitute the smallest part of the mind," if not to destroy them entirely. (See p. 457d.) It does this through attaching our love to God.

Moreover, it begets a love towards an immutable and eternal object (see Prop. 15, pt. 5) of which we are really partakers (see Prop. 45, pt. 2);

a love which therefore cannot be vitiated by the defects which are in common love, but which can always become greater and greater (Prop. 15, pt. 5), occupy the largest part of the mind (Prop. 16, pt. 5), and thoroughly affect it. (pp. 457d-458a)

All this, however, relates only "to this present life," says Spinoza, and he turns in the remaining propositions of Part V to "the duration of the mind without relation to the body" (p. 458a).

IV

Props. 21-23 are an argument that the mind, or something in the mind, has eternal existence. First, it is admitted that there can be no perception, and hence no imagination or memory, once the body ceases to exist. Next, it is pointed out that the body exists eternally as an idea in God, "*an idea which expresses the essence of this or that human body under the form of eternity*" (p. 458b); that is, as necessary existence. (For what Spinoza means by "the form of eternity," see Part I, Def. 8, and Explanation, and Part II, Prop. 44, and Corol. 2.) This idea is "something which pertains to the essence of the human mind," and being linked to the essence of God, "this something which pertains to the essence of the mind will necessarily be eternal" (p. 458b-c). This "something" is the intellectual part of the mind.

We do have a sense of eternity in our present experience, in the highest activity of the mind, that is, in the intuitive knowledge of God, which is the basis of our intuitive knowledge of all things. Such knowledge brings us to the peak of human perfection, to the greatest possible joy, to "the highest possible peace of mind" (p. 459b). Our delight in this intuitive knowledge is accompanied "with the idea of God as its cause" (p. 460b), and hence with "the intellectual love of God." Indeed this love, like the knowledge from which it springs, is eternal, and the joy bound up with it goes far beyond the pressure that arises from the transition to a greater perfection, for it is the "blessedness" which arises from the eternal possession of perfection.

Going still further, Spinoza sees man's intellectual love of

God as a part of the infinite intellectual love with which God loves Himself. It is *"the very love with which He loves Himself, not in so far as He is infinite, but in so far as He can be manifested through the essence of the human mind"* (p. 461a); that is, through the finite mode of God's infinite attribute of thought. This love is linked to the activity of contemplation, in which the mind contemplates itself, "accompanied with the idea of God as cause." But then it follows that God does love men, after all, for

. . . the love of God towards men and the intellectual love of the mind towards God are one and the same thing. . .

Hence we clearly understand that our salvation, or blessedness, or liberty consists in a constant and eternal love towards God, or in the love of God towards men. (p. 461a-b)

The knowledge which is at the root of this love is the most potent available to man, with its "beginning and foundation" in God (p. 461b), and nothing in the world can negate this love, which is rooted in eternal truth. Through the two higher kinds of knowledge (logical and intuitive) the mind comes to share more and more in eternity and to be unaffected not only by the passions but even by death.

. . . death is by so much the less injurious to us as the clear and distinct knowledge of the mind is greater, and consequently as the mind loves God more. (p. 461d)

Up to now, Spinoza has considered the intellectual activity of the human mind—specifically, intuitive knowledge—as the warrant of immortality. Now (in Prop. 39) he shifts the discussion to the state of the body as the precondition for the possession of "a mind of which the greatest part is eternal" (p. 462a). This, of course, is consonant with his own view of the parallelism between the order of the mind and the order of the body. Granted that the body may be fitted for many things, it is certainly possible that it is related to a mind which possesses the knowledge described above, a mind "whose greatest or principal part is eternal" (p. 462b). Spinoza sounds like Aristotle in the *Nicomachean Ethics,* as he calls upon us to "consider ourselves happy if we can pass through the whole period of life with a sound mind in a sound body"

(p. 462b); that is, with a body fit for many things. Our purpose in this life is to develop our bodies so that they are fit for many things and may be related to minds conscious of themselves, of God, and of objects, thus preparing us for immortality.

After this interlude on the body, Spinoza returns (in Prop. 40) to the action of the mind. Identifying perfection with action (as opposed to suffering), he terms the abiding, eternal part of the mind—the intellect, "through which alone we are said to act"—more perfect than the perishable part—the imagination, "through which alone we are said to suffer." He now considers it proved that "our mind, in so far as it understands, is an eternal mode of thought," and hence is part of "the eternal and infinite intellect of God" (p. 462c-d). The Scholium to Prop. 40, then, is a summary of what has been demonstrated in Props. 21-40.

V

After this demonstration of the eternal blessedness that marks the right order of the mind, Spinoza very vigorously counters (in Props. 40-41) any possible imputation that the ethics he has sketched is a "reward" ethics (based on the maxim "Act right and think right so that you will attain eternal joy"). Even apart from the eternality of the mind, moral virtue (which he calls "piety and religion" here) is of basic importance in human life. "Strength of mind and generosity" (fortitude and magnanimity, or "greatness of soul") would still be commanded by reason, and have been so demonstrated in Part IV, before the eternality of the mind was considered.

This point is directed against what Spinoza considers the popular religious attitude, which is to regard the divine moral commandments as a yoke, to be borne with the hope of freedom and eternal reward after death, or, even more, from fear of eternal torment after death. If the masses thought that there was no life after this one, "they would prefer to let everything be controlled by their own passions" (p. 463b). This Spinoza regards as utterly irrational, as if we should feed our body poisons instead of good food because the body is not immortal, or live insanely just because we thought the mind is not eternal. This is to disregard the basic truth:

Blessedness is not the reward of virtue, but is virtue itself; nor do we delight in blessedness because we restrain our lusts; but, on the contrary, because we delight in it, therefore are we able to restrain them. (p. 463b)

We must recall that for Spinoza, it is not "will power" but a stronger emotion that restrains the disordered emotions. Blessedness, the highest possible joy, is bound up with the active power of the intellect; and man restrains his lust insofar as he experiences this joy and possesses this power. This is the power of "intellectual love" to control and direct all things.

Thus Spinoza closes his discussion in the Scholium to Prop. 42 with a comparison of "the strength of the wise man" with the shakiness of the ignorant man. The latter is constantly disturbed by external causes, ignorant of God and things, and "as soon as he ceases to suffer ceases also to be" (p. 463d). His existence is suffering; when one ends, the other ends. The wise man, on the other hand, is almost completely impassive, "scarcely ever moved in his mind," but with his constant awareness of the eternal necessity of all things, "never ceases to be, and always enjoys true peace of soul" (p. 463d).

Admittedly, the way to this happy state is a difficult one, but the noblest things are always the most difficult; that is why they are so rarely attained. Earlier, however, Spinoza has said that, given the diligent practice of certain exercises, it is not difficult to act in accordance with the rules of reason. (See p. 456a.)

VI

If all things are determined, how are we free to throw off the yoke of the passions?

Spinoza is perhaps the first in the series of great modern thinkers, including Marx and Freud, who propose to lead man to freedom by showing him how he is necessarily determined in his actions and attitudes. He proposes a program for freedom from bondage to the passions, based on an analysis of the determining causes of human emotions. He speaks of "the power of the mind over the affects and its liberty" at the end of the *Ethics,* as he appeals to the reader to find and follow the high and difficult road to "salvation" which he has indicated. Yet this call to choose the way of virtue and happiness comes at the end of a work which is an argument for the necessary causation of all things and events.

We may be able to understand this apparent inconsistency if we recall what Spinoza has proposed as a cure for human ills. This remedy is simply adequate knowledge of the causes of things and particularly of the causes of human emotions. Through such knowledge, a man comes to accept consciously the whole scheme of things and his place in it, unaffected by disturbances from without and free from disturbances from within.

This prescription is not new in the history of philosophy and religion. It has existed in one form or another since ancient times, in both the East and the West. We have already considered one of the classic examples of such therapy in Epictetus' *Discourses.* You have probably already noticed many resemblances in the viewpoints of Epictetus and Spinoza. However, Spinoza is obviously much colder, harder, more objective, and more "clinical" in his approach than Epictetus, which perhaps indicates the difference between the modern and ancient temper in the study of human behavior.

In any case the world (or reality or God) is what it is, and we, who are part of it, are what we are, and happiness lies in accepting this, and in acting and reacting accordingly. Freedom is equivalent to the conscious acceptance of this necessity, reached through intelligence and knowledge. It is not equivalent to the capacity to act otherwise than we have acted in any particular case, through some process of deliberation and choice, since whatever happens is necessarily determined and deductible from the laws governing all nature (including deliberation and choice). How, then, do we choose "freedom" in Spinoza's sense?

Spinoza would reply that we "choose" freedom necessarily, not freely. The basic drive, endeavor, or "conatus" toward being ourselves is identical with our very essence, with what we essentially are. (See Part III, Prop. 7.) Our whole psychophysical organism is motivated and affected by this drive, and marked by feelings of pleasure and pain as we approach or recede from our natural perfection. Our natural impulse to be what we are, in accordance with our particular nature and the harmony of the whole of reality, becomes clear through reason, which is also a part of our nature. Virtue and perfection do not lie in making a choice between "good" and "evil," but in consciously following our nature. In doing this, we attain not only psychological ease but also many qualities that have traditionally been considered virtues, and avoid those that have been called vices. These traditional virtues and vices are, however, states of the psychophysical organism.

Such is Spinoza's view of the road to perfection. Though it is the natural and the only right way, it is a difficult one, and few, he admits, find it. The vast majority of men are weighed down by ignorance and by bondage to the passions. Most of us "are disturbed by external causes in a number of ways, and . . . like the waves of the sea agitated by contrary winds, we fluctuate in our ignorance of our future and destiny" (p. 416a). Admittedly, most men remain in this condition, and only a rare few attain the perfection and peace that are by nature available to all men.

Is there anything comparable to an act of will that accounts for our different destinies? Or is human destiny in each particular case predetermined by the natural mental and physical constitution or by more metaphysical factors? Looking back, in the light of Spinoza's analysis, all events are determined. Are they also predetermined and predestined? Or does Spinoza's rejection of design and purpose make predestination impossible?

Is each particular, concrete human being actually able to be free?

Is love toward one's fellows essential to Spinoza's ethical doctrine?

We have seen in the summary of Part IV that Spinoza defi-

nitely advocated a social ethics, on the grounds that men need
one another in order to attain their natural perfection. We have
also seen that he advocates returning love for hate, generosity
for injury. However, he prescribes against attaching our emotions to any finite being, to any external cause. Would particular human beings fit into this category?

On what grounds does Spinoza advocate loving our fellow
men? Is it because they are worth loving in themselves, as
brother human beings or the particular persons they are? Or
is it, on the one hand, for the sake of mutual aid and self-
perfection and, on the other, because love is a "positive" feeling, making for inner as well as outer peace? Do we love the
other man, according to Spinoza, for his good or for our peace
of mind? Is Spinoza's ideal "wise man" indifferent to the actual
persons with whom he has to deal?

Would Spinoza ever find any justification for "negative" emotions such as anger and hate in his ethical program?

How does Spinoza's "blessedness" compare with Aquinas' "beatific vision"?

Is the final good in each case attained through an act of
the intellect? If so, is this an act of contemplation? Is the
knowledge in each case intuitive, immediate knowledge? If
so, is the content of that intuitive vision the same? Is man
naturally necessitated to see the ultimate good in both cases?
What is the role of divine grace in the attainment of the
blessed state, for Spinoza? Is final blessedness possible in this
life, for Spinoza?

How does Spinoza's analysis of the effect of thought on our judgments of good and evil compare with Montaigne's?

In Spinoza's view, human judgments of good and evil are determined by our desires. Through clarification of our thoughts
we are able to transform our desires and attach them to their
proper and real objects, or the one single proper object—God
or Nature. We are then able to accept and affirm all that hap-

pens as necessary, to consider it good, if you will, or actually to see things in a realm in which judgments of good and evil have no meaning. Things simply are, and we know them in their being and causes.

How does Montaigne's emphasis differ from Spinoza's? Is Montaigne more concerned than Spinoza with the psychological aspect, with feelings of pain and pleasure? Or is this factor of equal importance in both views? Does Spinoza's analysis of the structure and causes of things make an important difference? Does such a vision of objective reality play any role in Montaigne's thought?

Is there an essential connection between Spinoza's analysis of the emotions and his analysis of the rest of nature which provides a greater rational cogency than is directly visible in Montaigne's argument? Would Spinoza's complete and precise world view offer a rational undergirding for Montaigne's argument?

If you are interested in comparing the thoughts of Spinoza and Montaigne on death, see Part IV, Prop. 67, of the *Ethics*.

What would Spinoza think of the following statement from a contemporary "mental health" psychologist?

Are there completely happy people? No. We find no one whose life is, and has been, without some hard-hitting frustration or some profound sorrow. When a beloved parent dies, or a just-grown child—what door of escape is there? There is no way out of the grief except to live through it.

For more than half of us, life is a matter of settling for a good deal less than we want. We know it; we've known it for years; and we are decidedly not happy at the many moments when we think about our losses, our disappointments and our never-will-be's. For such of us, life is *never* brilliantly happy. Unalloyed joy is an unknown or forgotten sensation. Too many hurts, big and little, have chipped the bright colors away.[5]

[5] Dr. Robert F. Peck, as quoted by Ernest Havemann in "Who's Normal? Nobody, But We All Keep on Trying," *Life*, August 8, 1960, p. 80.

What would Spinoza think of "The Spinoza of Market Street"?

"The Spinoza of Market Street" is a short story by the contemporary Yiddish writer Isaac Bashevis Singer, laid in the Warsaw ghetto about 1914. It tells the story of a philosopher who has been studying Spinoza's *Ethics* for thirty years and is a convinced Spinozist. He studies the stars with a telescope, joyful that he, too, is a mode of the infinite extension which is a divine attribute. He considers that the common people around him are ignorantly immersed in vain passions and desire, treading the road to suffering and frustration. Inspired by Spinoza's teaching, he is not afraid of dying, yet he is cruelly tormented by a stomach ailment, an ulcer, perhaps a cancer, and seems to be at the point of death.

At this moment, ordinary human love enters his life in the person of an ugly spinster, "tall and lean, and as black as a baker's shovel," with a broken nose and a moustache, too. The old bachelor and the old maid become interested in one another and get married. On their wedding night, the philosopher plans to read the *Ethics* as usual, and pleads that he is too old and weak to consummate the marriage. But when his bride enters, the book drops from his hands, and he is miraculously able to play the role of the ardent bridegroom. Later that night he goes to the window and looks out at the infinite expanse of the starry heavens, at the completely determined cosmos of which he and his destiny are a part, and murmurs, "Divine Spinoza, forgive me, I have become a fool."

If you can imagine Spinoza reading a work of fiction (indeed, a short story that first appeared in *Esquire*), what do you think he would say about his twentieth-century acolyte? Would he say that his disciple has strayed from the right way? Is repression or sublimation of sexual love a necessary consequence of Spinoza's philosophy? What would Spinoza say to the interpretation that the old maid is a mode of divine reality too, and that in loving her the "foolish" philosopher was loving God?

For Spinoza's views on sexual love, see the fragmentary remarks in Part IV, Appendix, Nos. XIX-XX on page 449a. For

Spinoza's own experience of the love of woman, see Lewis Feuer's *Spinoza and the Rise of Liberalism* (Boston: Beacon Press, 1958, p. 220 f.). Feuer reports that Spinoza fell in love with a witty, learned, and accomplished young lady, but failed to marry her because she insisted on being married in the Catholic Church. Feuer suggests that Spinoza's subsequent doctrine of the intellectual love of God was a compensation for this frustration of ordinary human love, and that his denigration of the erotic as compared with the intellectual was influenced by his early upbringing in a tradition that counted study of the Torah a much higher joy than sexual love.

Do you think that Feuer's interpretation is a likely one? Was Spinoza's view of love in a sense determined by his personal upbringing and experience? Or was the latter only the occasion for a system of thought that would have been constructed anyway? Is it possible that someone else, with a happy love life in the ordinary sense, might construct a similar philosophy, or concur in all essentials with Spinoza? What would Spinoza think of the kind of causal determinism suggested by Feuer? Would such determination be in accord with Spinoza's system?

For a fictional version of Spinoza's frustrated love for Clara Maria van den Ende, see Israel Zangwill's short story "The Maker of Lenses," which ends with the philosopher's contemplation of the cosmos, his realization of the endless reality of which he is a part, and the final peace through victory over the "enslaving affects." At that moment he composes the final sentences of the *Ethics*, about the immovable strength and peace of soul of the wise man. His personal anguish is transcended in a true vision of reality, a vision expressed in "the words that were not to die."

The following questions are designed to help you test the thoroughness of your reading. Each question is to be answered by giving a page or pages of the reading assignment. Answers will be found on page 304 of this Reading Plan.

1 How does the mind control the passions, according to Descartes?

2 Who inveighs the most vehemently against the vanity of glory, the abuses of wealth, and the fickleness of women?

3 How does death become less injurious to us?

4 What is "the primary and sole foundation of virtue"?

5 Are all men moved with the same intensity by the same emotion?

6 How does the subject matter of Part V differ from the subject matter of logic and medicine?

7 What is "an idea of an affection of the body"?

8 What type of ideas must desires arise from if they are to be considered virtues?

LOCKE

An Essay Concerning Human Understanding

"Epistle to the Reader"; Book I, Ch. 2; Book II,
Ch. 20, Ch. 21, Sections 42-44, Ch. 28; Book III,
Ch. 11, Sections 16-17; Book IV, Ch. 3, Sections 18-20

Vol. 35, pp. 87-92, 103-112,
176-178, 188-189, 228-233, 303-304, 317-319

In his "Epistle to the Reader," Locke makes a disarmingly humble judgment of this work and its author. He labels himself a mere "under-laborer" of the sciences, employed "in clearing the ground a little, and removing some of the rubbish that lies in the way of knowledge." The result of this "menial" labor, it turns out, was one of the most important works in the history of Western thought. With this work modern empirical philosophy begins, and the theory of knowledge becomes a central concern of philosophy.

Locke discusses ethical questions here in the light of his theory of knowledge. He affirms that we can attain true and exact knowledge in matters of right and wrong. Our moral judgments, he says, originate in experience and are solidly grounded in immediate intuition and demonstrative reasoning. This is what knowledge consists in, and moral knowledge is knowledge like any other.

The question of the validity and grounds of moral judgment is an ancient one. Plato's polemic against the Sophists revolved around this point, and a large part of his work was devoted to arguing that ethics has a rational basis and is not a matter of subjective preference or social custom. Locke's emphasis on sense experience, however, and his contention that ethics can be made a demonstrative science on the model of mathematics offer a sharp contrast with ancient moral philosophy. So also does his stress on the diversity of moral standards, beliefs, and practices among the peoples of the world.

This work is certainly written in the modern temper. Locke was deeply impressed by the creative genius of the great empirical scientists of his age, such as Boyle, Huygens, and Newton, whom he called "the masterbuilders." He also shared with Descartes and Spinoza the view that mathematics was the model for all exact knowledge. In an odd and unique way, he combined both the empirical and rational tendencies of seventeenth-century thought. He also combined in a unique way an emphasis on actual moral diversity with a stress on the natural or divine moral law which sets the absolute ethical standard by which human action is measured.

To some readers this work may seem highly theoretical and abstract. However, Locke's main purpose, repeated many times, was to be of practical use in human endeavors—not only in the advancement of the sciences, but also and especially in the conduct of life. Through his direct, unpretentious, and sometimes genial style he appeals to us to make use of our critical intelligence in dealing with moral principles and judgments.

Tenth Reading

I

John Locke's *An Essay Concerning Human Understanding* is a treatise on epistemology—the theory of knowledge. It deals with the nature, modes, and limits of human knowledge—with what we can know and how we know. Hence, the discussion of ethics in this work is primarily a consideration of the principles of moral knowledge—of the sources and validity of our ethical judgments. It might seem that such a discussion is tangential to the main subject matter of the *Essay*, which is largely concerned with our experience and knowledge of the physical world and which devotes only scattered sections to ethics. It will soon become clear, however, as we read the passages which have been selected here, how important Locke held moral knowledge to be and how much certainty he thought it possessed.

A clue to this concern, vitally connected with the writing of the *Essay*, may be indicated by his account in the "Epistle to the Reader" of the origin of this work. He tells how he and several friends were once engaged in a discussion of certain topics, but were unable to come to any conclusions. It occurred to Locke that they were approaching these problems in the wrong way,

. . . and that before we set ourselves upon inquiries of that nature, it was necessary to examine our own abilities, and see what *objects* our understandings were, or were not, fitted to deal with. (p. 87d)

That is, first find out what the human mind is capable of understanding before engaging in any inquiry. Or, putting his idea more precisely a few pages later, Locke announces his purpose as

. . . to inquire into the original, certainty, and extent of *human knowl-*

edge, together with the grounds and degrees of *belief, opinion,* and *assent.* . . . (p. 93b)

What were the topics that originally gave rise to this project? All that Locke says is that it was "a subject very remote from this" (p. 87d). However, James Tyrrell, a friend of Locke, wrote on his copy of the *Essay*: "I remember myself being one of those that met there when the discourse began about the principles of morality and of revealed religion." The historian of philosophy Harald Höffding concludes from this remark that "it was a discussion on ethical and moral questions which led to the closer investigation of knowledge."[1]

In any event, in order to understand Locke's discussion of the principles of moral knowledge, we must have some understanding of his account of knowledge in general. The primary materials of knowledge, the true objects of our understanding, says Locke, are "ideas," and the sources of our ideas are "sensation" and "reflection." By "ideas" Locke means not only the abstract concepts of thought but also what we apprehend through sense perception—"those *ideas* we have of *yellow, white, heat, cold, soft, hard, bitter, sweet,* and all those which we call sensible qualities" (p. 121c-d). Indeed, sensation is the "great source of most of the ideas we have."

The other primary source of our ideas is reflection, that is, "the perception of the operations of our own mind within us, as it is employed about the ideas it has got," which gives us ideas of "*perception, thinking, doubting, believing, reasoning, knowing, willing*" (p. 121d) and other actions and passions of the mind. (See pp. 121d-122a.) Reflection is a sort of "internal sense," dealing with inner mental operations, just as sensation arises from external material things. These two functions are the source of all our ideas. Hence, when Locke says our ideas arise from "experience," he means that they arise from sensation and reflection.

Human knowledge, of course, is concerned with more complex matters than the "simple ideas" mentioned above. But

[1] Harald Höffding, *A History of Modern Philosophy* (New York: Dover Publications, Inc., 1955), Vol. I, p. 380.

complex ideas, ideas of relation, and abstract ideas are based on the simple ideas of immediate perception and of reflection. The mind attains these higher-level ideas by combining, associating, or abstracting from simple ideas. Simple ideas are acquired passively, automatically; complex ideas require the active constructive work of the mind.

In any case, it is ideas that we perceive or know, not things; it is ideas, not things, that are the objects of our understanding. Or, putting it in another way, we perceive or know things only through the ideas that arise in sensation and reflection—not directly. Knowledge is basically the perception of the agreement or disagreement of ideas; for instance, the distinction between white and black, or the equality of the three angles of a triangle to two right angles.

The primary form of knowledge is "intuition," or immediate perception, which affords us certain knowledge. Another form of certain knowledge is "demonstration," which is attained through reasoning based on intuitive knowledge (as in mathematics). Intuition and demonstration are the only certain forms of knowledge, and the only modes by which we attain knowledge of general truths.

There is also a third kind of knowledge, which Locke calls "sensitive knowledge," which is not so certain as the first two but which goes beyond mere probability. It is the knowledge of "the particular existence of finite things without us," for instance, that it is wormwood, and not sugar, that we have tasted; or a rose, and not tar, that we have smelled; or a fire and not ice, that has burned us. In this sense, then, we can have a fairly certain knowledge of the external objects that give rise to the ideas in our minds.

In any event, all knowledge and the ideas upon which it rests are derived from experience. The basic principle of identity or non-contradiction, the abstract notion of substance, the category of quantity—all arise ultimately from sense experience and reflection. The same is true of basic moral ideas, such as justice, good, and right and wrong. None of these basic ideas, categories, or principles is an "innate idea," present in the mind before and apart from experience. The mind is originally bare and empty, like an unfurnished room, and it is through experience that it is filled with its "furniture," that is, ideas. Or, in another metaphor, the mind is originally an empty tablet, like a scratch pad ("white paper, void of all characters, without any ideas" [p.121b]), upon which, through experience, ideas are written.

Since knowledge is primarily a matter of the comparison of ideas, it is essential that our ideas and the terms that express them be clear and distinct. This emphasis, together with the polemic against "vague and insignificant forms of speech," runs all through the *Essay*. It connects Locke (along with Hobbes) with the emphasis on the analysis of language in present-day British and American philosophy.

I I

Locke opens his work with an attack on the theory of "innate ideas"; that is, a set of primary notions or principles, "stamped upon the mind of man" and present there at his birth. Locke grants that there are certain self-evident speculative or logical propositions, such as "Whatsoever is, is" and "It is impossible for the same thing to be and not to be"; but he holds that assent to such propositions requires an understanding of the terms involved, that is, thought and judgment. He also grants that there are certain practical or moral principles and rules which can be certainly known by the human reason; but again he holds that these are not present in the mind at birth, but are attained through thought.

His argument against the existence of innate ideas runs something like this:

If they were innate, then everyone would know them. But (1) it is obvious that children, idiots, illiterates, and primitives do not know them. And (2) even if the ideas were universally known, this might be explained adequately by some other cause than their innateness.

Locke's polemic against innate ideas is of interest to us here only as it is connected with his own theory of how men come to hold the moral beliefs that they do, with what one might call his "natural history" of moral opinions. In the first place, says

Locke, there is no moral principle (such as the Golden Rule) which is as generally assented to as self-evident speculative propositions. He challenges the proponents of innate moral principles to name just one that commands universal assent. And he will not accept the argument that such principles may be in our minds without constantly working on us and directing our actions.

The wide variety of moral rules and beliefs in different eras and cultures, says Locke, offers strong evidence that there are no innate moral principles. The fact is that "men have contrary practical principles" and approve such things as ritual murder, rape, infanticide, cannibalism, etc. Where whole peoples violate what we take to be innate moral principles, we must question whether such principles are innate.

> Where then are those innate principles of justice, piety, gratitude, equity, chastity? Or where is that universal consent that assures us there are such inbred rules? (p. 106d)

Locke grants that there are certain natural tendencies or inclinations, such as the natural urge toward the beneficial and profitable, but these are not innate characters, indelibly imprinted on our minds, not "principles of knowledge regulating our practice" (p. 104d). Moreover, many natural urges require the restraint of moral laws rather than provide a basis for them. (See p. 108b.) There is a natural moral law that we may come to know through the exercise of our reason, but this is distinct from an innate law in the mind. (See p. 108c.)

Locke's account of how men come to hold the moral beliefs that they do also explains why they consider them innate. Men are indoctrinated by their parents, nurses, and teachers with a certain set of beliefs from the time they are infants. Hence, they cannot remember a time when they did not believe as they do, and they consider their beliefs inborn. They accept these principles unquestioningly because they need some foundation upon which to base their judgments of truth and falsehood, of right and wrong. They take the easy way of mimicking the voices of parents, custom, and common opinion, rather than enduring the personal discomfort and public reproach which is the lot of those who challenge "received opinions."

It is this uncritical acceptance of "borrowed principles"—which are regarded as of natural or divine origin—that accounts for the scandalous diversity of moral beliefs among men and the dogmatic adherence to "contrary tenets" of morality. As long as such tenets are taken for innate ideas, "to be received upon their own authority, without examination" (p. 112b), anything may be believed by anyone. But their very diversity, the lack of universal assent, demonstrates that they are not innate (and hence not unquestionable). The obvious and irrefutable truth is "that there are no practical principles wherein all men agree; and therefore none innate" (p. 112c).

III

The above analysis of the way men come to their moral beliefs occurs in the context of Locke's polemic against innate ideas in Book I. A fuller and more positive account of the sources of moral principles is given in Book II, where Locke presents his own theory of how we get our ideas, namely, through sensation and reflection. His first approach to ethical problems in that book occurs in Chapter 20, in the context of a discussion of the "simple ideas" of pleasure and pain.

He starts with a simple hedonistic version of good and evil: our judgments of good and evil are merely expressions of the pleasure or pain caused in us by objects or the contemplation of objects. What pleases us we call good, what pains us we call evil. Pleasure and pain are also the sources of the passions—love, hate, desire, joy, sorrow, hope, fear, despair, anger, envy, etc.—which are simply "modes of pleasure and pain resulting in our minds from various considerations of good and evil" (p. 178a).

Happiness, the ultimate aim of human desire, is defined in the next chapter as "the utmost pleasure" and misery or unhappiness as "the utmost pain" (p. 188d). Since there are various degrees of pleasure and of pain, our judgments of good and evil are to a great extent comparative. We are not inclined to view a slight degree of pleasure as good when a more intense one is at hand. This is somewhat on the analogy of our calling weather "good" or "bad"—we may consider a twenty-degree temperature "bad" if it has just dropped from forty degrees, but "good" if it has just gone up from zero.

However, Locke makes it clear in Chapter 28 that specifically *moral* good involves something far more than a psychophysical reaction of pleasure. He defines a *moral relation* as "the conformity or disagreement men's *voluntary actions* have to a *rule* to which they are referred, and by which they are judged of" (p. 229b). If we add this definition to the previous definition of good and evil, we get this definition of moral good and evil:

> *Moral good and evil*, then, is only *the conformity or disagreement of our voluntary actions to some law, whereby good or evil is drawn on us, from the will and power of the law-maker;* which good and evil, pleasure or pain, attending our observance or breach of the law by the decree of the law-maker is that we call *reward* and *punishment.* (p. 229c-d)

Locke discerns three kinds of moral rules or laws, each with its own kind of sanction: divine law, civil law, and the law of opinion. (1) Divine law, which proclaims what our duties and sins are, is known either by natural reason or by revelation. It is the absolute measure of good and evil in human actions. (See also p. 109d.) (2) Civil law comprises rules set up by political societies to determine criminal guilt and innocence. (3) The law of opinion or reputation measures virtue and vice, not absolutely, but in accord with the code and custom of a particular time, place, and society. It is simply the expression of general "approbation or dislike, praise or blame" of certain actions in a particular community.

Locke feels called upon to discuss at length this third type of moral law and to defend against possible criticism his listing of it. He argues, on the one hand, on the grounds of historical fact, that "that passes for vice in one country which is counted a virtue, or at least not vice, in another" (p. 230d), and hence is held blameworthy in the one and praiseworthy or a matter of indifference in the other. He also argues, on the other hand, that praise and blame are, on the whole, distributed according to "the unchangeable rule of right and wrong, which the law of God hath established" (p. 231a). This law (which Locke also calls "the law of nature") is so obviously directed to the general good of mankind that most men are naturally disposed to recognize it; even when they do not obey it, they heed it when they condemn in others faults which they themselves are guilty of.

Thus the law of opinion generally reinforces the law of God or nature. Moreover its sanctions—public esteem or discredit—are very powerful, even more so than the penalties for breaking God's law or the civil law, as far as the immediate consciousness of most men is concerned. It is impossible to avoid awareness of the disapproval of one's fellows, and there are few men so callous that they can bear for long the dislike and contempt of their neighbors.

To sum up, then, the "moral rectitude" of human actions is measured by their conformity with one of three rules—the rule of God, or of the state, or of public opinion. *"Morality is the relation of voluntary actions to these rules"* (p. 231d), any one of which may serve as the touchstone whereby we may name and mark the value of our actions. In Locke's view, it is an easy matter to apply these rules to particular actions, relying only on the "simple ideas" derived from sensation and reflection.

In the case of murder, for instance, we can derive from reflection such simple ideas as willing, deliberation, purpose, life, perception, and motion, and from sensation, simple ideas of what goes on in a living human organism and of the action that will put an end to its perception, life, and motion. It is this action that we call "murder," and we may apply to it the moral valuation put on it by common opinion, divine law, or civil law.

It is only this relation of an action to a law that gives it a moral valuation. An action cannot be judged good or evil merely on the basis of what Locke calls its "absolute" characteristics, that is, from the mere objective fact of killing, stealing, etc. Taking away someone's property may not be judged wrong under any of the three laws in certain cases:

for instance, stealing a weapon from a madman so that he will not harm anyone. Such an act is not wrong, measured by the absolute law of God. The same might be said about killing a man in self-defense. The moral rule applies to the specific circumstances and factors involved. (See p. 232b-d; see also pp. 264c-265c, 286c.)

IV

Locke's acknowledgment of the general opinion of a particular community as a moral rule by which good and evil are measured did not go unopposed. He replies in the "Epistle to the Reader" to the criticism by a Mr. [James] Lowde of his presentation of this rule in an earlier edition of the *Essay*. His defense against Lowde's charge that he has made virtue vice and vice virtue, confusing "the eternal and unalterable nature of right and wrong" with local and passing customs and opinions, is as follows: first, that he has only described what actually takes place in human societies, without in any way confusing it with the absolute right and wrong established by divine or natural law.

For I was there not laying down moral rules, but showing the original and nature of moral ideas, and enumerating the rules men make use of in moral relations, whether these rules were true or false: and pursuant thereto I tell what is everywhere called virtue and vice; which "alters not the nature of things," though men generally do judge of and denominate their actions according to the esteem and fashion of the place and sect they are of. (p. 90b)

Secondly, he has indicated that, by and large, custom and opinion follow the dictates of the natural moral law, which is the absolute measure of virtue and vice. His aim has been

. . . not to prove that the general measure of what man called virtue and vice throughout the world was, the reputation and fashion of each particular society within itself; but to show that, though it were so, yet, for reasons I there give, men, in that way of denominating their actions, did not for the most part much stray from the Law of Nature; which is that standing and unalterable rule by which they ought to judge of the moral rectitude and gravity of their actions, and accordingly denominate them virtues or vices. (p. 90d)

Later, in Book IV, when he discusses the importance of

examining our basic principles, especially moral principles, because they determine the kind of lives we shall lead, it seems clear that he places himself with "those who take it for granted that we are under obligations antecedent to all human constitutions," and not with those who hold "that right and wrong, honest and dishonest, are defined only by [man-made] laws, and not by nature" (p. 359d). And he holds fast in the "Epistle" to his contention that the precepts of the natural moral law become known through the activity of the mind and are in no sense embedded in it as innate deposits before experience and the process of thought. (See p. 91a-b.)

Locke does not state explicitly in this work what precepts consist in; however, we may have an indirect indication of what some of them may be in his list of virtues and sins that should be universally known if the doctrine of innate moral ideas is to have any basis. These are the precepts

. . . not to kill another man; not to know more women than one; not to procure abortion; not to expose their children; not to take from another what is his, though we want it ourselves, but on the contrary, relieve and supply his wants; and whenever we have done the contrary we ought to repent, be sorry, and resolve to do so no more. . . . (p. 110b)

V

Finally, let us see how Locke argues in Books III and IV for his view that we may attain a science of morality that will afford us as certain and demonstrative a knowledge as the science of mathematics. Such certainty is possible, he says, because

. . . the precise real essence of the things moral words stand for may be perfectly known, and so the congruity and incongruity of the things themselves be certainly discovered; in which consists perfect knowledge. (p. 303c)

For instance, through an act of rational intuition, men may

. . . frame in their minds an idea, which shall be the standard to which they will give the name justice; with which pattern so made, all actions that agree shall pass under that denomination. . . . (p. 304a)

This is a simple matter of putting together "simple ideas" already in the mind and of the clear definition of terms, since clarity of terms and definitions is necessary for the attainment of certain knowledge. Certainty is assured because, like mathematics and unlike the natural sciences, the science of morality need not go outside the mind in its inquiry, but deals with mental archetypes—such as justice—which are adequate and complete ideas in themselves. (See pp. 303d-304a; see also p. 325b.)

Two basic ideas provide the foundation of this process of rational intuition and demonstration: the idea of a supreme and perfect Being who is our creator and ultimate resource, and the idea of ourselves as rational creatures. These ideas, if they are made clear and pursued rigorously,

. . . afford such foundations of our duty and rules of action as might place *morality* amongst the *sciences capable of demonstration:* wherein I doubt not but from self-evident propositions, by necessary consequences, as incontestible as those in mathematics, the measures of right and wrong might be made out, to any one that will apply himself with the same indifferency and attention to the one as he does to the other of these sciences. (p. 318a)

For instance, given the definition of "property" as a right to something, and the definition of "injustice" as the violation of such a right, we may demonstrate the truth of the moral proposition "Where there is no property, there is no injustice," just as certainly as we may demonstrate the truth of the mathematical proposition that the three angles of a triangle are equal to two right angles. Similarly, given the definition of "government" and of "absolute liberty," we may state with complete certainty that "No government allows absolute liberty."

Locke recognizes, however, that demonstration in the moral sciences is not as easy as in mathematics. For one thing, moral ideas cannot be represented by "sensible marks," such as diagrams and numbers. All we have at hand to express moral ideas are words, which mean different things to different people, or even to the same person at different times. (See, for example, pp. 109b, 110a-b.) Furthermore, moral ideas are far more complex than the ideas represented by mathematical figures; hence the meaning of moral terms is not always clear or precise. They do not always mean the same thing. (See for instance the remarks on murder, incest, and stabbing, pp. 264c-265a, and on murder and sacrilege, p. 286c.) This makes communication of moral ideas and propositions difficult and also hinders our own thought in moral matters.

The remedy for this situation lies first in the clarification of definitions, which already has been alluded to. Another is a completely scientific, impartial attitude, searching for objective truth in morality "with the same indifference" as in mathematics. But, Locke complains, men are still too much moved by more unworthy passions than the passion for truth, so that they merely parrot the moral opinions that are in fashion (and in power) in their place and time. There are vested interests in morality which, fortunately for scientific truth, play no role in mathematics. Yet there is still some hope, for God has put an unextinguishable light of truth in men's minds.

Whilst the parties of men cram their tenets down all men's throats whom they can get into their power, without permitting them to examine their truth or falsehood; and will not let truth have fair play in the world, nor men the liberty to search after it: what improvements can be expected of this kind? What greater light can be hoped for in the moral sciences? The subject part of mankind in most places might, instead thereof, with Egyptian bondage, expect Egyptian darkness, were not the candle of the Lord set up by himself in men's minds, which it is impossible for the breath or power of man wholly to extinguish. (p. 319c)

VI

How is the natural moral law known?

It is Locke's contention in the *Essay* that moral principles are known through experience, that is, through sensation and reflection, and are not innate in the human mind. But just how do we come through the process of experience to know the precepts of the natural moral law? Locke has shown how, through simple ideas derived from sensation and reflection, we may arrive at the concept of homicide, the killing of a man, as an empirical fact. But to judge such an act as murder, in a culpable sense, requires the application of a moral rule, furnished by common opinion, civil law, or natural (or divine) law, the latter being the absolute source of moral valuation. Just how do we know what the natural moral law declares to be right and wrong? If there are no "innate principles of justice, piety, gratitude, equity, chastity," then how does the natural law obtain a fairly general agreement of moral opinions, as Locke claims?

In the *Essay* he talks about "the light of nature" or the proper use of "our natural faculties" as the means to this basic moral knowledge. But just what does he mean by these terms? Does he mean simply "reason" in some traditional sense of the term? Or, in view of the doctrine laid down in this work does he also mean "sensation"? And if so, just how can the recognition of absolute moral obligation be derived from sense perception?

A series of essays on the law of nature written some time before the *Essay Concerning Human Understanding* indicates that Locke did consider sensation and reason as the sources of our knowledge of the natural moral law.[2] In these essays he rules out the possibility that natural law may be known innately or through tradition and declares sensation to be the sole original source of moral as of all other kinds of knowledge. "The light of nature," then, is sensation plus reason, which orders, distinguishes, and conjoins constructively the ideas furnished by sensation. If we add the contribution of "reflection," the sort of "inner sense" which has been discussed above, we have a close parallel to the theory of knowledge presented in the *Essay*.

Locke takes due account in the *Essay* of the role of reason as a constructive activity of the mind, necessary for discerning the logical connections and conclusions involved in the ideas contributed by "*outward sense* and *inward perception.*" See Book IV, Ch. 17.) He says "Sense and intuition reach but a very little way. The greatest part of our knowledge depends upon deductions and intermediate ideas" (p. 372a). Yet are not the basic principles on which moral judgment is based

---

[2] See *John Locke's Political Philosophy* by J. W. Gough (London: Oxford University Press, 1950), pp. 12-17.

the starting points rather than the conclusions of a process of reasoning? Locke apparently affirms this in his discussion of the truths that are known immediately through intuitive knowledge, needing no further proof. He says:

In this consists the evidence of all those *maxims* which nobody has any doubt about, but every man (does not, as is said, only assent to, but) *knows* to be true, as soon as ever they are proposed to his understanding. In the discovery of and assent to these truths, there is no use of the discursive faculty, *no need of reasoning*, but they are known by a superior and higher degree of evidence. (p. 378c-d)

Is this the way in which the precepts of the natural moral law are known? Does Locke mean to imply that we have a direct intuition of the nature of justice, equity, chastity, and other virtues, comparable to our perceptions of *"whiteness, hardness, sweetness, thinking, motion, man, elephant, army, drunkenness"* (p. 121a), etc.? But it is not enough in matters of morality to know what justice, etc. are. We must also know that we are *commanded, required, obliged* to be just, to do good and avoid doing evil. Can we have a direct intuition of moral obligation? Or is ethical duty to be inferred from some theoretical view of the world or God?

What about the specific moral precepts listed on page 110b and cited above (p. 195)? Do we know immediately, once we have attained a rational state, that we must not murder, commit adultery, steal, etc? Are these self-evident truths which we understand immediately, once we understand the terms? See Locke's remark on page 107c that such a precept is a command and not a proposition, a personal address and not an impersonal statement, and hence "not capable of truth and falsehood," that is, of being verified by ordinary intellectual procedures. This, of course, must be understood in a special sense, to distinguish moral commandments from theoretical statements, for, as we have seen, Locke constantly talks of "moral truths."

Can ethics be an exact science, like mathematics?

Obviously Locke, as an empirical philosopher, was just as aware as Aristotle of the shifting and uncertain character of human affairs; but he was also a rationalist, in the style of his time, who sought and saw demonstrative certainty in the field of ethics, on the model of mathematics. In this view, precision in moral judgments lies in the proper application of a general precept to a particular case, such as in applying the injunction against murder to a particular act of homicide. It also lies in properly putting together or separating terms that have been precisely defined, as in noting that property and justice are necessarily conjoined and that absolute liberty and government are necessarily opposite.

It can be and has been objected that the latter procedure reduces ethics to an analysis of terms and ideas, without any bearing on moral obligation, on the objective reality to which terms such as "justice" refer, or on the determination of what is right and wrong in a particular case. J. W. Gough, for instance, complains that Locke's examples "amount to no more than defining the meaning of certain terms and then drawing tautologous conclusions from their logical incompatibility."[3] He means that we learn nothing from the statements that is not already contained in the terms, once we accept their definition. To say "Where there is no property, there is no injustice" is like saying "You cannot descend upward." It might be argued, however, that the more fully we see the implications of ethical terms, the deeper our ethical insight may be. And it might also be argued that, for lack of time or capacity, Locke never undertook the task of constructing the precise ethical science he envisioned—which would by no means prove that it could not be done.

The whole discussion, then, goes back to the question of whether ethical matters are of such a nature that they cannot be precisely and certainly known. Aristotle, as we have seen, argued cogently that this was the case, that we can have only probable knowledge in ethics, since the whole point of ethics is action, which must always be particular and is not ultimately subject to general rules knowable in advance. How does Locke deal with the stubborn fact of the particularity of con-

[3] *Op.cit.,* p. 7.

crete existence? Does he take it into consideration in his ethical philosophy? How, then, does he set off the roles of the probable and the certain in ethics?

A significant passage on this subject appears in his *Journal* where he distinguishes between "physique, polity and prudence" (medicine, politics, and private affairs) on the one hand, and "the truths of mathematics and morality" on the other. On the one hand, we cannot know for certain "whether this course in public or private matters will succeed well,—whether rhubarb will purge or quinquina cure an ague"; such things are a matter of practical experience and astuteness. On the other hand, we can know for certain "whether men make true mathematical figures, or suit their actions to the rules of morality or no." We can certainly know that "it is every man's duty to be just, whether there be any such thing as a just man in the world or no," just as we can know for sure the equality between the three angles of a triangle and two right angles, whether there are any actual triangles in the world or not.[4]

Thus Locke separates the realm of the practical arts from that of ethics. The arts deal with empirical situations to attain certain objectives, while ethics furnishes a transcendent norm to be applied to human actions. It might be objected to this neat division that the practical arts have ethical ends, that they aim at human goods. It might also be objected that we must apply the absolute ethical norm to particular situations in everyday life. Can we be absolutely sure of what is right and wrong in a particular contingency? Are the rules of morality applicable with exact precision to every concrete case? Is the rightness or wrongness of our actions to be judged only when we are able to determine what their consequences have been? Can we learn from the results in ethical decisions, as in the practical arts, so as to establish a moral prudence and rough general rules of action? Or are the fundamental principles of ethics necessarily established before and apart from any experience and any results?

[4] *Ibid.*, p. 6.

Is Locke's moral theory hedonistic, defining good according to the criterion of pleasure?

Locke holds that there is an absolute moral law providing the norm for our actions. Yet he also holds that good and evil are matters of pleasure and pain; and he defines happiness as "the utmost pleasure." Is he therefore contradicting himself? Is it pleasure or right that is to be the guide of our actions?

Before answering these questions, we should remember that Locke did not make *moral* good essentially a matter of pleasure but rather of the conformity of action with a moral rule. We should also note that he recognized that there are various kinds of pleasures—intellectual as well as sensual. (See p. 189a-b.) He also emphasized the pleasure that is experienced in acting rightly in conformity with the natural or divine law.

If we examine again the definition of moral good and evil, cited above on page 191, we see that the rewards and punishments connected with the moral law are a matter of pleasure and pain. Conformity with God's law brings complete happiness, disobedience brings utter misery.

Does it necessarily follow from this that Locke is advocating a "reward" ethics and would be subject to Spinoza's criticism of this type of moral motivation? Does Locke advocate that men should be good in order to obtain pleasure and avoid pain? Or does he mean that "being good" is necessarily accompanied with "feeling good," that a perfectly good man would be a perfectly happy man, feeling "the utmost pleasure"?

How would the findings of contemporary anthropologists on the diversity of moral standards affect Locke's moral theory?

A recent work by an anthropologist and a philosopher[5] points out that acts we regard as unquestionably evil, such as cannibalism, stealing, and adultery, are regarded as positive

[5] May and Abraham Edel, *Anthropology and Ethics* (Springfield, Illinois: Charles C Thomas, 1959).

virtues or a matter of moral indifference in some primitive societies. On the other hand, acts that we regard as right or a matter of indifference, such as eating one's own crops or eating in the presence of someone who is not a close relative, are regarded as indecent in these cultures. Not only is there a marked difference between primitive ethics and our own, but there is also an extreme diversity among primitive societies as to what is right and wrong in character and conduct, so that they may enjoin opposite standards of action.

What would be Locke's response to this statement? Would he assent to it as a description of the facts of human culture? How would it affect his disbelief in innate moral ideas? How would it affect his belief in a natural moral law that is universally applicable and knowable by human reason? How would it affect his view that, by and large, there is general agreement among mankind as to what is right and wrong?

Are primitive societies, on the grounds that they have not attained full rationality and morality, to be taken as exceptions to moral standards that prevail well-nigh universally in advanced civilizations? Or is it the case that Western civilization, through philosophy and religion, has attained the absolute truth about right and wrong, that this has not been clearly seen by men in other cultures but that they are capable of perceiving it once it is presented to them? Would the primitives mentioned above, for instance, after some exposure to Western, Judaeo-Christian moral doctrine, recognize at once that it is their moral duty "not to kill another man; not to know more women than one; not to procure abortion; not to expose their children; not to take from another what is his," etc.?

Would it be possible to find some traces of the natural moral law in primitive customs? Let us suppose that murder or stealing is prohibited among fellow tribesmen or members of the same family group. Would that indicate a partial recognition of the natural law, lacking the essential characteristic of universality? Are *all* extra-marital relations in primitive societies merely a matter of the mutual desires of the couples involved? Is incest also a matter of individual preference?

Are incest lines drawn more rigorously or more loosely than in our society? Let us suppose that the prohibition against incest is universal. Would that demonstrate that it is a precept of the natural moral law? Or could its universality be interpreted in another way, not ethically, but historically and psychologically, as it is by Freud?

The following questions are designed to help you test the thoroughness of your reading. Each question is to be answered by giving a page or pages of the reading assignment. Answers will be found on page 304 of this Reading Plan.

1 Why does not the justice obtaining among thieves prove that justice is an innate moral idea?

2 What book in *Great Books of the Western World* is cited as Locke's source for the "idols" of the mind?

3 What are the two modes by which the divine law is promulgated?

4 What homely example does Locke use for his definition of love?

5 What two passions are not found in all men, and why?

6 What type of reader is this work intended for?

7 Why does Locke think the critics of his short Epitome of this work had not read it?

KANT

Fundamental Principles of the Metaphysic of Morals

Vol. 42, pp. 251-287

Kant's moral philosophy is one of the highest achievements in the history of philosophical ethics. It ranks with the efforts of the great ancient moral philosophers Plato and Aristotle. Kant's thought, like theirs, took as its central problem the rational justification of moral judgment and action. It did so more consistently, more rigorously, and more extremely than had ever been done before, and with due awareness of the new vistas opened up by modern philosophy and of the new problems it set for philosophical ethics.

Kant sought a basic principle of morality, an unconditional ground of moral obligation, that completely transcends the realm of sense experience and the specific characteristics of human nature. His aim was to construct an ethics which is completely abstracted from natural desires and ends, even from the generic human desire for happiness. He found the basis of such an ethics in the "good will," which wills only those actions which can, without contradiction, be made universal laws for everyone.

This avowedly trans-experiential and trans-human doctrine may seem extreme, irrelevant, and even ridiculous at first glance. But, on second thought, we may find that much of Kant's ethics echoes the basic moral judgment of the common man, although with a far more elaborate intellectual apparatus and terminology. Kant separated the essentially moral from what is merely self-serving, and he put the ground of morality in the will instead of in results. Ordinarily we do something like this in judging our own actions or those of others.

Kant started from this common distinction and proceeded to draw from it the basic principles of his moral philosophy: the universality of moral laws, the rational being as end in itself, the self-legislating moral will, and the moral kingdom of ends. And he ended with a grand vision of man as a being who operates in two realms: the moral realm of freedom and the natural realm of necessity. It is an incredible achievement to have included so much in such a small compass.

Eleventh Reading

I

It is not altogether accidental that Kant follows Locke in this series of readings. Athough very much a German, Kant is the great inheritor of the British empiricist school of philosophy. It was David Hume, the lineal descendant of Locke in the British tradition, said Kant, who woke him from his "dogmatic slumber," that is, who showed him the decisive importance of understanding the nature, modes, and limits of human knowledge. Kant's great contribution, like Locke's, was a theory of knowledge, and like Locke, he stressed the role of sense experience in providing the basic materials for our knowledge of the external world.

Kant, however, contributed a much more systematic and profound account of the constructive role of the mind in the act of knowing, through the pure forms of sensibility (space and time) and the categories of the understanding (such as cause and substance). Our knowledge of the world comes through sense experience, he said, but it is produced by *a priori* elements of the mind. What we know, then, is the product of our sensibility and understanding, wrought from the materials of sense experience. These mental constructions are all that it is possible for us to know about the world. We can never know the ultimate reality of a thing, what Kant called "the thing in itself," but only its appearance to the mind, "the phenomenon."

This analysis, however, comprises only the sphere of the "theoretical" reason, or the "understanding," which deals with *what is,* and makes judgments of fact—a sphere which is set forth in the *Critique of Pure Reason,* Kant's most famous work. This analysis was only a preliminary clearing of the ground, so that he could get on to what he considered even more important—a critique of practical reason and a metaphysics of morals, setting forth the rational grounds of moral judgment, that is, our judgments of *what ought to be*. With this we enter a sphere beyond the range of theoretical knowledge, which is limited to constructs based on sense experience. We are now seeking the absolutely unshakable grounds of moral obligation, decision, and action.

This must be found in the reason, that is, in the *practical* reason (or will). No amount of sense experience whatsoever, says Kant, can possibly be the moral ground of my will. It cannot place me under moral obligation. It cannot provide the moral sanction for my decisions and actions. Nor can I find the absolute ground of morality through an analysis of human inclinations, desires, and psychological characteristics; thereby we may arrive at an account of the way things are in fact, but not how they should be, what men ought to do, what they are obliged to do. Hence, Kant assigned himself the task of discovering the basic principles and structure of the practical reason.

He fulfilled this task mainly in the little work discussed in this guide, in *The Critique of Practical Reason,* and in *The Metaphysic of Morals.* Also important in the complete scope of his ethical philosophy are *Religion Within the Limits of Reason Alone, The Science of Right,* and *The Critique of Teleological Judgement* (Part II of *The Critique of Judgement*).

I I

Compared to most of Kant's famous works, the *Fundamental Principles of the Metaphysic of Morals* is a mere sliver. Its thinness, however, is disarmingly deceptive, for it is packed with ideas and analyses of the highest import; and within its small compass it contains an elaborate intellectual structure and a closeness of reasoning that will take more than a few hours (or days) to master. However, we should not let its formidable title and strange terminology deter us from appreciating one of the masterpieces of ethical thought. The Preface and Section I state in comparatively simple fashion the basic purpose, structure, and principles of the work. A close and careful reading of these early parts will help to orient us in the later, more difficult sections.

Kant tells in the Preface what he is going to try to do in this work, and where it fits into the whole of moral philosophy, as he sees it. Ethics, like physics, he says, has both an empirical part and a purely rational part. Just as we try to disclose the basic principles and conditions of the physical world through a "metaphysic of nature," so we may try to discover the fundamental principles and conditions of morality through a "metaphysics of morals." Kant labels the empirical part of ethics "practical anthropology" (apparently a philosophical psychology of human conduct). Only the pure, rational part has to do with the truly moral realm and deserves the name "morality."

Scientific precision requires a clear distinction of the empirical and purely rational (or moral) aspects of ethics. And the absolute necessity that is inherent in moral obligation requires a purely rational ground, apart from and prior to sense experience, and, indeed, apart from human nature and man's situation in the world. Absolute universality is implied in our common notions of duty and the moral law. The precept, "Thou shalt not lie," must apply universally to all conceivable rational beings, not to man alone. It must be rooted *a priori* "in the conception of pure reason." Precepts based merely on experience may yield a practical rule for conduct but never an absolutely binding moral law.

In addition to these scientific or speculative reasons, there are cogent practical reasons for developing the purely rational part of ethics. Clear and exact knowledge of the true basis of morality prevents the insidious moral corruption that is involved in doing the right thing for the wrong reason—out of self-interest and personal inclination rather than for the sake of the moral law.

For in order that an action should be morally good, it is not enough that it *conform* to the moral law, but it must also be done for the sake of the law, otherwise that conformity is only very contingent and uncertain; since a principle which is not moral, although it may now and then produce actions conformable to the law, will also often produce actions which contradict it. (p. 254b)

Hence it is in "pure philosophy" or "metaphysic" alone that we can attain the essential ground and motive for moral action.

The present work will attempt only a preliminary approach to a metaphysics of morals, expounding in "necessarily subtle discussions" the basic principles for such a study. Indeed, Kant narrows down the subject matter of this work to one topic: "the investigation and establishment of *the supreme principle of morality*" (p. 255c).

This inquiry is divided into three parts. Section I starts with common moral knowledge and proceeds to popular moral philosophy, which combines both empirical and rational elements. Section II starts with popular moral philosophy and proceeds to a purely rational metaphysics of morals. Section III starts with a metaphysics of morals and proceeds to a critique, or critical examination, of the pure practical reason. The first two sections are to proceed "analytically"—from common moral experience and judgment to the formulation of the basic principle of morality. The last section is to proceed "synthetically" —from this principle and its sources in pure practical reason to its operation in common moral knowledge.

III

The first basic notion which Kant obtains from common moral knowledge is that of *a good will*. Section I opens with this resounding proclamation:

Nothing can possibly be conceived in the world, or even out of it, which can be called good, without qualification, except a good will. (p. 256a)

It alone determines whether our actions are morally good or bad. It is good in itself, without regard for results—such as attaining or preserving well-being or happiness. It is the supreme condition of every other good. Without a good will, the highest human endowments and virtues, even happiness itself, would not be good. The first and highest purpose of the practical reason is to produce such a will (and only secondarily to attain happiness).

In developing this basic notion of a good will, Kant comes to the notion of *duty*. Under the actual conditions of human existence, there are "certain subjective restrictions and hindrances" to the operation of a good will—various forms of self-interest, inclination, and desire. A good will is manifested most notably, as far as man is concerned, in ignoring or overcoming all such appeals and proceeding from duty, that is, purely from the sense of moral obligation. We see again that it is the basic motivation that determines the moral worth of an action. An act is not good merely because it conforms literally with moral precepts. We must act not only *as* duty requires, but also *because* duty requires it, "for the sake of duty."

Kant takes for his example the merchant who treats all his customers honestly, charging fixed, fair prices alike to the naïve and to the shrewd buyer. This is a morally good action only if the merchant is acting *from duty* in obeying the precepts of honesty. If he is acting out of self-interest, because he thinks that honesty is the best policy to secure success and profit, then he is not acting morally. *Any* desire or pleasure, even the desire to do good to others, is not, strictly speaking, a moral motivation. The actions of kindhearted, sympathetic persons are not thereby moral. To be so, they would have to be done from a sense of duty.

Kant pushes this apparently paradoxical point home by citing as his extreme example of moral heroism the man who does good to others purely from duty, although he is by temperament callous and indifferent to other people's sufferings. Although he has no *inclination* to philanthropy he *acts* philanthropically, against or in spite of his nature, because moral duty requires it. Greater good hath no man, says Kant. Indeed, it is this "practical" kind of love, he avows, that is enjoined by the precept of love of neighbor in the Bible, not the "pathological" kind that is a matter of mere feeling. We are obliged unconditionally to do good to our neighbor even though we loathe him. It is our action that is commanded, not our sympathy.

Kant puts this basic principle of moral action somewhat differently by contrasting "formal" and "material" maxims. A "maxim" is simply a principle or general rule that determines our actions. It is a "subjective" principle that would prevail universally for all rational beings. Maxims determine all kinds of activity, not only moral activity, and they may be either good or bad. "Do unto others as they do unto you" and "Tit for tat" are morally dubious maxims that guide many people's conduct.

Kant's basic distinction here is between formal and material maxims. The latter type has a certain object or end in mind, which is the "matter" or "content" of the maxim. Being honest with people in order that we may become popular or successful is a material maxim. A formal maxim, on the other hand, has no results in mind, no content, but is based on the "empty" concept of duty. The will of a man who is honest in business solely from duty is determined in this case by a formal maxim. Neither inclination nor results can play any role in truly moral action.

In a further step in his formulation of the basic principle of morality, Kant introduces the notion of "respect" (or "reverence") for the moral law. An action done solely from duty (moral obligation) implies (1) objectively, universal moral law; (2) subjectively, a feeling or attitude of respect for the law, and hence (3) the formal maxim of duty that governs actions.

The pre-eminent good which we call moral can therefore consist in nothing else than *the conception of law* in itself, *which certainly is only possible in a rational being,* in so far as this conception, and not the expected effect, determines the will. This is a good which is already present in the person who acts accordingly, and we have not to wait for it to appear first in the result. (p. 259c-d)

In a significant footnote (see p. 259d), Kant admits that respect for the moral law is a feeling, but holds that it is "self-wrought by a rational concept" instead of produced by external influences working on the senses. If we consider the law in its objective majesty as something to which we are unconditionally subject, our feeling is analogous with fear. If we consider it as something that we impose on ourselves, our feeling is analogous with inclination. Respect, then, is a kind of rational fear and inclination produced by the holy worth of the moral law.

So far Kant has set forth these three propositions about duty as the criterion of moral value:

1. Only action done for the sake of duty is morally good. (Action done from inclination or self-interest is not morally good.)

2. An action done from duty derives its moral worth from the formal maxim or principle of the will that one must do one's duty—apart from any results that may or may not be attained.

3. Duty is the necessity of acting from respect for the law— an objective moral law which is present as a concept within the rational being and self-imposed by him.

It is at this point, after formulating in various ways the basic notion of duty and stressing man's response to the moral law, that Kant makes his first statement of the fundamental criterion of moral action—the "categorical imperative." Law connotes universality. Hence, the test of the morality of an action is whether it can be universalized, to become the law for all persons, in all times, places, and conditions.

I am never to act otherwise than so *that I could also will that my maxim should become a universal law.* (p. 260a)

This is Kant's first formulation of the categorical imperative. It is the simplest of the many formulations he makes in this work. It contains the essential idea of the imperative—universal law.

Kant is convinced that it provides us with a simple test, ready at hand, easily applicable, and requiring nothing beyond common moral knowledge. He takes as his example the dilemma of whether we may make a false promise when in distress (for instance, to obtain urgently needed money, transportation, or a job). If we apply the categorical imperative, it is clear that we may not do this. Any decision made on the basis of a calculation of consequences—even the decision not to tell a lie because it might ultimately harm us—cannot become a universal law. Only the decision to tell the truth which is based on duty alone can be a law for me and, hence, may become a law for all rational beings. In showing that a false promise cannot be made a universal law, Kant appeals to a practical law of non-contradiction.

. . . while I can will the lie, I can by no means will that lying should be a universal law. For with such a law there would be no promises at all, since it would be in vain to allege my intention in regard to my future actions to those who would not believe this allegation, or if they over hastily did so would pay me back in my own coin. Hence my maxim, as soon as it should be made a universal law, would necessarily destroy itself. (p. 260c)

IV

In Section II, Kant tells us what imperatives are, points out the essential distinctions between moral and non-moral imperatives, and provides new formulations of the categorical imperative. The basic ideas for this discussion are to be found in the following passage:

Everything in nature works according to laws. Rational beings alone have the faculty of acting according *to the conception* of laws, that is according to principles, i.e., have a *will*. Since the deduction of actions from principles requires *reason*, the will is nothing but practical reason. If reason infallibly determines the will, then the actions of such a being which are recognised as objectively necessary are subjectively necessary also, i.e., the will is a faculty to choose *that only* which reason independent of inclination recognises as practically necessary. i.e., as good. But if reason of itself does not sufficiently determine the will, if the latter is subject also to subjective conditions (particular impulses) which do not always coincide with the objective conditions; in a word, if the will does not *in itself* completely accord with reason (which is actually the case with men), then the actions which objectively are recognised as necessary are subjectively contingent, and the determination of such a will according to objective laws is *obligation*, that is to say, the relation of the objective laws to a will that is not thoroughly good is conceived as the determination of the will of a rational being by principles of reason, but which the will from its nature does not of necessity follow.

The conception of an objective principle, in so far as it is obligatory for a will, is called a *command* (of reason), and the formula of the command is called an *imperative*. (pp. 264d-265a)

The commands of reason, then, expressed in imperatives, are addressed to imperfect beings who do not always do what reason tells them they should. A perfectly good or "holy" will, which is in perfect conformity with objective laws, is not subject to moral commands and obligation. Such a will requires no "ought" or "shall," for it already wills subjectively what is objectively right. But here we are concerned mainly with the relation of finite, fallible man to the moral law and, hence, to moral obligations and imperatives.

Kant brings out the distinctive characteristics of the moral imperative by contrasting it with non-moral imperatives. There are, for example, "imperatives of skill" which direct us how to achieve desired ends in the arts. There are also "imperatives of prudence" which direct us how to achieve the common end of all mankind—happiness. Kant calls these two types of imperatives "hypothetical" because they command an action which is a means to something else. "Do this," they say, "if you want to attain that."

The "imperative of morality," on the other hand, is "categorical." It simply says, "Do this," without any "if" clause. It is absolute and unconditional.

It concerns not the matter of the action, or its intended result, but its form and the principle of which it is itself a result; and what is essentially good in it consists in the mental disposition, let the consequence be what it may. (p. 266c)

All imperatives involve necessity, "an obligation of the will." (See p. 265c-d.) However, the necessity is of a significantly different nature in the hypothetical and the categorical imperatives. Only the categorical imperative is absolutely necessary and can properly be called a "command." Technical "rules of skill" and pragmatic "counsels of prudence" are conditional and depend on various contingencies; for instance, on whether I want a certain good or consider it essential to my happiness. Only a moral command, "belonging to free conduct generally," is absolutely obligatory.

However, it is much easier to find the rational ground of necessity in the hypothetical than in the categorical imperative. As regards the imperatives of skill, it is quite clear that whoever wills the end must will the means that are necessary to attain it. If I want to draw a geometrical figure, build a bridge, or become a ballet dancer, I must do the things that are required to attain my objective; hence, when I will any of these ends I implicitly will the means necessary to them. As for the imperatives of prudence, the same thing holds true, except that we are not sure what happiness consists in, and hence we follow merely probable "empirical counsels" rather than the absolute "precepts of reason." But, in principle, willing the end here too implies willing the means.

Hypothetical imperatives are what Kant calls "analytical" propositions, that is, the predicate is implied in the subject; here, specifically, the means in the end. But the simple implication of the means in the end does not apply to the categorical imperative, which has no end beyond itself. We cannot find its rational ground by an analysis of the subject of the sentence. It must also, as we have seen, be an *a priori* proposition, completely apart from and independent of experience. To find the rational justification for the necessity of an "*a priori* synthetical practical proposition" is a difficult task, which Kant postpones to Section III. He proceeds here instead to a more specific formulation of the categorical imperative.

V

He begins by putting the categorical statement of Section I into the imperative form.

Act only on that maxim whereby thou canst at the same time will that it should become a universal law. (p. 268c-d)

Next, associating the universality of law with the essential "form" of nature, he puts the basic "imperative of duty" thus:

Act as if the maxim of thy action were to become by thy will a universal law of nature. (p. 268d)

Here Kant surprisingly joins "the laws of nature" and "the laws of freedom," which he originally assigned to two different realms. (See p. 253a.) He does so to show, by analogy, that moral action must be determined by a principle as universal and impersonal as the laws of nature. For example, committing suicide when one grows tired of life, borrowing money one has no intention of repaying, neglecting a valuable talent for the sake of pleasure and ease, or refusing to aid others in distress—none of these acts can be willed consistently and without contradiction within the whole of things and events; that is, none can become a law of nature. Whatever exceptions we may want to make for ourselves in particular circumstances, we cannot will that these acts should become universal laws.

Thus far Kant has formulated the categorical imperative in terms of an objective *principle* or form of action—universality. Next he formulates it in terms of an objective *end* or ground of action. This must be an end which has *absolute worth* in itself, independent of human needs and actions. Such an end is found in *persons*—man or any other rational being—who exist as ends in themselves and who may not be used *merely* as means. Hence we get this formulation of the categorical imperative:

So act as to treat humanity, whether in thine own person or in that of any other, in every case as an end withal, never as means only. (p. 272b)

In his next formulation, Kant emphasizes the active role of the will—"the idea of *the will of every rational being as a universally legislative will*" (p. 273b). The will of rational being is not merely obedient to the universal moral law but itself makes the law to which it is unconditionally subject. Kant here espouses "the principle of the *autonomy* of the will" as opposed to *heteronomy*—a law imposed from without. All attempts to base moral obligation on an external law are bound to fail, because they make duty depend on interest, that is, on the "attraction or constraint" of the external lawgiver, and hence make it conditional, not categorical. Only a universal law which is produced by a rational being's own will, "a will, however, designed by nature to give universal laws," elicits absolutely unconditional assent. The categorical imperative, then, becomes

. . . always so to act *that the will could at the same time regard itself as giving in its maxims universal laws.* (p. 274c)

Kant then proceeds from this imperative, stressing the will and action of the individual rational being, to the grand idea of a *kingdom of ends,* that is, a realm or order to which all rational beings belong as ends in themselves and which is ruled by universal laws. This ideal "systematic whole" includes "rational beings as ends in themselves, and also the special ends which each may propose to himself" (p. 274b). As a lawmaking member of the kingdom of ends, a rational being possesses *dignity*, that is, intrinsic absolute worth, as distinguished from mere market or aesthetic value. Morality alone— the condition of being an end in oneself—has dignity.

> Now morality is the condition under which alone a rational being can be an end in himself, since by this alone is it possible that he should be a legislating member in the kingdom of ends. Thus morality, and humanity as capable of it, is that which alone has dignity . . . their worth consists not in the effects which spring from them, not in the use and advantage which they secure, but in the disposition of mind, that is, the maxims of the will which are ready to manifest themselves in such actions, even though they should not have the desired effect. (pp. 274d-275a)

The lawmaking member of the kingdom of ends is, in this realm, free of natural laws and obedient only to those which he makes himself and which are at the same time universal laws. Such autonomous lawmaking possesses dignity and elicits respect from every rational being.

> *Autonomy* then is the basis of the dignity of human and of every rational nature. (p. 275b)

We may, then, reformulate the categorical imperative thus:

> "Act according to the maxims of a member of a merely possible kingdom of ends legislating in it universally" . . . (p. 276d)

This formulation is put more forcefully in H. J. Paton's interpretation:

> 'So act as if you were always through your maxims a law-making member in a universal kingdom of ends.'[1]

This is the fifth and last formulation of the categorical imperative in Section II. Kant, however, speaks of only three formulations—one stressing the laws of nature; one, the end in

---

[1] H. J. Paton, *The Categorical Imperative* (London: Hutchinson's Universal Library, 1953), p. 185.

itself; and the third, the kingdom of ends. The first, he says, stressing universal law, is the basic criterion of moral action. The others are of rhetorical value, making it easier for intuition or feeling to approach the idea of unconditional obligation.

All of the formulations set forth by Kant fill out and explicate the original common-sense idea of an unconditionally good will. It must be recognized, he adds, that the ideal kingdom of ends cannot be realized in actuality unless all rational beings conform to the categorical imperative and the natural order cooperates. But success or failure in achieving this is not of essential importance for the good will. No result, not even the highest, can be a motive for the perfectly good will, for which only disinterested respect for moral dignity and the idea of duty can be the spur.

And it is just in this that the paradox lies; that the mere dignity of man as a rational creature, without any other end or advantage to be attained thereby, in other words, respect for a mere idea, should yet serve as an inflexible precept of the will, and that it is precisely in this independence of the maxim on all such springs of action that its sublimity consists; and it is this that makes every rational subject worthy to be a legislative member in the kingdom of ends: for otherwise he would have to be conceived only as subject to the physical law of his wants. (p. 276d)

The essence of things is not altered by their external relations, and that which, abstracting from these, alone constitutes the absolute worth of man, is also that by which he must be judged, whoever the judge may be, and even by the Supreme Being. *Morality,* then, is the relation of actions to the autonomy of the will, that is, to the potential universal legislation by its maxims. (p. 277a)

Autonomy of the will, then, is the supreme and sole principle of morality. Heteronomy is the source of all the false principles of morality and of the basic form of the hypothetical imperative: "I ought to do something if I wish for something else." It places the ground of morality in some object outside the will. Any motive for moral action based on an object outside the will falls under the stigma of "heteronomy"—happiness, self-perfection, or the will of God. This, then, is the role of autonomy in a perfectly good will:

An absolutely good will, then, the principle of which must be a categorical imperative, will be indeterminate as regards all objects and will contain merely the *form of volition* generally, and that as autonomy, that is to say, the capability of the maxims of every good will to make themselves a universal law, is itself the only law which the will of every rational being imposes on itself, without needing to assume any spring or interest as a foundation. (p. 279b-d)

VI

In Section III, Kant deals with the fact of moral freedom in a world of natural necessity. It is in the idea of freedom that he finds the external third term that will justify the categorical imperative—which is an *a priori* synthetical proposition. Freedom of the will in all rational beings is the basic presupposition underlying the moral principle of autonomy.

As a rational agent, belonging to the intelligible world, man is free. As a physical being, belonging to the sensible world, man is subject to causal necessity. He must then view himself from two standpoints—both as naturally determined and as morally free. These are complementary, not conflicting, aspects of the reality of human experience. It is because I *also* belong to the sensible world that I am directed by the categorical imperative, telling me what I ought to do. It is to a will influenced, but not determined, by sensual desires that the categorical "ought" (derived from an *a priori* synthetical proposition) is addressed.

Kant's view of man as a member of both the physical-sensible and the intelligible-moral realms is discussed more fully in the next reading.

VII

Does the categorical imperative forbid us to choose the lesser evil or the higher good?

Suppose a friend of mind is in a state of rage and despair at being rejected by the woman he loves. I know that he is an emotional and impulsive man, and I also know that he has a revolver. I think it possible or even likely that he will kill the woman, himself, or both. Hence, under some pretext or other, I get into his apartment, take the revolver, and hide it where he cannot find it. If he asks me, I lie to him and say I don't know anything about it.

Have I acted according to the categorical imperative in this hypothetical case? I have acted to prevent murder and suicide. Kant himself has taken suicide as an example of an act implicitly forbidden by the categorical imperative, and obviously he would consider murder another prime example of transgression. May I then look on myself as an auxiliary of the categorical imperative and consider my actions approved by it?

To answer this question, we have to go back through Kant's whole argument, from the very beginning. For an action to be good it must be done by a good will, that is, a will which is moved by duty alone. Did I act from duty alone, out of conformity to the moral law? Or did I act out of compassion or prudence (in some large, good sense)? I acted in order to keep my friend from killing himself and from killing the woman (whom I may or may not also have liked). My act was a means of preventing him from hurting himself and from hurting someone else. If all this is granted, then my act was not moral, in Kant's view.

If the act were moral, it would not be motivated primarily by compassion and benevolence, and it would not be a prudential means of attaining an end beyond itself. Furthermore, I would be able to will that everyone should do the same as I, that is, steal and lie, without any qualifications or conditions. Obviously, none of us is able to will rationally that stealing and lying should be the universal moral law. And we are willing to grant that the essence of morality is a good will, motivated by strictly moral reasons, and that moral rules must be universal, not permitting us to make exceptions for ourselves.

Still, common moral judgment also takes into account the concrete circumstances of moral action, and thus tends not to view stealing, lying, or even homicide as wrong where the particular situation demands it—for instance, for the prevention of harm, for self-defense, and for similar reasons. Am I forbidden by the categorical imperative to steal and hide the weapons of a dangerous lunatic, to lie to an ugly mob as to where their intended victim has fled, or to wound or kill a man who is trying to kill me or someone else? Does the categorical imperative forbid men to assassinate tyrants in order to end their unjust rule and save thousands or millions of men from being harmed or murdered? Is it not possible that some of the Germans who plotted Hitler's assassination were ethically motivated and that their intent could be morally justified?

Would Kant concede that any of the acts mentioned are *moral* acts, that they are *morally* either good or bad? If they are *non-moral* acts, just what kind of good or evil do they possess? Is the good or evil that we may attribute to such acts relevant to human ethics? Doesn't the boy in the Masefield poem who lies to the hunters as to the direction in which the fox has fled possess some admirable quality? Weren't the men who participated in the unsuccessful plot to assassinate Hitler, at the cost of torture and cruel execution, possessed of a certain virtue?

Why are such "virtues" irrelevant to a Kantian ethics? What is the advantage of a strictly formal ethics, which rules out such motives and qualities? Why is it destructive to attach conditions and qualifications to moral imperatives?

Does Kant's argument rely in part on the consequences of moral actions?

The argument against lying was that if everyone were to lie, then lying would become useless, since no one would believe anyone else. The argument against suicide was that if everyone did it, there would be an end to human life. The argument against not helping others in distress was that if everyone behaved like that, then we would be depriving ourselves of any hope of aid in the future. All of these are arguments in terms of consequences. Is Kant therefore contradicting his view that moral action cannot be judged in prudential terms?

In order to answer this question, we should reread the arguments and judge them in the light of Kant's basic ethical theory, as presented here. Each of the arguments tries to show the practical impossibility or contradiction of willing that any of the acts in question be made a universal law for all men. Kant argues that we cannot *will* that any of these acts be a universal moral law, although in some cases (idleness or un-charitableness) it might be universally practiced, as a matter of fact. It is an argument from practical absurdity, a didactic device to enable the reader more easily to grasp Kant's formal thesis.

The relevant question is this one: Does Kant say that we should do or not do any of these acts *in order to obtain or avoid the results* which he has pictured? If he does, then he clearly contradicts himself and presents what is, in his view, a non-moral motivation for moral action.

Is Kant's ethics a "cold" one?

Clearly, Kant rules out any kind of feeling or desire, even benevolence, brotherly love, or the desire for happiness, as a motivation of moral action. Is his ethics, therefore, a cold, arid, detached one, fit only for men whose natural feelings have withered away?

In answering this question we must, of course, remember that Kant does single out one feeling, "respect" (or "reverence") for the moral law, as essentially involved in true moral action —that done from duty alone. Does pleasure or satisfaction in fulfilling the moral law also play a role in Kant's account of moral experience? Does he rule it out entirely? Could it without contradiction be included in his ethics?

Kant denies that kindliness, sympathy, or "pathological" love may be the moral motive for action. Does this mean that they can play no role at all in moral action? Does the essentially moral quality of benevolence require an attitude of indifference or loathing toward one's neighbors? Or is Kant's extreme example in his contrast between "practical" and "pathological" love merely a didactic, rhetorical device to bring out the essential moral motive—in abstraction from everything else that is involved in human life and action?

Granted the strictly moral point, is it psychologically possible for a callous man to act benevolently, or for a man who loathes his neighbor to act on the command of love? Can ethics be separated from psychology?—in theory?—in practice? How do Kant's views on this question compare with those of Aristotle, Epictetus, and Spinoza?

The following questions are designed to help you test the thoroughness of your reading. Each question is to be answered by giving a page or pages of the reading assignment. Answers will be found on page 304 of this Reading Plan.

1 What are the three ancient divisions of knowledge?

2 To which division does empirical psychology belong?

3 What leads men to fall into "misology"?

4 Is it a moral duty to seek our own happiness?

5 Can the principle of moral perfection be taken from the example of Christ?

6 How does Kant define the term "pragmatic"?

7 Can we conceive the neglect of natural gifts as a universal law?

8 How do teleology and ethics, respectively, view nature?

KANT

Critique of Practical Reason

Part I, Book II
Vol. 42, pp. 337–355, esp. pp. 337–343

T he concept of the philosopher as an abstract thinker is utterly wrong, says Kant in this reading. The "wisdom" that is traditionally associated with the term "philosophy" is a practical wisdom, and the true philosopher must exhibit his love of such wisdom in his own person and activity. Indeed, the central mission of philosophy is to teach men what the supreme end—the *summum bonum*—of human life and action is and how to attain it.

It is within the framework of this concept of philosophy and the philosopher that Kant investigates the meaning of happiness and its relation to moral virtue, as well as the relative order of the speculative and the practical—the scientific and the ethical—in human reason and aspiration. In a startling reversal of the traditional order in these things, he attributes to the practical reason or moral experience a wider range of apprehension than is attainable through the operations of the intellect. The practical reason, according to

Kant, provides the speculative reason with basic metaphysical ideas which it cannot reach by itself and which it needs for its own work.

With the aid of two of these ideas—God and immortality—Kant provides a dramatic answer to the perennial question of how happiness and morality are possible in an apparently recalcitrant universe and in a finite human existence.

Twelfth Reading

I

According to Kant's announced plan in the *Fundamental Principles of the Metaphysic of Morals,* that preliminary ethical work was to be followed by a "popular" metaphysics of morals, and then by a critical examination of the pure practical reason. (See p. 255a-d.) He considered this the best order, in view of the practical need of applying the "fundamental principles" to ethical life, postponing the fundamental theoretical task of a critique of the practical reason until a later stage. Actually, however, the next work after the *Fundamental Principles* (1785) was the *Critique of Practical Reason* (1788), and the long-planned and long-awaited *Metaphysic of Morals* was not published until 1797. Kant apparently felt that important questions had been raised in the *Fundamental Principles* which could be dealt with only in a critique of practical reason; and that the strictly *a priori* foundations of the ethical theory presented in the earlier work required a critical analysis of practical reason to match the critique of speculative reason.

Assuming as a given fact of common human experience that we do apprehend the requirements of the moral law, Kant endeavors to examine just how the human mind comes to apprehend them and why the will is unconditionally commanded to act in conformity with them. This cannot be explained by the same type of analysis that applies to our knowledge of nature, for this is a matter not of knowledge but of action, involving moral freedom, not natural necessity. Furthermore, we require an absolute certainty as the basis of moral action which it is impossible, in Kant's view, to achieve in speculative knowledge, limited as it is by sense experience and mental constructions. Morality, it turns out, must necessarily assume certain basic ideas—namely, God, freedom, and immortality—which cannot possibly be demonstrated by sense experience and speculative reason. We cannot know them for sure, as a matter of objective theoretical knowledge, but we must be sure about them through a kind of rational faith in order to have an absolute rock for morality.

Hence, we must harmonize not only "the two standpoints"— nature and freedom—but also the speculative and practical functions of the reason. Otherwise, the certainty about the basic ideas which underlies our obedience to the moral law might be undermined by the agnostic conclusions of the critique of speculative reason. However, according to Kant, this cannot happen, because there is only one human reason, whether it is being exercised in the speculative or in the practical sphere; and instead of the practical reason being undermined by speculative agnosticism, the speculative reason is strengthened by the practical certainty to which it cannot attain by itself.

In its pure *a priori* state (undetermined by inclinations, results, etc.), the practical reason, then, has primacy over the speculative in any act of cognition where they are conjoined. The reason for this is that practical activity has primacy over theoretical knowledge. The "interest" of the practical reason is "in the determination of the *will* in respect of the final and complete end," whereas the "interest" of the speculative reason is in objective knowledge—a lesser, subordinate, and partial end. (See p. 343a.) Furthermore,

. . . all interest is ultimately practical, and even that of speculative reason is conditional, and it is only in the practical employment of reason that it is complete. (p. 343d)

Book II, entitled "Dialectic of Pure Practical Reason," provides an excellent example of Kant's approach to the questions raised above. The discussion of the *summum bonum* ("highest good") in Chapter 2 shows how the Kantian analysis is applied to one of the principal points of ethical theory since ancient times.

II

In *The Critique of Pure Reason*, Kant presented his view that man is both causally determined as a part of nature and volitionally free or self-determining as a part of a realm beyond that of sense experience. (See pp. 140-143.) This apparent contradiction is, in Kant's terminology, one of the "antinomies" of the pure speculative reason. The critical examination of these antinomies he called "dialectic."

This dialectic was still within the framework of a critique of the pure *speculative* or scientific reason, and provided a formal, theoretical justification for moral freedom. In the present reading, Kant develops and fills out this solution within the framework of a dialectic of the pure *practical* or ethical reason. He seeks specifically for the objective ground or end of pure practical reason (the moral law being the *subjective* ground, or principle determining the will), for the unconditioned object of moral action—the *summum bonum*.

He cautions us, however, to remember that the *summum bonum* as such cannot be the *determining principle* of the pure practical reason (or will), because it is an "object," an external end, and if it determined our will we would then fall into "heteronomy," which is non-moral. Only the moral law can be the determining principle of the pure will. However, if the moral law is thought of as the supreme condition of the *summum bonum*, then the idea of the realization of the highest good through the practical reason would also be the determining ground of the will, fulfilling the requirement of "autonomy." The *summum bonum* in this case is not an external object determining the will, but is subordinate to its supreme condition, the moral law, which determines the will according to the principle of autonomy. (See p. 338b-c.)

After this cautionary remark, Kant proceeds to a critical definition of the *summum bonum*. The term *summum*, or "highest," may mean either an unconditioned and primary condition ("supreme") or a whole which is not part of a larger whole ("perfect"). Virtue is the *supreme condition* of happiness, which is a necessary component of *perfect good*. Hence, the *summum bonum* must include both virtue and happiness, the one as the condition, the other as the content of the highest good.

Kant is convinced that these two elements are quite distinct and that moral action or quality and the pursuit of happiness are two different things, which must, however, be combined to constitute the *summum bonum*. He disagrees both with the Epicureans, that the pursuit or attainment of happiness is virtue, and with the Stoics, that the conscious possession of virtue is happiness.

The *summum bonum*, then, is a *synthesis* of two distinct concepts, a practically necessary synthesis which is made apart from experience. Its "deduction" (rational justification) must therefore be "transcendental"—based on a principle transcending sense experience.

It is *a priori* (morally) necessary to *produce the summum bonum by freedom of will:* therefore the condition of its possibility must rest solely on *a priori* principles of cognition. (p. 340a)

III

Kant states the problem presented by the "antinomy" of practical reason thus: Since the two elements of the *summum bonum* are not connected "analytically," by identity, they must be connected "synthetically," by a cause-and-effect relation. One, then, must be the cause of the other. However, we are faced with an impasse, for neither, according to Kant's ethical theory, can be the cause of the other.

The desire for happiness cannot be "the motive to maxims of virtue," because it is not a moral motive. (See the preceding argument in Book I, "The Analytic of Pure Practical Reason," pp. 304-307.) Nor can the maxim of virtue be "the efficient cause of happiness," because that depends "on the knowledge of the laws of nature and the physical power to use them for one's purposes" (p. 340b), not on moral disposition. The moral law, then, seems to be a vain command to attain what it is impossible to attain "by practical rules."

To extricate us from this impasse, Kant has recourse to the same procedure with which he harmonized the antinomy of the pure *speculative* reason, namely, to distinguish between man as a "phenomenon" (appearance) in the realm of natural causality and man as a "noumenon" (thing-in-itself) in a purely intelligible realm, which transcends the sensible world and at the same time provides it with its principle of causality. Man as noumenon in the *intelligible* world, then, contains a principle whereby natural causality is determined, a principle which is "free from all laws of nature." Similarly, in the *practical* realm, man has "a purely intellectual determining principle" of the causality he exercises in moral action, namely, the *moral law.* Hence,

. . . it is not impossible that morality of mind should have a connection as cause with happiness (as an effect in the sensible world), if not immediate yet mediate (viz., through an intelligent author of nature), and moreover necessary. . . . (p. 340d)

Therefore, while it is absolutely false to say that the pursuit of happiness produces a virtuous disposition, it is true to say that the latter produces happiness, provided we think of virtue as grounded in a noumenal realm that transcends the merely sensual world.

Kant grants that ancient moral philosophers, such as the Stoics and Epicureans, did not seek for the connection of happiness with virtue in a "transcendental" realm, finding them instead harmoniously joined in the life of the sensible world and marked by a feeling of pleasure, contentment, or peace of mind. However, he finds this view defective, for, granted that the virtuous man is happy only if he is virtuous, why is he virtuous in the first place? Why must he be moral? Why must his peace of mind depend on his consciousness of moral worth? Ordinary experience can provide no justification for this connection.

Kant gives an evaluation of the elements of moral experience which is quite different from that of the Stoics and Epicureans. For him, the pleasure that accompanies or follows moral activity is the result of a determining moral principle that transcends all sensible feelings (including those of the "inner" senses).

. . . the determination of the will directly by reason is the source of the feeling of pleasure, and this remains a pure practical not sensible determination of the faculty of desire. (p. 341c)

We must, however, avoid confusing the determination of the will by the moral law with the feelings of pleasure that result from it. Only the former can be the "spring" of moral action, never the latter.

IV

In an effort to get away from the connotation of "enjoyment" that is usually involved in the term "happiness," and to avoid the error of making "feeling good" the motive of moral action, Kant seeks an alternative term. He finds it in "self-contentment," which expresses the satisfaction that accompanies virtue or the consciousness of being virtuous. It indicates "a negative satisfaction in one's existence, in which one is conscious of needing nothing" (p. 342a). By "negative" Kant means that self-contentment is not the consciousness of the fulfillment of certain desires and inclinations, for instance, health, wealth, sex, or benefaction (this would be "positive" satisfaction). Self-contentment is "a negative satisfaction with one's state, i.e., *contentment*, which is primarily contentment with one's own person" (p. 342c).

More specifically, this is an *intellectual* contentment as distinguished from the *sensible* contentment that accompanies the satisfaction of the inclinations. It is based on the *consciousness of freedom*, "as a faculty of following the moral law with unyielding resolution," *independently of all inclinations*. (See p. 342a.) With this consciousness goes the "consciousness of mastery over one's inclinations, and therefore of independence of them, and consequently also of the discontent that always accompanies them" (p. 342c). Such consciousness brings a kind of enjoyment and even a kind of bliss, analogous to that attributed to God Himself.

Freedom itself becomes in this way (namely, indirectly) capable of an enjoyment which cannot be called happiness, because it does not depend on the positive concurrence of a feeling, nor is it, strictly speaking, *bliss*, since it does not include complete independence of inclinations and wants, but it resembles bliss in so far as the determination of one's will at least can hold itself free from their influence; and thus, at least in its origin, this enjoyment is analogous to the self-sufficiency which we can ascribe only to the Supreme Being. (p. 342c)

This completes Kant's solution of the antinomy of pure practical reason. He believes he has shown that virtue or the consciousness of virtue can produce a proportionate happiness, and hence, that virtue is the primary element of the *summum bonum*, with happiness its second element, dependent on the former for its existence. Thus conceived, the *summum bonum* is "the whole object of pure practical reason," which commands us to realize it with all our power.

Freedom, the basis of this solution, is one of the three "postulates of practical reason." The other two are immortality and the existence of God, which are discussed in Sections IV and V of Chapter 2. By a "postulate" here, Kant means a *practically necessary presupposition of moral action,* for such action assumes that the necessary conditions of obedience to the moral law do exist.

To obey the moral law requires a free will, unshackled by any empirical influences and inclinations. It also involves a perfect conformity of the will to the law ("holiness") that requires "an *endless* duration of the *existence* and personality of the same rational being" (p. 344a). Finally, obedience to the moral law involves happiness as the result of virtue, a result which can be assured only by the existence of a Supreme Being who has the power to harmonize the physical world with the *summum bonum* and establish an "exact harmony of happiness with morality" (p. 345b). Hence freedom, the immortality of the soul, and the existence of God are the three necessary postulates of the practical reason.

V

Can moral freedom be stifled by natural determination?

Kant recognizes the hindrances to external action and concrete fulfillment presented by the physical world, and hence he postulates a supreme, intelligent "author of nature" who will assure that good will ultimately triumph. Kant always holds fast to the principle that "what we ought to do, we can do." He also maintains the principle of absolute freedom of the will, unaffected by any natural causality, whether from within or from without. Hence, although man as a physical being is subject to mechanical causality, as a moral being he is absolutely free and self-determining. Moral freedom always has the preponderant power to overcome all physical determination, including psychological inclinations.

Freedom has a "transcendental" basis, beyond the reach of sense and speculative reason. Yet it is present in human conduct along with natural determination. This raises some highly significant moral and legal questions. To take an extreme example, damage to the brain which is serious enough to cause a highly distorted wave pattern on electronic recording devices is held by some medical and legal authorities to be a predisposing cause of violent and anti-social behavior. The Governor of California has called for tests on all men condemned to death for murder and similar offenses, to make sure that no one is executed for acts beyond his control—acts in which absolute freedom of the will is lacking. Can a man lose his effective "noumenal" freedom through disease or injury, so that natural "phenomenal" causes become the decisive factor in his conduct?

In such a case, where the power of practical reason has been short-circuited by physiological deterioration, we may say that the person is no longer a person in the Kantian sense, is no longer a rational being, and hence that no moral theory is applicable. However, there are less extreme cases, in which conduct seems to be connected with innate character, upbringing, or psychological development and complexes. Why, if man is a physical being subject to natural determination, does the Kantian ethics warrant a condemnation in such cases, which seemingly is "quite opposed to all equity" (p. 333d)?

For Kant's discussion of this question, see the "Critical Examination of the Analytic of Pure Practical Reason," especially pages 331a-334b.

Is Kant's view of happiness hedonistic?

After the *Fundamental Principles*, which frequently inveighs against a eudemonic (happiness) ethics, it comes as a surprise to see Kant devoting so much attention to happiness as an essential element of the moral life. In the present reading, morality is bound up with happiness in the *summum bonum,* the ultimate end or good of human existence. Happiness now is presented as the seal of human fulfillment. Although we do not act virtuously in order to attain happiness, but only out of conformity to the unconditional moral law, nevertheless virtue is the necessary condition of happiness. In this sense, then, happiness does have a moral, and not merely a prudential, significance.

Moreover, Kant does admit the element of pleasure, contentment, or peace of mind in happiness that is stressed by the ancient moral philosophers, seeing it as an accompaniment or consequence of the determination of the will by the moral law. He identifies happiness with a sense of self-fulfillment, the consciousness that one lacks nothing, accompanied by an almost divine joy or bliss. When Kant talks like this, we seem to hear echoes of Aristotle and Aquinas.

Where does the difference lie between Kant and the earlier writers? In the definition of the highest good? In the role of natural human powers and ends? In the emphasis on specific human goods in virtue and happiness?

Do Aristotle and Aquinas see moral virtue as a means of attaining happiness as an end? Would Aristotle disagree with Kant's "negative" definition of happiness, as something open and "global," not describable by any specific content? How does Kant's use of the "transcendental" compare with Aquinas' use of the supernatural? In what way does the role of God differ in Kant and Aquinas?

Is the doctrine of the *Critique of Practical Reason* on happiness and pleasure at variance with that of the *Fundamental Principles,* or complementary to it? Are there any passages in the latter work that indicate the positive moral role of happiness and pleasure? Would it be possible to describe Kant's moral theory in the present selection as hedonistic? Why or why not?

What is the philosophical significance of the primacy of the practical reason?

Moral action has a high place in the ethics of Aristotle and Aquinas, but it is ultimately subordinate to contemplation, which is regarded by them as the highest power of the human soul. Kant, however, puts the practical function of the reason at the top, with the speculative function subordinate. He puts deeds and acts above theoretical knowledge, even of the highest order.

Is the will, then, placed above the intellect? But how can we clearly distinguish between the will and the intellect, if "all interest is ultimately practical," including that of the speculative reason? Is the one human reason, then, essentially practical, essentially will, with speculation as one of its expressions? Is intellectual cognition, the act of knowledge, a department of human conduct, ultimately subject to the will determined by the moral law? Is the awareness of the "transcendental ideas" of freedom, immortality, and God a kind of knowledge attained through moral action and experience?

Is this primacy of the practical or moral more in line with the Biblical view of man or with that of the Greek moral philosophers and later thinkers directly influenced by them?

Are the postulates of God and immortality at variance with Kant's fundamental ethical theory?

Kant's basic emphasis in the *Fundamental Principles* is on the power, as well as the duty, of the human person to conform with the moral law, which is a matter of self-legislation as well as an objective command. The *Critique of Practical Reason* builds on this basic framework. In the earlier work, Kant is well aware of the limitations placed on the achievement of the kingdom of ends by the natural order and the moral failure of other persons. But he is quite clear that everyone must and can act from duty alone, in such a manner that he can will that his act be made a universal law; that everyone must and can have a good will, whatever the state of the external world and other persons.

However, in the present reading he emphasizes the perfection of will and the harmony of nature and morality, a perfection and harmony which require an "endless duration" of personal existence and a supreme cause which will assure that virtue and happiness always go together. Has Kant illegitimately or perversely introduced concepts which clash with his central emphasis on the autonomous operation of human will and reason? Is he inserting the "pie in the sky" lure which he castigates as immoral in every "reward" type of ethics? Is he linking morality to an external legislator and thus bringing back the specter of "heteronomy" which he has labored to exorcise?

Before answering these questions, we should reread those passages in the *Fundamental Principles* that distinguish between the merely *good* will and the *holy* will, which conforms with the moral law without the need for duty and commands. We should also reread the passages about the kingdom of ends and the brief references to its "sovereign." Then we may return to the passages in the *Critique* about the immortality of the soul and the existence of God, and make up our minds on the question whether they fit in with the argument in the *Fundamental Principles* and whether they do violence to Kant's basic principle of autonomous conformity with the moral law without regard to results or rewards.

Is the acceptance of the postulates of immortality and of God's existence necessary for the achievement of moral virtue in the Kantian sense in the day-to-day life of the individual person? Is their acceptance necessary to affirm a proportionate relation between morality and happiness? Is their acceptance necessary for a coherent view of the moral order within the whole scheme of things?

Does the introduction of these postulates add anything to the presentation of the argument in the *Fundamental Principles?* Which is more easily understandable to you in grasping Kant's argument—the idea of a kingdom of ends or the postulates of an immortal soul and a divine harmonizer of the natural and moral orders?

The following questions are designed to help you test the thoroughness of your reading. Each question is to be answered by giving a page or pages of the reading assignment. Answers will be found on page 304 of this Reading Plan.

1 What is the "inevitable illusion" of human reason?

2 What school of philosophy identified prudence and morality?

3 What was the common misinterpretation of Epicurus' ethical teachings?

4 Why are inclinations "burdensome" to a rational being?

5 What kind of practical reason should the speculative reason *not* depend on?

6 Why is the postulate of immortality salutary both ethically and religiously?

7 What is the main difference between Christian morality and Greek moral philosophy?

HEGEL

The Philosophy of Right

Part III, Sub-section I, "The Family," with Additions 101-115
Vol. 46, pp. 58-63, 133-135

Georg Wilhelm Friedrich Hegel believed that thought is the essence of reality, manifesting itself in the concrete course of things and events. Certainly his own thought has been embodied in cultural and political movements in our time. Two of the most influential schools of thought today, Marxism and Existentialism, although opposed to Hegelianism, arose out of it. Some historians of culture believe that Fascism, Communism, and the totalitarian spirit generally grew out of Hegel's doctrine that the state is the fulfillment of human existence.

However, a careful reading of *The Philosophy of Right* and *The Philosophy of History* indicates that whatever historical accuracy such views may have, the intellectual and political movements in question were not consciously intended by Hegel, and he would undoubtedly have disowned them.

Hegel identifies the ethical with the universal and concrete—both at once. He acknowledges the partial

241

validity of the sense of duty and the important factor of individual conscience in moral matters, but, unlike Kant, he refuses to accept what he calls mere "morality" as the central aspect of ethics. For Hegel, ethics in its perfection is social, not individual.

This reading discusses the primary manifestation of "ethical life"—the family. Hegel deals with marriage as an ethical union, the respective ethical roles of parents and children, the right and wrong sharing of family property, the ethical purpose of education, the nature and effects of divorce, and the ethics of sexual relationships.

Thus, the thinker with a reputation for the most abstract and abstruse thought provides us with the most concrete ethical topics. Far from being paradoxical, this is in accordance with Hegel's whole philosophy. What is most abstract becomes most concrete in his system, where the speculative reason—on a cosmic scale—is restored to its throne and its dominion is extended to all things, including the ethical realm.

I

The key terms in Hegel's thought are "idea" and "development." Reality, in Hegel's view, is essentially ideal or rational. It is actualized through a process of development called "dialectic." This dialectical development moves through three stages, phases, or "moments": a primary positive stage ("thesis"), a secondary negative ("antithesis"), and a final positive stage ("synthesis"), which becomes the basis for a new dialectical development.

For instance, if we think an abstract concept such as "being" deeply enough, we reach the opposite concept of "nothing" or "non-being," and if we keep on thinking through this concept we reach the concept of "becoming," which is a synthesis of being and non-being. But the dialectic is not merely a process of abstract thought; indeed, the whole point of Hegel's philosophy is that thought is energizing, productive, fulfilled in concrete actuality. Thought makes the world go around. Human history and culture are the fulfillment of thought—universal thought at the core of reality, not merely human thought.

The dialectical development of an idea, such as right, is a development both in thought and in things, for the ideal and the real are ultimately one. *The Philosophy of Right,* for instance, discusses the idea of right, which in its pure concept is absolute freedom of the will. Its development comprises a primary stage of abstract or formal right, a mediate stage of subjective, individual morality, and a final stage of social, ethical life. An idea, for Hegel, is not something merely mental, identical with a bare concept. Its fullness as an idea requires actualization, as here in the individual will and social life.

Each stage does not merely leave the preceding stage behind, but includes it and perfects it. To describe this transition, Hegel uses a German term (*aufheben*) which literally means "raise up." As he uses it, it means "annul," "preserve," and "elevate" at the same time, for all three actions occur when one stage is succeeded by another. The earlier stage is done away with, but at the same time it is preserved and perfected in the later stage, as a seed in a flower, or a chrysalis in a butterfly. In the work under discussion, ethical life includes and fulfills the earlier stages of abstract right and morality; and within ethical life, the state is the fulfillment of the earlier sub-stages of the family and civil society—and thus of the whole idea of right.

This may be and has been called a 'spiritual evolutionism," based on the working out of ideal principles at the core of reality. Hegel scornfully rejected the merely naturalistic type of evolutionism, which has become familiar to us through Darwin, and certainly would have reacted in the same way to the "materialistic dialectic" of his most famous student, Karl Marx. Reality, for Hegel, is essentially ideal and developmental at the same time.

At the end of the Introduction (see p. 20b-d), Hegel tells us how he has applied this method to the idea of right and why he has divided it exactly the way he has. A glance at the Table of Contents (see p. ix) shows immediately how systematically and consistently he has applied his three-stage pattern. There are three main parts to this treatise—no more, no less. Each of the parts is, in turn, divided into exactly three sections. In some cases, the sections are themselves divided into three sub-sections; and sometimes the sub-sections are also divided into three parts.[1] These systematic boxes within boxes require an apparatus of Roman numerals, capital letters, and Greek letters to keep things neat and orderly. Hegel's orderliness makes Kant,

[1] The "Additions," numbered from 1 to 194, on pages 115-150 are derived from the lecture notes of Edward Gans, a student of Hegel's and an early editor of this work. They are indicated in our text by an [A.] at the end of a "paragraph," that is, of one of the 360 numbered sections which constitute the book. For instance, at the beginning of our reading an [A.] appears after Paragraph 158. Looking back in the Additions, we see that it is Addition 101. (See p. 133b.)

with his famous "architectonic" mind, seem haphazard in comparison.

Unlike Kant, Hegel was convinced that we can know everything and know it certainly, that it is possible to create a thought system that will reflect and predict the whole of reality. Such a grandiose ambition certainly requires systematic orderliness for its fulfillment by the merely human mind.

II

The Philosophy of Right, as we have noted, is divided into three parts. Part I deals with abstract or formal right, comprising legal rights and wrongs (property, contract, torts, fraud, crime, etc.). Part II deals with the sphere of individual morality and conscience—of "duty" in the Kantian sense. Part III deals with concrete ethical life, as embodied in the social institutions of the family, civil society, and the state. It reconciles the merely formal stage of *rights* and the merely subjective stage of *duties* in the fullness of corporate human life, where the good becomes concretely actual or "real."

Seen in relation to this concrete wholeness of ethical life, moralistic as well as legalistic right is abstract and formal. "Duty" is a purely formal principle; no specific precepts can be drawn from it. "Conscience" is merely individual and subjective. Duty and conscience are concerned with what *ought* to be; the *realization* of what ought to be in concrete reality requires a transition to another stage of the development of the will. This is the stage of *the objective ethical order,* where the good is actualized through social groups and institutions.

The family is the first "moment" in this stage of development. It is, says Hegel, "ethical mind in its natural or immediate phase" (p. 57d). It is "natural or immediate" because it arises directly out of natural biological impulses and the human feeling of love. The ethical here takes form in a concrete relation between individuals, in which they go beyond the lesser stage of being independent and self-subsistent individuals to become interdependent members of a larger whole. Rights and duties are inseparable here and are defined by the person's function in this primary ethical group—as husband, wife, parent, or child.

Marriage is the first of the three phases of the family. It is an immediate ethical relationship or bond, based on the sexual union between man and woman, which is transformed into love—"unity of an ethical type" (p. 133b). As natural, it functions to carry on the race. As ethical, it is based on the free consent of the two persons involved, and is realized in their mutual fulfillment—"in their love, trust, and common sharing of their entire existence as individuals" (p. 58d).

Hence Hegel rejects the idea that marriage is a contract, similar to a business agreement, between two independent individuals. The so-called "marriage contract" is actually a contract between the two persons to transcend the contractual level of their relations with one another and to become one person. This identification is the expression of "the ethical mind" and was revered in ancient forms of religion.

Hegel also rejects the view that marriage is merely a sexual relationship as well as the view that the love between a man and a woman can completely transcend the physical relation. The first view ignores the fact that marriage is an ethical bond, in which love is the central feeling. The second view ignores the fact that the sexual relationship is an essential natural condition of there being any marriage or family at all.

Hegel, however, distinguishes between "concubinage," or extra-marital sexual relationships, in which sexual satisfaction is the main motive, and marriage, in which it is secondary. In a true marriage, as he sees it, "the sensuous moment" or aspect becomes increasingly subordinate to the essentially ethical aspect, expressed in "reciprocal love and support" (p. 59b).

Despite his repeated emphasis on the factor of love, Hegel does not think that love by itself is enough to make marriage an ethical relationship. Or, more precisely, he does not think that love as a mere subjective feeling, contingent and perhaps ephemeral, is enough to make marriage a solid ethical bond. Marriage is *ethico-legal* love, as distinguished from a merely "transient, fickle, and purely subjective" feeling (p. 133c). That is why he thinks the formal wedding ceremony is an indispensable element of a real marriage, not a mere superfluous formality or legal requirement. Marriage, the immediate ethical tie, is not a matter of surrendering to subjective inclinations, feelings, and desires, but rather of restraining and subordinating them to the objective, substantial ethical union which is its content.

Hence, despite his stress on free consent, Hegel chooses the extreme of marriages arranged by benevolent parents in preference to the other extreme of marriages inspired merely by the subjective inclinations of the man and woman. Particularity cannot be ethical, for Hegel; only the universal has an ethical character. ("Particularity" here is expressed in sentimental "crushes" or erotic "yens.") Hence Hegel is sardonic about the romantic emphasis on passion and the state of being in love in contemporary literature.

A "double standard" for men and women seems to operate in sexual morality, but that is simply the practical effect of the distinctive sexual characteristics, which are intellectual and ethical as well as physical. A girl, says Hegel, is ethically ruined by submitting to pre-marital sexual relations, because her essential sexual role is as a wife and mother within the family. With a man, however, the consequences of extramarital intercourse are not so serious, for he has a wide sphere of ethical activity outside the family—in economic, academic, social, and political life.

Man, according to Hegel, is a thinker and a doer by nature, with a capacity for abstract thought and the will to productive action in the world. Woman is more passive and subjective in relation to the world of thought and action, more concrete and intuitive in her thinking, and more integrated mentally than man. "Woman . . . has her substantive destiny in the family, and to be imbued with family piety is her ethical frame of mind" (p. 60a). That is so true that when family piety conflicts with the law of the land, woman feels impelled by allegiance to a higher law to disobey the civil law, as illustrated in Sophocles' tragedy *Antigone*.

III

The second phase of the family is property or capital. Family capital is permanent property, which is the common possession of all the members, not merely a means of satisfying the needs of a particular individual. Just as marriage transcends individual inclinations and satisfactions, so property in the family transcends merely material needs; it is "transformed into something ethical, into labour and care for a common possession" (p. 60d). The husband has the specific function of providing for the economic needs of the family and controlling and administering its wealth, but he controls and administers it for the good of all the members, not solely for his own benefit.

This leads to the third phase of the family—the education, care and upbringing of children. Children are the objective manifestation of the essential unity, of the "one person" formed by the union of man and wife. They are not things or slaves, but, as full members of the larger "person" constituted by the family, they are endowed with ethical personality, which is to be developed and fulfilled through parental care. The culmination of this development is the exit of the children from the parental family to form families of their own.

Mutual rights and duties are involved in the relations between parents and children. It is the duty of the parents to support, care for, and bring up the children—the child has a right to these things. The parents have the right to demand services from children, and to discipline and punish them, for the sake of developing their moral character, not in deference to abstract justice. The child has the duty to obey their commands.

The ethical significance of the education of children lies in the fact that their potential freedom is actualized through parental care and upbringing. Education, then, has two aims: (1) Its *positive* aim is to instill ethical principles "in the form of an immediate feeling," through love, trust, and obedience, thus establishing "the foundations of an ethical life" at an age when the basic principles cannot yet be grasped through the intellect. (2) Its *negative* aim is to raise the children out of this early natural dependence to a stage where they can stand on their own and have reached a level of freedom and personality which permits them to leave the family. Thus, paradoxically, the fulfillment of the family, achieved through the education of its children, results in its dissolution.

Several complementary themes are interwoven in Hegel's account of the educational process. On the one hand, feeling is of the utmost importance, especially in the early stages. For his ethical development, the child absolutely requires the warm, healthy atmosphere engendered by love and trust— "rationality must appear in him as his very own subjectivity" (p. 135a). On the other hand, an authoritarian directiveness is essential. Indeed, the purpose of discipline, an important factor in education, is "to break down the child's self-will and thereby eradicate his purely natural and sensuous self" (p. 134d). It is because the child is at the stage of mere feeling, subject to "immediate fancies and caprices," that he requires firm discipline and direction in order that he may develop into a free, independent personality. For these reasons Hegel opposes what he calls "the play theory of education."

The necessity for education is present in children as their own feeling of dissatisfaction with themselves as they are, as the desire to belong to the adult world whose superiority they divine, as the longing to grow up. The play theory of education assumes that what is childish is itself already something of inherent worth and presents it as such to the children; in their eyes it lowers serious pursuits, and education itself, to a form of childishness for which the children themselves have scant respect. The advocates of this method represent the child, in the immaturity in which he feels himself to be, as really mature and they struggle to make him satisfied with himself as he is. But they corrupt and distort his genuine and proper need for something better, and create in him a blind indifference to the substantial ties of the intellectual world, a contempt of his elders because they have thus posed before him, a child, in a contemptible and childish fashion, and finally a vanity and conceit which feeds on the notion of its own superiority. (p. 61c-d)

IV

The fact that the family dissolves, whether through the development of the children or through other causes, indicates that although it is the first it is not the highest aspect of ethical life. Since it originates in marriage, which is grounded in subjective feeling and free consent, it depends on what is a very uncertain and alterable thing—what Hegel calls "contingency." A family can become sundered when the two persons upon whose union it is based become totally estranged from one another; that is, when a marriage ends in divorce. It can also be broken by the death of a parent, particularly that of the father.

Hegel calls the breaking up of the family through the coming of age of the children "ethical dissolution" and the destruction of the family through death "natural dissolution." He has no name for its sundering through divorce but, following his description of marriage as "ethico-legal" love, we may call this dissolution "ethico-legal," since it requires the sanction of an ethical authority—the church or the state. He does not go into the ethical problems of divorce at length, merely insisting that it must be based on real estrangement, not on mere whim or passing mood. He grants that marriage *ought* to be indissoluble, but that since it essentially involves feeling, it is necessary in practice to permit divorce—"for the hardness of your heart," in the words of the New Testament. (See pp. 133d-134a, 135a-b.)

The death of the father, however, does involve important ethical problems, principally that of inheritance, "the transfer to private ownership of property which is in principle common" (p. 62a). If the family property were merely an individual possession, then the father could squander it in any way he chose or could will it to his favorite friends. Hegel denies that such arbitrariness can in any sense become "the principle underlying the right to make a will, especially if it runs counter to the substantive right of the family" (p. 62c). He extends this rejection of arbitrary freedom to willing property outside the family in order to preserve the larger blood group of the "clan" or *gens,* or to favoring sons or the eldest son as against the other children. The substantive group at this level of ethical life is the family; its members alone possess first claim to the family capital and, in principle, it should be shared among them equally. Hegel castigates the ancient Roman legal system, which violated these principles, as "harsh and unethical," and "a legal road . . . to the corruption of manners." (See pp. 62d-63c.)

In any case, that ethical unit, the family, breaks up for one reason or another into a number of new families. These new families act as independent units or "persons" in relation to other families similarly produced, and thus enter the phase of "civil society." The latter association is not based on common ancestry as in the "clan" type of belonging; indeed, it becomes effectually an association among individuals, based on the principle of difference rather than that of unity and apparently on the principle of particularity rather than that of universality. (See p. 135c.) It is an association based on the private needs and interests of individuals, which are satisfied by mutually accepted accommodations and restraints, something like the society envisioned by the social contract theorists or the *laissez faire* economy described by Adam Smith. Unlike the social contract theorists, however, Hegel does not identify civil society with the state.

The state, for Hegel, is not a grouping designed for the convenience of individuals. Like the family, it emphasizes the principle of unity, the good of the whole, and the individuals within it are fulfilled as members of the whole. Unlike the family, it is permanent, even "eternal," and the full development of its members entails the life, not the death, of the state. Unlike the family, it is based on reason, not feeling. While the family is the primary embodiment of the ethical idea, the state is its ultimate fulfillment.

V

Is the predominance of the social over the individual in Hegel's thought destructive of ethics?

R. Mackintosh has the following to say on the place of ethics in Hegel's thought:

Hegel himself is evidently less interested in the moral consciousness than in the moral institution. He finds deliverance in the latter from the defects and from the sharp antitheses of the former. Sociology, Politics, Economics, Ethics, all enter into his "Philosophy of Right"— the very name is significant. If there is a stepchild in the family, it is ethics.[2]

[2] R. Mackintosh, *Hegel and Hegelianism* (Edinburgh: T. & T. Clark, 1913), p. 207.

Noting this directly after our readings in Kant, which emphasize the centrality of the individual moral consciousness, we may feel that Hegel is belittling the very element which is essential in both common and philosophical ethics.

Sören Kierkegaard, not long after Hegel's death, voiced what has become the most influential criticism of this aspect of Hegel's thought. For Kierkegaard, man is essentially an individual, not a member of a species or race; and ethical and religious truth is known through individual existence and decision —through subjectivity, not objectivity. Systems of thought and a dialectic such as Hegel's are matters merely of thought, which cannot comprise individual existence and decision. Such systems leave out, said Kierkegaard, the unique and essential "spermatic point, the individual, ethically and religiously conceived, and existentially accentuated."

Similarly in the works of the American author Henry David Thoreau, writing at the same time as Kierkegaard, there is an emphasis on the solitary individual as the bearer of ethical responsibility, who, when he is right, carries the preponderant ethical weight against the state, the government, and a united public opinion, when they are wrong. The solitary individual with right on his side is always "a majority of one." Against manifest evils, such as slavery or an imperialistic war against a neighboring country, he acts to subvert what is iniquitous, never cooperating with it, even indirectly. He does not wait until unjust laws are revoked or altered; he disobeys them. He does not merely vote; he acts, exercising the virtue of "civil disobedience." The moral health of the community rests on the acts of such prophetic individuals, who, in their ethical quality, are greater than any state or government.

Can the individual rightfully set up his "hearing" of the command of right against the authoritative voice of state power, speaking for the community as a whole? Is it wrong for him actively and overtly to oppose something which may be acceptable at one stage of historical development (for instance, slavery), although it may be revealed as, or become, wrong at a later stage? Does the individual attain his ethical personality only as belonging to the larger whole of the family, society, or the state? Is the fully human person a "social self" rather than a "private individual"? Why is the moral consciousness and decision of the individual necessarily abstract and unfulfilled by itself? Is the passive resistance of an isolated individual or a handful of individuals necessarily without any concrete ethical effect? Or is it only when society and the state incorporate the moral sense of such individuals in institutions and laws that their resistance becomes ethically concrete and real?

Are all extra-marital sexual relationships lacking in a central ethical quality?

Don't love affairs between men and women normally involve a specifically human or ethical quality? Aren't personal love and physical desire interwoven in most normal sexual relations? Can't mutual tenderness and care be as much present, sometimes more so, in such relations as in a legally sanctioned union? Or is it permanence and the inclusion of the future (and potential children) in the present moment of joy that make the difference, ethically speaking?

But what of the lifelong extra-legal unions of certain anarchists in the late nineteenth and early twentieth centuries, which were marked by impeccable fidelity between the partners and the responsible care for off-spring? What of the lifelong extra-legal union of the writer James Joyce and his wife, which established a fairly solid family life in the most trying conditions? Or are these unions of free consent formed on the model of what should obtain in regular marriages?

But isn't the formal ceremony itself a significant difference, according to Hegel? Doesn't this symbolize, if not make, all the difference? Aren't the anarchists or the Joyces deliberately flouting the common bond and good, in Hegel's view? Are they therefore doing wrong?

Is the sexual relationship ethically good, or contributory to ethical (as distinct from aesthetic) good, only within the Western institution of monogamous marriage? Would an affirmative answer amount to attributing absolute worth to relative values which are bound up with a particular social order and pattern of human relations? Or would it be based on some universally ethical ground? Can continuity of the social order or the human race be an ethical ground for limiting sexual relations within some form of marriage? Can the view be defended that sexual relations are something essentially private, with which the state and the laws have no right to interfere?

How would Kant deal with sexual matters? If he were to place restrictions on sexual intercourse, what would his grounds be, as distinct from those of Hegel?

Does an unmarried girl "lose her honor" through a sexual relationship?

Hegel says that an unmarried "girl in surrendering her body loses her honour" (p. 134a). This conclusion is based on the division of the sphere of ethical fulfillment for man and woman, involving a double standard in sexual ethics, since man does not lose his honor by engaging in extra-marital sexual relations. Is Hegel merely reading into his supposedly rational ethics the common views and attitudes of his time, or is he making a significant and permanently valid ethical distinction?

Is a woman's "honor" involved in one type of action alone, the sexual? Could a woman also lose her honor through dishonesty, deceit, fraud, and other common moral lapses? Or is it her honor specifically as a woman, rather than generally as a human being, that is in question here? Would any and every voluntary act of extra-marital intercourse, then, defile a woman ethically, no matter what the motivation or who her partner was?

Why would Hegel reject the possibility that any pre-marital experience could leave a girl with her "honor" intact? What would he say if the girl gave "love" as a reason?

Is love merely a feeling?

Hegel attributes a good deal of ethical value to love, but love is essentially a feeling for him, and therein lie its ethical limitations. But admitting that we have a feeling of love for someone, or that certain feelings accompany a love relation, is love thereby reduced to a feeling? Some present-day philosophers see love as a relation between beings, that is, between personal beings, in which feeling is an accompaniment but not central. If this more substantial interpretation of love were granted, what effect would it have on Hegel's theory of the more developed manifestations of "ethical life"? Would it follow that society, the great community, could be based on love, rather than on law?

Can authoritarian directiveness produce a free, independent personality?

Would such directiveness produce the kind of free personality that would fit in with the American type of society and personal relationships? If not, would that indicate that there was something wrong with Hegel's view or with American society? What present-day tendencies in American education support or oppose Hegel's educational theories? Is there any cultural or educational value in "play"?

Would a child-centered permissiveness result in a free, independent personality or a dependent, uncertain one? Which type of education would more likely produce an authentic, individual moral sense—the authoritarian or the permissive? Which would be more likely to produce an aggressive, dominating personality type? Which of the two extremes of education would you prefer, if you had to choose, for the strengthening of your children's moral character?

The following questions are designed to help you test the thoroughness of your reading. Each question is to be answered by giving a page or pages of the reading assignment. Answers will be found on page 304 of this Reading Plan.

1. What is the significance of marriage settlements?

2 Why did Cicero divorce his wife?

3 What is the natural way of education for women?

4 Why do parents love their children more than children love their parents?

5 What ancient practice was a "gangrene of the ethical order"?

6 What right is based on the fact that man has to attain his desired status by himself?

7 Why is marriage essentially monogamous?

MILL

Utilitarianism

Vol. 43, pp. 443-476

Mill says of utilitarianism in effect what William James later said of pragmatism—that it is merely a new name for an old way of thinking. At the very start of this essay, Mill traces utilitarianism back to Socrates, or at least to the Socrates created by Plato in his dialogues. Certainly the determination of the rightness or wrongness of human conduct by the good or bad consequences it leads to goes back at least that far. And the coupling or identifying of the useful or expedient with the good is to be found in Aristotle and in Spinoza. The linking of the good and the pleasant, as well as of pleasure and happiness, goes back to the early days of the Western tradition, not only to Epicurus and his followers, but also to Aristotle. And this theme is repeated, with a different emphasis, by modern philosophers such as Hobbes and Locke.

We may say, then, that the elements of utilitarian ethics—based on the principles of pleasure and utility— were present in many of the great philosophical writings of the past. However, for the most part, they appeared in ethical theories constructed in the ancient mode, based on a metaphysical view of things, and emphasizing nature and reason in the classical sense. The utilitarianism of Jeremy Bentham and John Stuart Mill arose out of a markedly different intellectual environment, and was more closely related to the empirical philosophy of a David Hume than to the metaphysical vision of a Plato. Because of this accord with the modern temper, utilitarianism had a decisive effect on ethical, social, and political thought in the past century and a half, as well as on social and political developments.

Alfred North Whitehead, noting the effects of Bentham's utilitarianism and Comte's positivism on thought and action during this period, said:

Most of what has been practically effective, in morals, in religion, or in political theory, from their day to this has derived strength from one or other of these men. Their doctrines have been largely repudiated as theoretical foundations, but as practical working principles they dominate the world.[1]

John Stuart Mill's *Utilitarianism* is the best-known exposition of one of these two dominant doctrines in the present-day world.

[1] Alfred North Whitehead, *Adventures of Ideas* (New York: Macmillan, 1933), p. 46.

Fourteenth Reading

I

The first truly utilitarian view of ethics by an important modern thinker is to be found in the writings of David Hume, most succinctly in his *Enquiry Concerning the Principles of Morals.* Hume set out to construct a theory of ethics based on human experience and psychology. In his view, our judgments of "good" and "bad" are simply reflections of the emotions of approval or disapproval we feel toward actions and events. We approve of what we feel to be pleasant or useful—either to ourselves or to others. The basic "moral sentiment" is guided by the "social virtues" of benevolence and justice, which aim at the good of the human race, or "public utility." The social feeling of "sympathy" is central in Hume's ethics. Moreover, public utility, or the happiness of others, is pleasant and agreeable to the individual moral agent. And pleasure, says Hume, is the ultimate end of human action.

When Jeremy Bentham, in the next generation, sought a basic criterion whereby good laws could be distinguished from bad laws, he found it in Hume's principle of utility. In Bentham's hands, Hume's principle was used as an intellectual tool in a radical program of political and social reform, whence the name "Radicals" for Bentham and his followers.[2] Bentham's utilitarianism, unlike that of his Tory predecessor Hume, was universalist and egalitarian.

Moreover, it was quantitative. Bentham held that we can measure the amount of pleasure in any act, that is, its utility.

[2] See the excellent account of English utilitarianism and radicalism in *The Growth of Philosophic Radicalism,* by Elie Halévy (Boston: Beacon Press, 1955).

Through this hedonistic calculus we may determine whether an act is right or wrong, or rather its degree of rightness or wrongness. It is the *amount* of pleasure rather than its kind or quality that makes the difference. One of his provocative statements is that "[the child's game of] push-pin is as good as poetry." Also, the *extent* to which pleasure or utility is enjoyed is of basic importance in his theory. The basic utilitarian criterion, he says, is "the greatest good of the greatest number" (a phrase apparently borrowed by Bentham from Cesare Beccaria, the great eighteenth-century Italian economist, jurist, and criminologist).

In his *Introduction to the Principles of Morals and Legislation*, Bentham says that man is governed by "two sovereign masters"—pleasure and pain. He defines "utility" as that which "tends to produce benefit, advantage, pleasure, good or happiness" (all of which amount to the same thing)—either for the individual or for the human community. The good of the latter—of the greatest number—must be the determining criterion of the rightness or wrongness of conduct.

It was this kind of utilitarianism that John Stuart Mill undertook to expound, defend, and also modify in his pamphlet *Utilitarianism*. Mill was born and bred in this doctrine. His father, James Mill, was one of the great proponents of utilitarianism and a great admirer as well as a good friend of Jeremy Bentham. The latter was a close neighbor of the Mill family and a frequent visitor in their household. So also were David Ricardo, the great utilitarian economist, and many other prominent English Radicals of the time. J. S. Mill's rigorous early education, which is described in the Biographical Note on page 263, was modeled on Bentham's own education and influenced by Bentham's educational theories. It is highly significant, as regards both the character and the educational philosophy of James Mill and Bentham, that the latter's writings were not made a part of J. S. Mill's curriculum and were not read by him until much later, on his own initiative. As it turned out, however, it was the younger Mill who wrote the most succinct, persuasive, and best-known presentation of utilitarianism.

Mill claims in a footnote that he was probably "the first person who brought the word utilitarian into use," having discovered it in a novel by John Galt, a Scottish writer. (See p. 477d.) The *Encyclopædia Britannica* article on "Utilitarianism," however, credits Bentham with having been the first to suggest the term.

II

Mill's *Utilitarianism* is an essay of persuasion. It is an argument for the defense of utilitarianism, intended to convince its opponents, most of whom consider it an immoral moral philosophy, an unethical ethics. Hence the essay takes the form of a dialogue with the anti-utilitarians, answering their objections, actual or possible. It is a device, as Mill himself notes, of telling us what utilitarianism is by making clear what it is not. This defensive-offensive, which takes up most of the first three chapters, is climaxed by an attempt (in Chapter 4) to "prove" the truth of the utilitarian principle, in so far as proof is possible as regards ultimate ends. And it is completed by the exposition (in Chapter 5) of Mill's crowning thesis, that the transcendent ethical virtue of justice is itself a form of expediency and, hence, is supported rather than opposed by utilitarian ethics.

In Chapter 1, Mill tells us that utilitarianism has discovered the long-sought ultimate standard of right and wrong, for which moral philosophers have vainly searched since the beginning of our tradition. This utilitarian moral criterion is that the rightness or wrongness of human conduct is to be determined by its effect on happiness—ultimately, on the happiness of the greatest number of persons. It is this criterion, Mill claims, that has been operative without acknowledgment or recognition in all sound moral philosophies.

In Chapter 2, Mill begins his task of telling us what utilitarianism is not, and thus removing common misconceptions about it. First, he deals with the accusation that this doctrine advocates the satisfaction of base, sensual desires as the criterion of good. Mill makes it clear at the start that the "useful," in this view, is what brings pleasure and averts pain, and that happiness here is identified with pleasure.

The creed which accepts as the foundation of morals, Utility, or the

Greatest Happiness Principle, holds that actions are right in proportion as they tend to promote happiness, wrong as they tend to produce the reverse of happiness. By happiness is intended pleasure, and the absence of pain; by unhappiness, pain, and the privation of pleasure. (p. 448a)

As to the accusation that this reduces human good to animal satisfactions, Mill points out, as the Epicureans did before him, that man has the capacity to enjoy specifically human pleasures—intellectual, aesthetic, imaginative—and, departing significantly from his great predecessor Bentham, he asserts that *quality* as well as *quantity* (that is, intensity) is important in assaying the ethical worth of pleasures. There are qualitative kinds and levels of pleasure.

It is quite compatible with the principle of utility to recognise the fact, that some *kinds* of pleasure are more desirable and more valuable than others. (p. 448c-d)

It is a fact of common experience and observation, says Mill, that those who are capable of enjoying both "low" and "high" pleasures always prefer the high ones. The higher type of person always prefers precarious human happiness to sure animal fulfillment, or the uncertain fulfillment of an intelligent man to the secure bliss of a moron. Underlying this preference is the "sense of dignity," without which no truly human happiness is possible. All this is expressed forcefully in the famous epigram:

It is better to be a human being dissatisfied than a pig satisfied; better to be Socrates dissatisfied than a fool satisfied. (p. 449c)

How do we know that "it is better"? How do we know which pleasures are "higher"? Mill answers this question much as Socrates, Plato, and Aristotle answered it. The competent judge in these matters is the wise and good man who, having experienced both, chooses one pleasure above another, in spite of the comparative disadvantages and "discontent" that may accompany the former. He alone can judge, since he has experienced both kinds of satisfaction. The fool or the pig cannot, since he knows only one kind.

However, the objection may arise that seeking one's own pleasure and happiness, however high the quality of the enjoyment, is an ignoble and selfish aim. On the contrary, replies Mill (and here he is in line with Bentham's doctrine), the utilitarian standard "is not the agent's own greatest happiness, but the greatest amount of happiness altogether" (p. 450b). Even if a certain discontent and unhappiness be the price of a noble character, its nobility may benefit other persons and increase their happiness, thus according with the criterion of "Utility or Happiness . . . as the directive rule of human conduct" (p. 450b). Far from making one's own happiness the end of moral action, utilitarianism requires a strictly impartial and benevolent attitude in considering one's own happiness and that of others. Indeed, the precepts of Jesus of Nazareth, to do unto others as you would be done by, and to love your neighbor as yourself, "constitute the ideal perfection of utilitarian morality" (p. 453a).

As to the long-standing objection that perfect happiness is not attainable in this life, Mill retorts that utilitarianism aims at the limited kind of happiness that is possible in human life—not constant rapture and euphoria, but a predominance of pleasure over pain, of activity over passivity. Like Aristotle, he recognizes that certain external ills—"such as indigence, disease, and the unkindness, worthlessness, or premature loss of objects of affection" (p. 451d)—shut off a man from happiness. However, good utilitarian that he is, he is convinced that most external evils are removable through individual effort and social progress.

All the grand sources, in short, of human suffering are in a great degree, many of them almost entirely, conquerable by human care and effort . . . (p. 452b)

The spirit of Radicalism also inspires his sharp reply to the objection that renunciation is the highest ethical virtue and that the best thing is to learn to do without happiness. "Humbug!" retorts Mill, in effect—practically everybody, the "nineteen-twentieths," the underprivileged masses of mankind, are involuntarily practicing that virtue all over the world. As for voluntary self-sacrifice, utilitarianism counts it a great virtue, provided it is done "to increase the amount of happiness in the world" (p. 452c). Otherwise it is nothing but pathological, masochistic asceticism.

Mill also deals with the contrary objection, that utilitarianism establishes an impossibly high requirement—that individual action must always be motivated by the general good or interest. This objection gives Mill the opportunity to emphasize one of the basic points of utilitarian ethics—that the objective results, not the personal motivations of action, make the ethical difference. In this view, it does not matter what motive inspires a man who saves another from drowning—the action is good. Nor does it matter what motive inspires a man who betrays a friend—the action is bad. It is not necessary that an action be motivated by the desire to accomplish the greatest good of the greatest number in order to be good, as measured by the utilitarian standard—"the motive has nothing to do with the morality of the action, though much with the worth of the agent" (p. 453c-d).

Nevertheless, utilitarians are inclined, on the whole, to connect the moral quality of the action with that of the agent; they believe

> . . . that in the long run the best proof of a good character is good actions; and resolutely refuse to consider any mental disposition as good, of which the predominant tendency is to produce bad conduct. (p. 454c)

Mill also makes the common-sense observation that even when a person's conduct is motivated by the principle of the "general good," this does not mean that he must think of the whole human race. He need not think of anyone beyond the particular persons involved in the situation in which he is acting, of their good and their happiness, first making sure, however, that no one else will thereby be harmed.

But the whole human race and its experience is involved when it comes to calculating the effects of our action on the general happiness. It is not true, as some anti-utilitarians say, that we do not have the time to weigh the consequences of our actions before we act. We do not have to start off *de novo* at every moment, says Mill, as if nobody had ever existed, experienced, or learned before us. With the experience of the ages behind us, we have reached some general agreement as to what is useful and good, and this provides us with the rules of morality that we apply to particular cases—with the "secondary principles" which intervene between the fundamental principle of morality and the concrete instances of action. Granted that these secondary principles may be modified and extended through new experiences, still we do not have to start from scratch whenever we encounter a particular question of right and wrong (for instance, whether lying, stealing, or killing will work for or against the general good).

A reiterated theme in these replies to objections is that of the "long-run" as opposed to the "short-run" or immediate utility. A man is justified by the utilitarian criterion, says Mill, if, out of moral considerations, he refuses to do something that may be obviously beneficial *at the moment.*

. . . it would be unworthy of an intelligent agent not to be consciously aware that the action is of a class which, if practised generally, would be generally injurious, and that this is the ground of the obligation to abstain from it. (p. 454a)

Hence the fallacy of dismissing utility as "expediency," which is popularly taken to be the opposite of "principle" or "right." This assumes that expediency is limited to "the particular interest of the agent himself," and has to do only with "some immediate object, some temporary purpose" (p. 455c). But such limited expediency is actually inexpedient, that is, harmful, in the large-scale sense of expediency; for instance, a politician's sacrificing the good of his country for his own immediate political advantage. If I tell a lie in order to gain some present advantage, I am weakening one of the most expedient human feelings, the sense of veracity, upon which human communication, the social bond, and ultimately human happiness itself rest. Far from being expedient, the violation of "such transcendent expediency" is the most inexpedient and harmful act possible against mankind and the common good.

Like many previous moral philosophers, Mill admits exceptions to these transcendent obligations, but these are always granted for the sake of a greater utility. One may lie, or commit other acts generally considered harmful, to prevent a greater harm in a particular case (for instance, to prevent a lunatic from getting possession of a dangerous weapon, or evildoers from harming themselves or others). The guiding principle, however, the ultimate criterion, is still utility or expediency.

III

Whence does this utilitarian standard—the greatest good of the greatest number—derive its binding force? Why do we feel obliged to measure the right and wrong of our actions by this guide? Like any other moral standard, says Mill, it has external sanctions and may be developed by external influences—law, social structure, education, and public opinion. It also has the internal sanction of "conscience"—a subjective feeling which registers pain when we violate what we conceive to be our moral duty, culminating in "remorse."

Mill is convinced that this inner sense or "moral faculty" is natural, inasmuch as it has developed out of our basic human nature. However, he holds that it is acquired rather than innate, and extremely adaptable, admitting a wide variety of moral imperatives, as society and custom may direct. Hence the moral faculty is "artificial" as regards its specific orientation, and awareness of this may lead, in a developed state of culture, to moral skepticism (as in the case of the Greek Sophists). The utilitarian standard, then, like any other, might be regarded as merely arbitrary "if there were no leading department of our nature, no powerful class of sentiments" to provide "a natural basis of sentiment for utilitarian morality" (p. 459d).

This natural basis is provided by "the social feelings of mankind," the natural human impulse to associate with one's fellows. Man is naturally compelled to see himself as part of a social group. Hence he naturally comes to identify his own good with that of his fellow men, and this identification is reinforced by the development of social equality and the influence of education and other social institutions. Thus this basic social feeling, rooted in human nature and developed by organized society, is "the ultimate sanction of the greatest happiness morality" (p. 461b).

The exposition of the natural basis of the utilitarian criterion in Chapter 3 prepares us for the utilitarian interpretation of justice in Chapter 5. Justice, says Mill, is a branch of utility or expediency, not opposed to it, as is commonly believed. Justice is a particular form of expediency, associated with a unique feeling of absolute obligation.

First Mill lists various connotations of the term "justice." This involves the meanings of personal "rights" or "claims," of "due" or "desert," of "faithfulness" to commitments, and of "impartiality" or "equality." But more important for our purposes here is the notion of *punishment* or "penal sanction" which is involved in any judgment of ethical wrong. Whenever we judge an act to be wrong, we also think that the person responsible should be punished—if not by law, at least by public censure or by his own conscience. This distinguishes the realm of specifically moral obligation from that of expediency in general, which includes acts that are useful, desirable, and admirable but not absolutely obligatory and not requiring punishment if not done.

Mill then divides the realm of moral obligation into two spheres: "perfect obligations" and "imperfect obligations." Justice belongs to the sphere of perfect obligations, where particular persons have specific rights or claims, as distinct from the sphere of imperfect obligations, where the specific application of a moral duty, such as charity or benevolence—to *whom* and for *what*—is left open. In justice, we may owe a particular person a certain payment for his services, a specific interest on his capital, or the performance of a certain act; but we do not owe any particular person acts of charity or benevolence, although these too are morally required of us. An unjust act, therefore, involves a wrong done to a particular person, who has a particular right or claim which is violated by the act.

Whence, however, arises the unique feeling of absolute obligation which is always bound up with the idea of justice? It derives originally, says Mill, from the natural impulses of self-defense and sympathy, from the natural instinct of retaliation. While operative in animals only where harm has been done to themselves or their young, it is extended in human beings to harm done to any human or sentient being, and thus becomes moral. Resentment is a moral feeling when it is a response to an act that has been judged blamable *as a general rule* and as affecting all men—not merely a response to the harm that a particular individual has suffered in the immediate case.

The idea of justice, then, implies (1) a rule of conduct for the good of all mankind, and (2) a desire to punish those who violate the rule. The latter, which Mill calls "the sentiment of justice," derives its peculiar force from the natural animal instinct of retaliation, and its morality from the universal extension to all mankind.

A basic utility is involved, an "extraordinarily important and impressive kind of utility," which provides society with its sanction for enforcing personal rights or claims and punishing their violation. This basic utility is security, man's most vital interest, without which he cannot be protected against evil or conserve what is good. The absolute necessity of security gives to justice its absolute quality, which distinguishes it from all ordinary expediency.

. . . *ought* and *should* grow into *must*, and recognised indispensability becomes a moral necessity, analogous to physical, and often not inferior to it in binding force. (p. 471b)

The utilitarian interpretation accounts for all that has commonly been ascribed to justice. "Justice is a name for certain classes of moral rules, which concern the essentials of human well-being" so vitally that they have the character of absolute obligation. (See p. 473d.) They are the "rules which forbid mankind to hurt one another," and are fundamental in the establishment of social harmony. We all need to be assured of not being harmed by our fellows—through wrongful aggression, domination, or withholding of what is our due. This common interest obliges us to return evil for evil and good for good—to retaliate against those who violate the "primary moralities" and to provide deserved and promised benefits.

The traditional formulation of justice, "Render unto each his due," is essentially utilitarian and expedient. So are the accompanying principles of impartiality and equality, "that we should treat all equally well . . . who have deserved equally well of *us*," which Mill calls "the highest abstract standard of social and distributive justice" (p. 475a). It rests ultimately on the utilitarian Greatest Happiness principle, which implies that one person's happiness counts the same as another's. "Everybody to count for one, nobody for more than one," Bentham said. This means, says Mill, that every person has an equal claim to happiness and to the means of happiness, aside from the superior claim of some greater social expediency.

And hence all social inequalities which have ceased to be considered expedient, assume the character not of simple inexpediency, but of injustice, and appear so tyrannical, that people are apt to wonder how they ever could have been tolerated; forgetful that they themselves perhaps tolerate other inequalities under an equally mistaken notion of expediency, the correction of which would make that which they approve seem quite as monstrous as what they have at last learnt to condemn. The entire history of social improvement has been a series of transitions, by which one custom or institution after another, from being a supposed primary necessity of social existence, has passed into the rank of a universally stigmatised injustice and tyranny. So it has been with the distinctions of slaves and freemen, nobles and serfs, patricians and plebeians; and so it will be, and in part already is, with the aristocracies of colour, race, and sex. (p. 475c-d)

IV

In Chapter 4 Mill provides his promised "proof" that the general happiness is actually the ultimate end of human conduct. He repeats his warning, given at the start, that there can be no demonstrative proof where ultimate ends are concerned. All that can be done is to show that the desirable end is actually desired and that it is an end in itself, to which all other ends or goods are means. In this case, where happiness is the ultimate end, it must also be shown that it is the *general* happiness that is desired. Mill's "demonstration" of this affords him an opportunity to set forth his views on the nature of happiness and its relation to other goods, particularly virtue.

Mill's first point is that happiness is a desirable end. Certainly happiness is desired as a good by men—this is a matter of common experience. Assuming that whatever is *desired* is *desirable*, then happiness is a desirable end. However, all that this argument may demonstrate is that *individual* happiness is a desirable end, for experience merely shows us that individuals pursue their own happiness. How do we jump from this proposition to the conclusion that the *general* happiness is a desirable end? Here is Mill's answer:

No reason can be given why the general happiness is desirable, except that each person, so far as he believes it to be attainable, desires his own happiness. This, however, being a fact, we have not only all the proof which the case admits of, but all which it is possible to require, that happiness is a good: that each person's happiness is a good to that person, and the general happiness, therefore, a good to the aggregate of all persons. (p. 461d)

Still, all that the preceding arguments may show is that happiness—the general happiness—is *a* desirable end. It still remains to be shown that happiness is the *ultimate* end, good in itself, and the *sole* criterion of morality. For it is also a matter of common experience that persons desire other things beside happiness—virtue, health, fame, power, money, being well-liked, etc.

Virtue in particular has been considered a good, indeed a good in itself and not merely a means to an ultimate end. The utilitarians, according to Mill, readily agree to this "as a psychological fact," while still holding that virtue is prized originally because it brings pleasure and that its ultimate worth lies in its conduciveness to the general happiness. In order to contribute to the general good, the individual must pursue virtue as an end in itself, even when the immediate consequences may be inconvenient or undesirable. Moreover, if we examine the concept of happiness more closely, we see that virtue—as well as every other good—is a constituent part of the end in itself.

Happiness is not an abstract idea, but a concrete whole; and these are some of its parts. (p. 463a)

In any case, if man desires whatever he desires as a part of or as a means to happiness, then happiness is "the sole end of human action" and "the criterion of morality" (p. 463c).

Mill believes that the "if" clause here involves a "psychological truth," which is proved by common experience, that is, by introspection and observation of others. Hence at this point he sketches a psychological basis for the utilitarian ethics. It turns on the close relation between desire and pleasure. Happiness and virtue, as well as other goods, we recall, are valued because they bring pleasure or avert pain. We desire what gives pleasure or averts pain. Indeed, says Mill,

. . . desiring a thing and finding it pleasant, aversion to it and thinking of it as painful, are phenomena entirely inseparable, or rather two parts of the same phenomenon; in strictness of language, two different modes of naming the same psychological fact: that to think of an object as desirable (unless for the sake of its consequences), and to think of it as pleasant, are one and the same thing; and that to desire anything, except in proportion as the idea of it is pleasant, is a physical and metaphysical impossibility. (p. 463d)

The importance of this psychological thesis for the utilitarian ethics is indicated by Mill's remark in the next chapter "that 'happiness' and 'desirable' are synonymous terms" (p. 475b).

It has already been indicated, however, that virtue may and should be pursued, even where the immediate consequences are undesirable. Does not moral virtue require a firm will to do the right, rather than the pursuit of the desirable for the sake of pleasure? Mill admits the important psychological distinction between will and desire, as that between the active and the passive, and maintains that in a person of fully developed and fixed moral character the will predominates over immediate desires. But if we look back to the genesis of this firm moral will, he says, we find that it originated in a desire that was associated with pleasure and that became a fixed will only through a long process of habituation. Hence, if we want to make a person's will virtuous when it is weak and unstable, we must first make "the person *desire* virtue" by making him associate it with pleasure.

Thus pleasure in the desirable or desire for the pleasurable remains basic in the development of moral virtue and the attainment of happiness. However, habit—the right kind of habit —is required to assure constancy "in feeling and in conduct," by developing independence of pleasure and pain—"the will to do right ought to be cultivated into this habitual independence" (p. 464c). Nevertheless, this state of the will is only a means to what is ultimately good, pleasurable, and desirable— happiness. Hence Mill considers the utilitarian principle demonstrated, in spite of the qualifications made by the factors of habit and will. He holds it proved that

> . . . nothing is a good to human beings but in so far as it is either itself pleasurable, or a means of attaining pleasure or averting pain. (p. 464d)

V

Does it follow that what is desired is desirable?

The basic assumption in Mill's "proof" of utilitarianism is that what is desired is desirable. Just what does he mean here by "desirable"? Does he mean "capable of being desired"? But this would reduce his starting assumption to the mere truism that what is actual is possible, a proposition seemingly without ethical significance. Or does he mean "fit to be desired"? Then his basic assumption is that what *is* desired *should* or *ought* to be desired.

Is this jump from "is" to "ought" legitimate? Or is Mill confusing natural capacity with ethical fitness? Or does he hold the tacit sub-assumption that what is desired in accord with man's nature is a proper end of human activity—in line with the older "teleological" views of Aristotle and Aquinas? Or should we seek a more modern "hedonistic" linkage of the desirable and the pleasurable—in the spirit of Hobbes, Locke, and Hume—as underlying his statement that the desired is desirable?

Assuming either the teleological or the hedonistic viewpoint, is Mill's statement ethically valid? Must an ethical "ought" necessarily be supported by a natural "is"? Is the linking of natural capacity with ethical fitness proper or is it confused?

Do the desirable and the pleasant always go together?

Mill says that to desire a thing and to find it pleasant are inseparable aspects of the same experience. The British moral philosopher Henry Sidgwick has pointed out, however, that there is an ambiguity about the English word "please." It may, for instance, "please" the martyr to choose martyrdom; in that sense his martyrdom "pleases" him, but that does not mean that he finds it "pleasant."

But would Mill say that it is the martyrdom (or any other type of sacrifice or hardship) that is desired, desirable, and pleasant? What is it, according to Mill, that the martyr desires and finds pleasant? Does Mill's psychological analysis of the pleasure-desire correlation account for the martyr's desire for the pleasure he takes in his sacrifice?

Writing elsewhere on Plato's *Gorgias*, Mill agrees that it is better to suffer wrong than to do wrong, and goes on to say:

The step marked by the Gorgias is one of the greatest ever made in moral culture,—the cultivation of a disinterested preference of duty for its own sake, as a higher state than that of sacrificing selfish preferences to a more distant self-interest. (*Dissertations and Discussions*, vol. iii, p. 340)

Is this statement concordant with Mill's use of the pleasure principle as the basis of conduct? If so, how so? Is it concordant with Mill's emphasis on "long-run" utility?

Does the desirability of individual happiness imply the desirability of the general happiness?

If we grant that each person desires his own happiness, says Mill, it follows that happiness is a good to the individual, and, as a corollary, that the general happiness is a good to "the aggregate of all persons." But how does it follow that the latter is a good to the individual, and that it should be the ultimate end of personal conduct and the sole criterion of individual morality? This is a crucial point, for generality or universality is essential to utilitarian ethics, which, in Mill's view, does not sanction merely individual pleasure-seeking—hedonism in the ordinary sense. Is it dubious to ground the pursuit of the general happiness in that of the individual happiness? Is Mill illegitimately trying to deduce a "Universalistic Ethical Hedonism" from a "Psychological [Egoistic] Hedonism," as C. D. Broad has charged?

Mill assumes, says Broad, that the general happiness is a whole composed of all the individual happinesses as parts. Since each of the parts is desirable, it follows, according to

Mill, that the whole is desirable. Not so, says Broad—"it does not follow from the fact that every part of this whole is desired by someone that the whole itself is desired by anyone."[3]

Now, we might argue, in behalf of Mill and against Broad, that the general happiness functions as the *criterion* rather than the *motive* of action in Mill's ethics. However, he does attempt to show that the general happiness is desirable and desired, just as individual happiness is desirable and desired. And he emphasizes throughout the essay that the general good is involved in personal happiness.

Perhaps we can find the clue to this coupling of personal and general happiness in Mill's appeal to "the social feelings of mankind," which he himself calls "the ultimate sanction of the greatest happiness morality." Is this organic social belonging of man with man more basic in Mill's ethical thought than the purely discrete pleasures, the "atomistic" happinesses that are central in any doctrine of "psychological hedonism"? If so, then is his dwelling on individual desire, pleasure, and happiness irrelevant to his main argument and not essentially connected with his conclusions?

After all, Mill does say that it may be necessary to sacrifice one's own happiness for the sake of the happiness of others, and that the capacity to do this "gives the best prospect of realizing such happiness as is attainable." It is this sort of thing that made Henry Sidgwick remark on the "curious blending of Stoic and Epicurean elements" in Mill's ethics.

Why do men choose the general happiness as their end? Is it a kind of natural and normal result of widening awareness, the development of moral consciousness? Could a man possibly know that the greatest happiness is the ultimately desirable end of human action without desiring it? Does desire for the general happiness require a moral choice, a decision which we are free to make one way or the other?

[3] C. D. Broad, *Five Types of Ethical Theory* (London: Routledge & Kegan Paul, Ltd., 1930), p. 184.

Can we estimate adequately the consequences of our acts for the general happiness?

How do we know whether an act will contribute to or impair the greatest happiness of the greatest number? On the one hand, says Mill, we have the whole experience of the human race upon which to draw for our judgments of consequences. On the other hand, unless we are community leaders, we need not take more than a limited view of circumstances and consequences, and may concentrate on merely "private utility, the interest or happiness of some few persons" (p. 454a).

But it is the greatest good of the greatest number in the absolute sense that is the ultimate end and criterion of right and wrong in conduct. How can we be sure that what we are doing for "private utility" is good for "public utility"? Mill himself warns that we must make sure that we do not violate the rights of anyone outside the persons immediately concerned. But how can we be sure of this?

Mill's reply is that we cannot be sure, and that this uncertainty is one of the conditions of human existence: "Our foresight of consequences is not perfect. Is anything else in our constitution perfect?" We have to live with this condition and make the best judgment that is open to us in the human condition. John Dewey calls this uncertainty or dimness of awareness about the ultimate import of our actions the "poignancy" of human situations.

Is an ethics based on this admittedly uncertain estimate of consequences a satisfactory guide to human conduct? Or must we have recourse instead to an ethics based on fixed and absolute principles, such as Kant's? Does an ethics like Kant's afford us a surer and more precise guide to particular ethical judgments and decisions than an ethics like Mill's?

Do motives have nothing to do with the morality of actions?

Mill says that utilitarianism is concerned only with the rightness or wrongness of actions, not with the moral qualities of the person who performs them. The latter's motive, intent, disposition, etc., do not matter for the utilitarian ethics. All that matters is what actually occurs, the overt action.

This view not only contradicts Kant's view that motive is the central factor in morality, that it is what makes an action moral, but it also seems to conflict with our common-sense view of right and wrong. Even cold, hard law, which deals with specific acts clearly and objectively classified, takes account of personal motivation and disposition in its judgments. Does it do justice to the concrete reality of moral situations to separate the act and the agent?

John Dewey says that, although "consequences fix the moral quality of an act . . . in the long run but not unqualifiedly, consequences are what they are because of the nature of desire and disposition."[4] Is Mill's qualification "that in the long run the best proof of a good character is good actions" (p. 454c) in basic agreement with Dewey's view that the will is "something practical and moving," the personal cause of the objective consequences, with which it is inextricably involved? Mill's qualification certainly implies a negative judgment of a disposition, "of which the predominant tendency is to produce bad conduct." Is not this the kind of judgment of personal moral quality which utilitarianism is supposed to eschew?

Does Mill's choice of the wise and good man as the human measure of which pleasures are higher and which are lower indicate an emphasis on the person rather than on the act?

[4] John Dewey, *Human Nature and Conduct* (New York: Modern Library, 1930), pp. 44-45.

The following questions are designed to help you test the thoroughness of your reading. Each question is to be answered by giving a page or pages of the reading assignment. Answers will be found on page 304 of this Reading Plan.

1 Are most of our actions done from a sense of duty?

2 What is the only sensible meaning of Kant's fundamental principle of morals?

3 What are the essential differences between the "intuitive" and the "inductive" theories of morals?

4 Is tranquillity or is excitement the main element in a happy life?

5 Why is not the belief in the transcendental objective reality of moral obligation more effective than the force of subjective feeling?

6 Can money be desired for itself, as part of the ultimate end of life?

7 What are the two main views on whether or not a bad law may be disobeyed?

DARWIN

The Descent of Man

Part I, Ch. 4-5

Vol. 49, pp. 304-330

Charles Darwin belongs to the small group of thinkers, including Copernicus and Newton, whose thought has revolutionized man's conception of the natural world. Because his interest was in organic life, in both its mental and its physical aspects, his influence has been even more far-reaching than that of his great predecessors. There are few fields of inquiry during the past hundred years that have not been affected in one way or another by Darwin's theory of evolution, and this applies to the human as well as to the natural sciences. The century that has elapsed since the first presentation of his theory has been an era of stress on positive empirical facts; and Darwin's thought has been a guide, acknowledged or unacknowledged, to the illumination and interpretation of the welter of positive facts for three generations of empirical inquirers.

The present reading demonstrates that Darwin's theory and, hence, his influence were not restricted to the explanation of how the diverse forms of life originated and survived. What we have here is nothing less than a natural history of morals—a theory of how the moral sense developed, based on observations of animal life, and the connected inferences and hypotheses. Out of the struggle for existence, in which animal species compete for survival with one another, Darwin sees emerging among individuals the social virtues and feelings—mutual aid, sympathy, self-sacrifice, and fidelity. It is these morally elevated qualities and affections which he finds biologically essential to the survival of the species—among the lower animals and among men.

This theory of the origin and development of morals provided a naturalistic, positive, empirical explanation, as against so-called transcendental, metaphysical, or idealistic analyses, which the thinkers of the late nineteenth century considered lacking in substance and reality. The temper of the age demanded that everything be explained in terms of natural processes, including ethics and perhaps religion too. Darwin's theory, after the initial shock, was a great success.

However, the ethical doctrine which most social and political thinkers drew from it was not that intended by its author. What they emphasized was the struggle for existence and the survival of the fittest, which when applied to man living in society became the right of the stronger—physically, mentally, socially, or economically—against the weaker. Evolutionary ethics, especially in England and the United States, was used to justify the doctrine of unrestricted economic competition and "rugged individualism."

This kind of "social Darwinism" is regarded much less favorably today, by conservatives as well as by liberals, than it was in Darwin's time. The tendency now is to emphasize the elements of mutual aid, sympathy, and social institutions, which were present in Darwin's theory but were neglected by most of the social thinkers of his time.

Fifteenth Reading

I

Many of the moral philosophers whom we have considered in these readings have speculated on correspondences between the mental and moral qualities of men and those of the lower animals. Aristotle, for example, like Darwin, was a biologist. He too saw man as a social or political animal, who essentially exists in association with his fellows and is distinguished by the moral sense from all other animals. (See Vol. 9, p. 446b-c.) But, for Aristotle, there is a definite "jump" or "gap" between man and the lower animals. Speech, rationality, and the moral sense are signs of a difference in kind, not merely of degree, in the same basic potentialities. For Aristotle, the natural world is made up of fixed kinds and species.

Darwin broke with this conception of traditional philosophical naturalism as well as with the traditional religious doctrine of the uniqueness of man. In his view, organic nature is a united whole, with the various types of organisms connected by lines of descent. Variations in form and development are explainable by natural causes, which account for the survival and expansion of the species best adapted to the prevailing environment. The mental faculties, found in their highest state in man, have developed by a natural process from the crude state in which they are found in the lower animals. "Perfection," for Darwin, means the capacity to change, to adapt to environment, not the capacity to remain what one is.

Darwin's theory of evolution is a theory of the development of the mental as well as of the physical faculties, and hence also of the moral faculties. Long before he had completed his theory and presented it to the world, he realized that it had ramifications far beyond the scope of biology proper. "My theory will lead to a complete philosophy," he noted in 1837, more than twenty years before the appearance of *The Origin of Species*. In later years, he investigated various psychological phenomena, such as instinct, sexual feelings and behavior, and the expression of the emotions.

As for Darwin's own intellectual and moral character, he was a paradigm of the honest inquirer, the man of science, always eager to form a hypothesis to account for observed phenomena but ever ready to give up a favorite hypothesis when the facts obviously contradicted it. Like all critical thinkers, he foresaw most of the weighty objections to his theory before others presented them, and he took them seriously. Unlike some of his followers, he was not arrogantly dogmatic about the theory of evolution, and did not claim that it had been proved directly or that it was amenable to direct proof. The only "proof" of his theory, as he saw it, would be "whether it is, or is not, able to group together and explain phenomena." He himself was convinced that his theory did adequately account for the appearances in the organic world.

As a young man, Darwin had many interests, including poetry and music. As he grew older and devoted himself singlemindedly to his chosen vocation, he lost his capacity to appreciate good literature and art, a failing for which he expressed regret in later life. His conclusion about himself in his *Autobiography* is an honest and humble one:

As for myself I believe that I have acted rightly in steadily following and devoting my life to science. I feel no remorse for having committed any great sin, but have often and often regretted that I have not done more direct good to my fellow-creatures.

Such a frank avowal gives credence to the eulogy of Harald Höffding, the Danish historian of philosophy:

As we learn to know him from his *Autobiography* and his letters, he stands out before us, a Socratic figure, unique amid the inquirers of modern times; to be honoured alike for his energy, his love of truth and his feeling for humanity.[1]

[1] Harald Höffding, *A History of Modern Philosophy* (New York: Dover Publications, Inc., 1955), Vol. II, p. 438.

II

The selection which constitutes this reading assumes that the reader is already acquainted with the main elements of Darwin's theory of evolution. Let us, therefore, sum them up briefly before going on to a discussion of the reading.

Darwin's theory attempts to account for the origin and development, and the survival or extinction of the organic forms that exist or have existed in the world. The key terms in this explanation are "the struggle for existence" and "natural selection." According to Darwin, a particular environment will support only a certain number of organisms and certain types of organisms; hence, there occurs a struggle for existence, for survival, which involves not only a tooth-and-claw conflict among species but also adaptation to the environment.

Adaptation occurs through variations in characteristics among the individuals of a species. Through a process of natural selection (on the analogy of the artificial selection of the human plant grower or stock breeder), those variations survive which are best adapted to the particular conditions, and thus they become part of the racial inheritance of a species or become links in the transition from one species to another. Natural selection emphasizes both the genetic factor—the variations and their hereditary transmission—and the environmental factor, which makes the demands, so to speak, that organisms must fulfill in order to survive.

As distinguished from the Lamarckian theory of evolution, the Darwinian theory holds, however, that only changes in the hereditary stock can be handed down, and that these cannot be produced by environmental conditions. The environment selects what has already been produced through genetic variation. (Natural selection explains the process whereby variations are handed down or blotted out, not how the variations originate.) Evolutionary inquiry in this century has investigated the effects of radiation on genetic stock; but the discovery that variations and mutations are effected in this way does not contradict Darwin's theory, since radiation affects the essential inheritance bearers, the genes, and not peripheral and obvious physical or mental acquirements. According to the Darwinian theory, acquired characteristics, such as the development of the body or mind through exercise or culture, cannot be transmitted to one's descendants.

III

In this reading, Darwin is seeking the natural, biological basis of what he considers to be the distinctively human characteristic—"the moral sense or conscience." He sets himself the task of elucidating "from the side of natural history" that unique feeling of "right" or "duty" which impels a man to sacrifice his biological well-being—even life itself. He sees this inquiry as

. . . an attempt to see how far the study of the lower animals throws light on one of the highest psychical faculties of man. (p. 304b)

Darwin's fundamental assumption is that man and the lower animals share in the same mental powers, with only one difference—that in man these powers are more fully developed. In other words, animals differ *in degree,* but not *in kind* from man. (See p. 319c.) Thus, in Darwin's analysis, the sense of right and wrong that is found uniquely in man is based mainly on two factors: (1) social instincts and (2) intellectual development. Animals possess social instincts and mental powers similar to those of man; it is only his more highly developed intellect that accounts for man's peculiar moral sense. Hence, Darwin proposes the following proposition as quite plausible:

. . . that any animal whatever, endowed with well-marked social instincts, the parental and filial affections being here included, would inevitably acquire a moral sense or conscience, as soon as its intellectual powers had become as well, or nearly as well developed, as in man. (p. 340b-c)

(Darwin also adds language and habit, in "obedience to the wishes and judgment of the community," as specifically human means of developing the moral sense and guiding conduct.)

That the moral sense is theoretically possible among the social animals does not mean, however, that the other animals would develop the same sort of ethics as man has. On the contrary, Darwin points out, the content of their ethics would be quite different from, and might even clash quite sharply with, human ethics. For instance, if we were reared in the same conditions of life as the bees, our spinsters would kill their brothers and our mothers would kill their fertile daughters, but this would be done as "a sacred duty," that is, out of a sense of what is good or bad for the species. If the bee or any other social animal had this sense, "an inward monitor" would inform the individual whether it had done right or wrong. "Right" action, then, would be action performed in accordance with the more enduring social instincts, even when they clash with urgent immediate desires, such as hunger.

Darwin acknowledges that John Stuart Mill has already recognized the basic ethical importance of natural social feelings in his *Utilitarianism*. But Mill erred gravely, says Darwin, by conceiving the moral sense as acquired rather than innate. It is a central theme of Darwin's evolutionary doctrine that mental qualities, including the moral sense, are racially transmitted, that is, are inherited, not individually acquired.

After the opening announcement of this thesis, he proceeds to analyze the nature of "sociability" in general, to show its importance in human morals, and to describe in detail the social virtues. (See pp. 305-316.)

IV

First of all, Darwin points to the obvious, observed facts of mutual aid and service among the lower animals, and infers mutual affection and even sympathy (fellow feeling) in some cases. Animals cooperate to warn each other of danger, to procure food, and also to scratch one another's itches and to remove parasites and thorns. However, the main aim of mutual aid is the survival of the group. Hence, a wounded animal may be driven from the herd or gored to death in order to save the group, a deed which may seem to be "the blackest fact in natural history" if we do not realize its purpose. However, to balance this "black" fact there are many cases of animals heroically confronting danger on behalf of a fellow animal in distress, and even of loving sympathy and charity for animals grown too old, weak, or blind to take care of themselves.

In addition to these basic feelings of love and sympathy,

Darwin notes certain moral qualities in animals akin to human virtues: self-command, fidelity, and obedience. These qualities are required and demonstrated in the main activities of the group and are necessary for its sustenance and survival. Among baboons, for instance, "if an imprudent young animal makes a noise, he receives a slap from the others to teach him silence and obedience" (p. 307d). Also notable is the obvious satisfaction and pleasure which many animals find in mutual association and their obvious discomfort when separated from the group.

According to Darwin's theory, the social instincts probably arose from parental and filial affection through a process of *natural selection,* which favored the survival of those who lived together and liked it. He claims to find evidence of parental affection all the way down the scale to starfishes, spiders, and earwigs. With the case of the bees in mind, however, he also must admit hatred between the next of kin as an impulse favoring the survival of the group—"the desire to destroy their nearest relations having been in this case of service to the community" (p. 308d). Nevertheless, he maintains that the major factor in preserving and expanding groups of social animals must have been mutual aid and sympathy.

Self-preservation is not always the most powerful instinct. Sometimes the migratory or the maternal instinct proves stronger; the former makes a salmon leap out of fresh water at the migratory season, which results in its death, and the latter leads mothers to defend their young against powerful and ferocious marauders at the cost of their own lives. Moreover, the migratory and maternal instincts often conflict, and sometimes the former proves stronger, so that mother birds leave their young to die in their nests unattended. Darwin, however, doubts whether in the long run the migratory is more beneficial than the maternal instinct for group survival, although it may prove stronger at a certain season.

V

After showing the sociability of animals, Darwin proceeds next to the demonstration that man is a social animal, motivated by the same basic social instincts as the lower animals and sharing with them certain feelings and moral qualities— although in a higher degree of development. Man too is impelled by love and sympathy, possesses the moral qualities of self-command, fidelity, and obedience, which are reinforced by habit and experience. His moral sense is distinguished from that of the lower animals mainly because of his highly developed reasoning power and his awareness, through language, of the opinions of his fellow men. The natural impulse to mutual love and sympathy is conducive in man to his being "influenced in the highest degree by the wishes, approbation, and blame of his fellow-men, as expressed by their gestures and language" (p. 310d). Like Willy Loman in Arthur Miller's play *Death of a Salesman*, he wants to be "well-liked."

Under all these influences, man reaches a state where he can choose his conduct on purely ethical grounds, apart from any consideration of immediate pleasure and pain. He may then say, "I am the supreme judge of my own conduct," and, after Kant, "I will not in my own person violate the dignity of humanity" (p. 310d).

After tracing summarily this rise from the social instincts acquired by our "early ape-like progenitors" to the pure Kantian morality, Darwin pauses to question why man feels he ought to follow his altruistic social instincts even when they clash with the selfish instinct for self-preservation. Would it not be more natural to put self-preservation above the good of others? Why should a man feel regret or remorse if he follows this apparently more natural policy?

Darwin answers this all-important question in terms of man's special capacity for *reflection* and of the distinction between the more enduring and the more transitory instincts or needs. The social instincts—and along with these the need for approval by one's fellows—are persistent and enduring. The selfish instincts and needs are momentary, ephemeral—hunger, sexual desire, retaliation, cupidity, and even self-preservation (which "is not felt except in the presence of danger"). Through reflection, man can look back on his past conduct and compare the images and impressions of immediate satisfaction with the persistent sympathy he feels for his fellows and the constant need for their approval. If he has chosen to satisfy hunger, wreak vengeance, or save his own skin at the expense of his fellows, he will not be able to avoid the consciousness that he has done so or the pain—in the form of "regret, shame, repentance, or remorse"—that accompanies his awareness.

It is a man's higher development—the capacity to reflect and compare—that brings this pain. The mother bird who leaves her young, impelled by the more immediately powerful migratory instinct, would also feel agonizing remorse at the thought of the awful fate to which she has condemned her little ones—if she possessed the capacity for this thought. This capacity finally takes form in the moral sphere as *conscience*, whereby man looks back toward his past deeds and judges them, and forward to his future deeds—an inner monitor that impels him always to follow his social instincts and fulfill his need for approval, in preference to immediate, selfish satisfactions. It is because of this inner monitor that a hungry man is inhibited from stealing food and a wronged man from wreaking vengeance. (Darwin ascribes a similar "conscience" to a well-trained and obedient dog; see p. 307c.)

However, this development of the capacity to follow one's more enduring impulses in preference to the immediate, urgent instincts implies no particular ethical content—for instance, a Christian or present-day Western morality. All that "the imperious word *ought*" implies, says Darwin, is "the consciousness of the existence of a rule of conduct," whatever it may be, that we feel bound to obey. It is such a rule, held sacred by his tribe, that compels a West Australian aborigine to kill a woman of another tribe in compensation for the natural death of his wife. When he does not do so, he wastes away through anxiety and guilt; when he does kill a foreign woman, his health of mind and body is restored—his "conscience" is clear, so to speak. (See p. 313b-c.) Indeed, certain primitive peoples consider it a far more horrible crime to marry a woman of one's own tribe than to kill a woman of another tribe. And among certain classes in European society, until very recently, it was regarded a moral duty for a man to fight a duel if insulted or challenged by a social equal.

For a man to have a clear conscience and to be free of anxiety, then, he must avoid "the disapprobation, *whether reasonable or not,* of his fellow-men" (p. 314b). [Italics added.] However, Darwin also adds that he must not violate "the fixed habits of his life, especially if these are supported by reason," and must avoid the reprobation or punishment of the deity or deities in whom he believes.

VI

Darwin now goes on to consider "the strictly social virtues." These are the virtues which hold men together even in a primitive state. In such a state they are practiced almost exclusively toward the members of one's own group. Murder, robbery, and deceit are forbidden among the members of the same tribe but permitted or even required against strangers. Actions are regarded "as good or bad, solely as they obviously affect the welfare of the tribe" (p. 315d).

The "social virtues" in a primitive state are those that help to maintain the group—courage, "self-sacrifice, self-command, and the power of endurance"—not those that are salutary or edifying for the individual. The latter are the "self-regarding" virtues—among which are prudence (apparently meaning here a careful regard for one's own interests), temperance, and chastity. Darwin, a good Victorian, speaks of the "utter licentiousness and unnatural crimes" practiced among primitive peoples, and of "the low morality of savages, as judged by our standard" (pp. 315c-316a). He enters into a good many details of the shocking practices of primitive peoples—infanticide, slavery, oppression of women, torture of their enemies, cruelty to animals—and concludes that among these peoples "humanity is an unknown virtue" (p. 315a). He does so to stress the fact that the social virtues among savages are limited in their application to the group or the tribe, and thus to avoid the sentimental myth of the gentle and noble savage.

He ascribes the "low morality" of savages to three factors: (1) "the confinement of sympathy to the same tribe"; (2) inadequate stress on the self-regarding virtues as conducive to the general welfare; and (3) "weak power of self-command." (The last apparently contradicts the inclusion on page 315c of self-command as among those virtues necessary for the tribal welfare.)

After this excursion into primitive morality, Darwin presents his conclusions as to the import of these investigations for ethical theory. First, he takes issue with the utilitarian doctrine that our actions are determined by the pleasure or happiness (individual or general) that we think will result from them. Although in theory this is a criterion rather than a motive, Darwin finds that most utilitarians write as if we must have "a distinct motive for every action," associated with anticipated pleasure or pain, and he feels that this is not true of many moral actions, especially of our most noble, self-sacrificial ones—where we act "impulsively, that is from instinct or long habit, without any consciousness of pleasure" (p. 316c). A man who risks his life to save another from danger acts instantly, not after due calculation of possible pleasures and pains, for

. . . there lies within him an impulsive power widely different from a search after pleasure or happiness; and this seems to be the deeply planted social instinct. (p. 316c)

In his earlier discussion of the associative instinct, Darwin has already referred to the causal relation between pleasure and pain on the one hand and conduct on the other. He points out that many actions are performed instinctively, apart from any feeling of pleasure or pain involved. Hence, we need not assume that men need the carrot of pleasure and the stick of pain to guide their conduct; they may automatically follow inherited patterns of action. However, it seems probable that pleasure and pain have been linked by nature with association and dissociation, respectively, in order to induce animals to associate and aid one another for the sake of survival. (See p. 308a-c.)

Darwin has earlier taken issue not only with utilitarian but also with traditional emphases on deliberation as essential to moral conduct. On the contrary, he says, our most perfect and noble actions are

. . . done impulsively, without deliberation or effort, in the same manner as by a man in whom the requisite qualities are innate. (p. 311c)

It is the habit of virtue that marks truly moral actions. We do not call an animal's actions moral because he apparently goes through a process of deliberating between different courses of action. Hence, we classify as moral certain actions, whether they are done deliberately, impulsively, or habitually, provided they are done by a moral being, that is, a being who can reflect, compare, and respond to approval or disapproval.

Continuing his polemic against the utilitarians, Darwin says it is the general *good* and not the general *happiness* that is supported by the social instincts, distinguishing between "welfare" and "happiness," which he apparently associates with "selfish" feelings of pleasure. It is the social instinct and sympathy that serve as "the *primary* impulse and guide" of conduct, granted that the greatest happiness does enter in as a *secondary* guide. Notwithstanding the absurdities and barbarities inculcated by common opinion as tending to the common good, Darwin is convinced that men develop both the social and the self-regarding virtues through the influence of public approbation, reason, and experience. With the advancement of civilization, man extends his social instincts and sympathy to larger and larger groups, taking in nations, races, all mankind, the lower animals, and all sentient beings. "Humanity," that is, humaneness, toward the animal kingdom is a late development in the history of moral culture. Finally man reaches the highest moral stage, where not only acts but thoughts are controlled, and he is inhibited against thinking, as well as doing, evil.

How do biological factors enter into this ethical development? Darwin hypothesizes a genetic transmission of "virtuous tendencies" through a gradual process of modification of the emotions and dispositions, passed on from generation to generation. He points to what he believes is strong evidence that vicious tendencies are inherited in certain families, and hence concludes that good tendencies also may be thus transmitted. He sees the physical basis for this in the obvious physical connection between the brain and the rest of the body, and the apparent effect of psychosomatic states on moral tendencies and conduct. Furthermore, only the inheritance of moral tendencies can explain the moral differences that are believed to exist "between the various races of mankind" (p. 318b).

The inheritance of virtuous tendencies would provide an important biological mechanism to support the primary impulse of the social instincts, and even the development of the elevated virtues of chastity, temperance, and humaneness to animals—apart from the survival value of such virtues in the struggle for existence. Here is how Darwin envisions the way in which they are transmitted:

. . . they become first impressed on the mental organization through habit, instruction and example, continued during several generations in the same family, and in a quite subordinate degree, or not at all, by the individuals possessing such virtues having succeeded best in the struggle for life. (p. 318c)

Meanwhile, the social instincts follow the path of higher and higher development, of wider and wider sympathy, and gain greater and greater strength and efficacy in the struggle between the enduring and the immediate impulses. Man has grown better and better in each succeeding stage of history. Darwin sees this progress continuing into the future, as it has from barbarism to civilization.

Looking to future generations, there is no cause to fear that the social instincts will grow weaker, and we may expect that virtuous habits will grow stronger, becoming perhaps fixed by inheritance. In this case the struggle between our higher and lower impulses will be less severe, and virtue will be triumphant. (p. 319a)

VII

In Chapter 5, Darwin takes up the problem of the mechanism whereby variations in the intellectual and moral qualities in the human race are inherited. It seems highly probable that the intellectual faculties were perfected through a process of natural selection, favoring the most intellectually developed individuals and tribes in the struggle for survival. Similarly, the social virtues seem to have developed "through natural selection, aided by inherited habit" (p. 321c), first among our animal ancestors and then among primitive man. The tribe best endowed with the cohesive virtues of fidelity and obedience, as well as courage and confidence, was bound to win in the struggle for existence.

It does not seem, however, that the same holds good for the individual. If he sacrifices his life for others, he is less likely to reproduce himself, compared with less courageous or less noble individuals. However, Darwin points out, the social virtues are of mutually pragmatic value to all members of the tribe, and become reinforced through habit, approbation, and blame, so that they become social, rather than merely individual, patterns of behavior. Furthermore, the extraordinary moral hero may do more for the edification of his tribe by his example than by producing numerous offspring. In any case, whatever the effect of his moral qualities on the individual's stock, Darwin maintains that the tribe with the most members possessing the social virtues would be the most likely to survive— "this would be natural selection" (p. 322d). Hence, since the most moral tribes would be the most successful, "the number of well-endowed men will thus everywhere tend to rise and increase" (p. 323a).

The effect of natural selection on intellectual and moral qualities is not so clear among civilized nations as it is among primitive tribes. The very moral advancement of civilizaton tends to the artificial encouragement and survival of people who are in a low physical, intellectual, and moral state. And nations do not exterminate one another entirely—or did not in prenuclear days. Nevertheless, there are certain counterchecks to these artificial hindrances on the operation of natural selection, and, on the whole, individuals who are more highly developed intellectually and morally do win out in the struggle for existence under the conditions of civilized society. Where these counterchecks do not work, "the reckless, the vicious and otherwise inferior members of society" will increase "at a quicker rate than the better class of men, and the nation will retrograde" (p. 327a).

Progress, that is, development toward greater perfection, is by no means inevitable. "Natural selection acts only tentatively" (p. 327c). All kinds of cultural factors play a part— a good educational system or a high standard of excellence, for instance. And certain biological conditions are required—such as a rapid increase in numbers and a rigorous struggle for existence. If the conditions of life are too easy, a people may stagnate or even retrogress rather than advance, says Darwin, preceding Toynbee by a century. Nevertheless, Darwin maintains that, on the whole and in the long run, there has been progress all along the line in man's path from savagery to civilization—in the mental and mechanical arts, as well as in morals and religion.

It is apparently a truer and more cheerful view that progress has been much more general than retrogression; that man has risen, though by slow and interrupted steps, from a lowly condition to the highest standard as yet attained by him in knowledge, morals and religion. (p. 330a-c)

VIII

Is survival the main value in Darwin's ethical theory?

One of the commonest objections to Darwin's moral analysis is that it is founded on the idea of the struggle for existence, and hence sanctions the philosophy of tooth-and-claw, of dog-eat-dog, of the supremacy of brute force. Judging by the present reading, this interpretation caricatures and falsifies Darwin's essential doctrine, for he stresses the biological value of the other-regarding virtues, even of the sacrifice of the individual for the sake of the group. But doesn't this merely extend the sphere of "sacred egoism" from the individual to the clan, the tribe, or the nation, locked in the war of each against all that was envisioned by Hobbes? Granted that survival in the struggle for existence is a biological good, why is it an ethical good? Is natural history also the history of the advancement of right?

Apparently this is what Darwin contends, with various qualifications, and his biological account is intended to furnish an empirical, natural basis for man's ethical development firmly rooted in his animal nature. In Darwin's view, what survives, on the whole and in the long run, is not better because it survives, but survives because it is better—measured on the scale of liberal nineteenth-century values, within the moral tradition of Western Christendom. It is those tendencies and qualities which contribute to the common good that make for the survival of the group, not the grasping for immediate and individual satisfaction; and these include the private virtues of temperance and chastity, as well as the social virtues of obedience and fidelity and the impulses of sympathy and mutual aid. Darwin insists that he is giving us the biological background for the Golden Rule of the Gospels. (See p. 319d.) He envisions a natural extension of the operation of the social virtues and feelings to the whole human race, indeed, to the whole of sentient life; and he even envisions a stage where a man acts from a supreme moral *ought*, not for pragmatic biological reasons, and where even his thoughts are purified.

Still, we may entertain doubts about whether things actually work out this way and for these reasons. Are we to believe that all is for the best in the best of all possible worlds? Do chance variations, the struggle for existence, and natural selection bring the triumph of right over wrong? Are there good things—ideas, values, individuals, and nations—that are overwhelmed by evil things, so that the loss of the good is never compensated by the onward "advance" of history? It is difficult to see how the sacrifices of martyrs and the lone and often vain struggles of prophets against the ruling morality of their own groups can be justified by biological considerations. Yet, admittedly, getting rid of the helplessly weak and wounded is biologically salutary for the group in the animal kingdom, "black" fact though it be. The application of such measures to human beings during the Nazi regime in Germany was justified on biological grounds—to better the German race in its struggle with other races. Darwin himself admits that the protection of the weaker and inferior types in civilized groups frustrates the process of natural selection and may even lead to retrogression. Yet the inhibition against getting rid of the weak and inferior is part of the morality which is the aim of the evolutionary process and which Darwin himself accepts. But can such inhibition be justified on biological grounds?

Thomas Huxley, although he was the doughty protagonist

of Darwin's theory of evolution ("Darwin's Bulldog"), nevertheless maintained that the realm of nature, with its ferocious struggle for existence, is utterly opposed to ethical values; that man's ethical progress is accomplished by struggling against natural processes, not by imitating them, and by setting up an artificial ethico-political order. The human conscience, in Huxley's view, is "an artificial personality . . . built up beside the natural personality . . . charged to restrain the anti-social tendencies of the natural man within the limits required by social welfare."[2] Other famous contemporaries of Darwin, such as John Stuart Mill and William James, also contrasted the cruel, reckless, wasteful, and meaningless realm of nature with the ethical realm in which man must operate as a moral being.

Darwin himself was not indifferent to the cruelty and suffering involved in the process of natural selection. Indeed, it was his awareness of the existence of evil in the world that gradually turned him from a belief in revelation to a philosophical theism, and finally to agnosticism. He was unable to accept either the belief that such a world was the work of a good and wise Designer or Providence, or the alternative belief that it was the result of mere chance or brute material force. He concluded that man cannot solve this problem through his intellect, but that, nevertheless, he can and should do his moral duty.

For a maintenance of the view that natural selection, aided by rational and social selection, does, in the long run, bring a steady progress toward the ethical ideals of the true, the good, and the beautiful, see the article on "Evolutionary Ethics" written by the British biologist J. A. Thomson for *Encyclopædia Britannica* in the late 1920's.

Are there genuine analogies or parallels between animal behavior and human conduct?

There are instances, as indicated in this reading, of what J. A. Thomson calls "the raw materials of morals" in the ani-

[2] Thomas Huxley, *Evolution and Ethics and Other Essays* (New York: D. Appleton & Co., 1898), p. 30.

mal kingdom. In addition to all the expressions of the social virtues among animals in a wild state, Darwin indicates that domesticated animals, such as the dog, exhibit signs of conscience, duty, and a response to praise or blame, accompanied by correlative feelings of satisfaction or shame. (See, for example, pp. 307c, 314a, and 322b.) He also notes that animals exercise a kind of deliberation, when they seem to be torn between opposing instincts, and choose between different courses of action. (See p. 311c.)

Yet we must ask ourselves whether we are not interpreting animal behavior in terms of human mentality and speaking figuratively when we talk of moral behavior of animals. Darwin himself notes that we do not call the apparently deliberated actions of animals moral, even when they are done for the good of others. And Thomson, the protagonist of an evolutionary basis of ethics, makes a significant distinction between "behavior" and "conduct." Behavior in this view is the mere physical manner of action, a positive fact; whereas conduct is something that is either good or bad.

Animals have behaviour, which hardly ever touches the level of conduct; man has always the possibility of conduct, though he often subsides into mere behaviour.[3]

This distinction is all the more interesting now because of the present-day use of the term "behavioral sciences" for what used to be called the "human" or "social" sciences. This usage implies, at least methodologically, the blotting out of the distinction between the physiological and ethical levels of the meaning of human action. (See also the various meanings of "behave" and "behavior" in any good unabridged dictionary.)

Animal behavior is a matter of organic response to immediate conditions, to the present environment or "field." Human conduct, in the moral sense, is regulated by the conscious sense of right and wrong, which involves generality or universality, extending beyond particular circumstances. Or, as Thomson says, "a truly ethical action implies control in reference to a moral ideal."

[3] *Encyclopædia Britannica*, Vol. 8, p. 931. (1962 printing.)

Darwin recognizes this distinction in principle. He emphasizes the specifically human character of rationality and morality. However, he is convinced that mentality and morality, rare though they be in the natural order, arise from that order and can be made understandable only by tracing their growth and development out of their animal beginnings or prefigurations. As Darwin sees it, we must account for the similarity as well as the difference, for the continuity as well as the discontinuity, between man and the lower animals—and this applies not only to bodily but also to mental and moral endowments. This does not mean, as Thomson notes, that morality in man is merely "the kin-sympathy . . . of the wolf" raised to a higher power, for there are jumps in the evolutionary process; but it does mean that there are potentialities in the lower animals that are developed to their fullest extent in man.

In short, it means that fundamentally man differs from the animals only in degree, not in kind; and this is still the crucial philosophical point of disagreement between the protagonists and antagonists of the idea that man evolved from the lower animals.

In his more polemical moments, when goaded by his detractors, Darwin held that some animals were morally superior to some men. He said that he would be prouder to acknowledge descent from an ape that risks its own life to save its keeper than from a savage who tortures his enemies, kills his children, and enslaves his wives.

Are moral advances inherited?

Darwin is, of course, the great exponent of the theory that only what is rooted in the genetic stock can be handed on, never acquired characteristics. This is his position in the great historical debate with Lamarck on the mode by which the process of evolution takes place. It would also seem to pit him against Herbert Spencer in the field of moral development; for Spencer, a good Lamarckian, held that mental and moral characteristics acquired by the individual can be handed down to his descendants. Yet it is not clear from this reading that Darwin holds consistently to an anti-Lamarckian position.

He states at the beginning the principle that the social instincts and feelings are innate, not acquired. However, throughout he puts much emphasis on such factors as habit, experience, and education in the development of the moral faculties and virtues. And at least once he affirms the possibility of "inherited improvement"—in the domesticated dog. (See p. 319c.) In the case of the heroic persons who sacrifice their lives for others, he does not solve the question of how their virtues are genetically transmitted to future generations; admitting the broad social and cultural effect of their example, just how do the virtues thus engendered in their fellows get transmitted to their offspring?

Thomson acknowledges this difficulty and affirms the distinction between "moral peculiarities that express germinal variations" and "moral peculiarities that are impressed as nurtural modifications." He agrees that only the former can be genetically transmitted; while the latter affect only "the extra-organismal or social heritage." However, he speculates that what is essential for human moral development may be not the selection of inborn variations in certain moral qualities but rather the quality of *susceptibility* to the socio-ethical heritage, customs, and institutions. Then those individuals would be "preferred" by the selective process who have the highest degree of susceptibility to the extra-organismal heritage; and buttressing the essential ethical elements in this heritage would serve to foster the maintenance of those stocks that are most susceptible to moral values.

Darwin himself recognized that, although natural selection of inherited variations originally plays the main role in the development of the moral sense out of the social instinct, other factors are more important in the development of man's higher qualities—culture, education, religion, etc.

Does Darwinism inculcate an ethics of mutual aid, or the right of the stronger?

We have already noted the remarkable emphasis on love, mutual aid, and self-sacrifice in an ethics derived from an evolutionary process based on a competitive and ferocious struggle for existence and survival. Competition and cooperation are complementary aspects of Darwin's theory of moral development, which he sees as eventually culminating in altruistic impulses and the fulfillment of the Golden Rule. Social and political theorists who applied Darwin's theory to human society could emphasize either the element of competition or that of mutual aid. Prince Kropotkin, the anarchist-philosopher and a younger contemporary of Darwin, emphasized mutual aid. Almost all other theorists at the time, however, emphasized the survival of the fittest and believed that society was improved through the rise of the stronger and most fit at the expense of the weaker and less fit. Darwin himself said that "open competition" must be maintained, and "the most able should not be prevented by laws or customs from succeeding best and rearing the largest number of offspring." This gave rise to what has been called "social Darwinism"—a defense of "rugged individualism" and the painful processes of nineteenth-century capitalism, based on an analogy with the biological struggle for existence and the survival of the fittest.[4]

On the basis of Darwin's remarks in Chapter 5, do you think he would agree that there are mentally and morally inferior races—that is, inferior by inheritance, not in culture?

[4] See the excellent work *Social Darwinism in American Thought*, by Richard Hofstadter, published by the Beacon Press, Boston, 1955.

The following questions are designed to help you test the thoroughness of your reading. Each question is to be answered by giving a page or pages of the reading assignment. Answers will be found on page 304 of this Reading Plan.

1 How do the Hamadryas baboons hunt insects?

2 Does sympathy characterize the feeling of a mother for her infant, or a man for his dog?

3 What attests to the "noble fidelity" of the Indian elephant sunk in the mud?

4 What are the most intense and persistent feelings?

5 What "lapse" did an Indian Thug "conscientiously regret"?

6 What Stoic philosopher does Darwin cite as support for the basic moral role of the social instincts?

7 What is the effect of wealth on natural selection among men?

8 Who bear more children—the poor and reckless, or the frugal and careful?

ANSWERS
to self-testing questions

First Reading
1. 30a
2. 28c-d
3. 36a, 37b
4. 28b-c
5. 29c-d
6. 31a

Second Reading
1. 253a-b
2. 254b
3. 261d-262a
4. 264d-265a
5. 270d
6. 276c
7. 281d
8. 286c-d

Third Reading
1. 339c, 347c
2. 340c-d
3. 344b-c
4. 345b
5. 347a-b
6. 426c-d
7. 431a-b
8. 432a
9. 435a

Fourth Reading
1. 349a-b
2. 350c
3. 352b-c
4. 353c-d
5. 355a
6. 357b
7. 358b
8. 358d
9. 359c-d

Fifth Reading
1. 108c
2. 110b
3. 111a-c
4. 113d
5. 114c, 119d, 122c
6. 124a-125a, 133b-d
7. 132b

Sixth Reading
1. 610a
2. 612b
3. 615a
4. 618b-c
5. 621a-b
6. 624b
7. 626a
8. 630a
9. 631c
10. 636b

Seventh Reading
1. 61d
2. 62d
3. 63c
4. 68b
5. 73b
6. 77b-c
7. 78b-c
8. 89b-c
9. 89d-90a
10. 94c

Eighth Reading
1. 29c-d
2. 31a
3. 89d
4. 95c-d
5. 97d-98a

6. 120c-d
7. 162c
8. 165b
9. 304b
10. 306d-307a

Ninth Reading

1. 451b-452c
2. 455d
3. 461d
4. 462d
5. 457c
6. 451a
7. 453b
8. 453c

Tenth Reading

1. 104b
2. 112a-b
3. 230a
4. 176d
5. 177c
6. 87c, 88b
7. 89c

Eleventh Reading

1. 253a
2. 271b
3. 257b
4. 258d
5. 263a-b
6. 266d
7. 269c
8. 275d

Twelfth Reading

1. 337a-c
2. 339b
3. 341a-b
4. 342b
5. 343c
6. 344b-c
7. 346d

Thirteenth Reading

1. 61a
2. 63b
3. 134b
4. 135a
5. 61c
6. 134d
7. 60b

Fourteenth Reading

1. 453c
2. 470b
3. 446a
4. 451b
5. 458d-459b
6. 462c-d
7. 465d-466a

Fifteenth Reading

1. 306a
2. 308d
3. 307c-d
4. 312b-d
5. 314d-315a
6. 319d
7. 324a-b
8. 325b-326c

ADDITIONAL READINGS

I. Works included in *Great Books of the Western World*

Vol. 7: PLATO, *Charmides; Lysis; Protagoras; Symposium; Meno; Euthyphro; Apology; Crito; Phaedo; The Republic; Statesman; Philebus; Laws*

      9: ARISTOTLE, *Nicomachean Ethics,* Book III, Chapters 6-12, Books IV-IX; *Politics,* esp. Books VII-VIII; *Rhetoric,* esp. Book I, Chapters 5-14, and Book II, Chapters 1-17

  12: EPICTETUS, *The Discourses,* Books II-IV
     MARCUS AURELIUS, *The Meditations*

  14: PLUTARCH, *The Lives of the Noble Grecians and Romans*

  17: PLOTINUS, *The Six Enneads,* esp. Enneads I, III, and VI, Tractates VIII-IX

  18: AUGUSTINE, *The Confessions; The City of God,* esp. Books V, XII-XIV, XIX; *On Christian Doctrine,* Book I

  19: AQUINAS, *Summa Theologica,* "Treatise on Man" (Part I, QQ. 75-102); "Treatise on Human Acts" (Part I-II, QQ. 6-48)

  20: "Treatise on Habits" (Part I-II, QQ. 49-89); "Treatise on Law" (Part I-II, QQ. 90-108); "Treatise on Faith, Hope and Charity" (Part II-II, QQ. 1-46); "Treatise on Active and Contemplative Life" (Part II-II, QQ. 179-182); "Treatise on the States of Life" (Part II-II, QQ. 183-189); "Treatise on the Last Things" (Part III Supplement, QQ. 87-99)

  21: DANTE, *The Divine Comedy*

  23: MACHIAVELLI, *The Prince*

  24: RABELAIS, *Gargantua and Pantagruel,* Book I, Chapters 52-58

  25: MONTAIGNE, *The Essays,* Book I, Essays 3, 4, 7, 8, 9, 12, 27, 35, 38, 43, 53; Book II, Essays 1, 5, 6,

8, 15, 20, 21, 23, 28, 32, 35; Book III, Essays 1, 4, 5, 9, 10

30: BACON, *New Atlantis*

31: SPINOZA, *Ethics*, Parts III-IV

32: MILTON, *Paradise Lost; Areopagitica*

33: PASCAL, *The Provincial Letters; Pensées*

35: LOCKE, *A Letter Concerning Toleration; Concerning Civil Government, Second Essay*

38: MONTESQUIEU, *The Spirit of Laws*, Books VII, XIX
    ROUSSEAU, *On the Origin of Inequality*

40: GIBBON, *The Decline and Fall of the Roman Empire*, Chapter XV, esp. pp. 191-200

41: GIBBON, *The Decline and Fall of the Roman Empire*, Chapter XLIV

42: KANT, *The Critique of Pure Reason*, II, "Transcendental Doctrine of Method," Chapter II, "The Canon of Pure Reason" (pp. 233-243); *The Critique of Practical Reason* (complete); *Preface and Introduction to the Metaphysical Elements of Ethics, With a Note on Conscience; General Introduction to the Metaphysic of Morals; The Science of Right; The Critique of Judgement*, Introduction and Part II

46: HEGEL, *The Philosophy of Right*, Preface and Introduction

53: JAMES, *The Principles of Psychology*, Chapters IV and XXVI

54: FREUD, *Beyond the Pleasure Principle; Group Psychology and the Analysis of the Ego; The Ego and the Id; Thoughts for the Times on War and Death; Civilization and Its Discontents; New Introductory Lectures on Psycho-Analysis*, Lecture 35

II. Other Works

A. Histories of Ethics and of Morals

ALBEE, ERNEST, *A History of English Utilitarianism*. New York: The Macmillan Company, 1957

ARNOLD, EDWARD VERNON, *Roman Stoicism,* reissue. New York: Humanities Press, Inc., 1958

BREASTED, JAMES H., *The Dawn of Conscience.* New York: Charles Scribner's Sons, 1934

HALÉVY, ELIE, *The Growth of Philosophic Radicalism,* trans. by Mary Morris. Boston: Beacon Press, Inc., 1955

HEARD, GERALD, *Morals Since 1900.* New York: Harper and Brothers, 1950

HOFSTADTER, RICHARD, *Social Darwinism in American Thought,* rev. ed. Boston: Beacon Press, Inc., 1955

JAEGER, WERNER, *Paideia: The Ideals of Greek Culture,* 3 vols., trans. by Gilbert Highet. New York: Oxford University Press, 1939-45

KROPOTKIN, PETER, *Ethics: Origin and Development,* trans. by Louis S. Friedland and Joseph R. Piroshnikoff. New York: Tudor Publishing Co., 1937

RILEY, WOODBRIDGE, *Men and Morals: The Story of Ethics,* reissue. New York: Frederick Ungar Publishing Company, 1960

SIDGWICK, HENRY, *Outlines of the History of Ethics for English Readers.* Boston: Beacon Press, Inc., 1960

WARNOCK, MARY, *Ethics Since 1900.* London: Oxford University Press, 1960

WESTERMARCK, EDVARD A., *The History of Human Marriage,* 3 vols., 5th ed. New York: The Macmillan Company, 1921; *The Origin and Development of the Moral Ideas,* 2 vols. New York: The Macmillan Company, 1906-08

B. Philosophical Ethics

ARISTOTLE, *Ethics: Ethica Nicomachea, Magna Moralia, Ethica Eudamia* (Aristotle's works: the Oxford translation, Volume IX), ed. by J. A. Smith and W. D. Ross. New York: Oxford University Press, 1915

AYER, A. J., *Philosophical Essays.* London: Macmillan & Co., Ltd., 1954; ed., *Logical Positivism.* Glencoe, Ill.: Free Press, 1959

BARNES, W. H. F. *et al., Logical Positivism and Ethics* (Supplementary Volume XXII, The Aristotelian Society). London: Harrison and Sons, Ltd., 1948

BAUMGARDT, DAVID, *Bentham and the Ethics of Today.* Princeton: Princeton University Press, 1952

BENTHAM, JEREMY, *A Fragment on Government; and an Introduction to the Principles of Morals and Legislation,* ed. by Wilfrid Harrison. New York: The Macmillan Company, 1948

BOSANQUET, BERNARD, *Psychology of the Moral Self.* London: Macmillan & Co., Ltd., 1904; *Some Suggestions in Ethics.* London: Macmillan & Co., Ltd., 1918; *The Value and Destiny of the Individual.* London: Macmillan & Co., Ltd., 1913

BOURKE, VERNON J., *Ethics: a Textbook in Moral Philosophy.* New York: The Macmillan Company, 1951

BERGSON, HENRI, *The Two Sources of Morality and Religion,* trans. by R. Ashley Andra *et al.* New York: Doubleday Anchor Books, 1956

BRADLEY, F. H., *Ethical Studies,* 2nd ed. rev. New York: Oxford University Press, 1927

BRAITHWAITE, R. B., *Moral Principles and Inductive Policies.* New York: Oxford University Press, 1953

BRANDT, R., *Ethical Theory: the Problems of Normative and Critical Ethics.* Englewood Cliffs, N.J.: Prentice-Hall, Inc., 1959

BROAD, C. D., *Ethics and the History of Philosophy.* New York: Humanities Press, Inc., 1952; *Five Types of Ethical Theory,* reprint. Paterson, N.J.: Littlefield, Adams & Co., 1959

BUTLER, JOSEPH, *Fifteen Sermons and a Dissertation Upon the Nature of Virtue,* ed. by W. R. Matthews. London: G. Bell & Sons, Ltd., 1950

CAHN, EDMOND N., *The Sense of Injustice: an Anthropocentric View of Law.* New York: New York University Press, 1949

CARRITT, E. F., *The Theory of Morals: an Introducton to Ethical Philosophy.* New York: Oxford University Press, 1928

COATES, J. B., *The Crisis of the Human Person.* New York: Longmans, Green and Co., Inc., 1949

COHEN, FELIX S., *Ethical Systems and Legal Ideals.* Ithaca, N.Y.: Cornell University Press, 1959

COMTE, AUGUSTE, *A General View of Positivism,* trans. by J. H. Bridges. New York: Robert Speller & Sons, Inc., 1957

CROCE, BENEDETTO, *Philosophy of the Practical,* trans. by Douglas Ainslie. New York: The Macmillan Company, 1913; *The Conduct of Life,* trans. by Arthur Livingston. New York: Harcourt, Brace and Co., Inc., 1924

DEL VECCHIO, GIORGIO, *Justice: an Historical and Philosophical Essay,* ed. by A. H. Campbell, trans. by Lady Guthrie. New York: Philosophical Library, 1954

D'ENTRÈVES, ALEXANDER PASSERIN, *Natural Law: an Introduction to Legal Philosophy.* New York: Longmans, Green and Co., Inc., 1951

DEWEY, JOHN and JAMES H. TUFTS, *Ethics,* rev. ed. New York: Henry Holt and Co., Inc., 1938

DEWEY, JOHN, *Outlines of a Critical Theory of Ethics,* 2nd ed. New York: Hillary House, Inc., 1957; ed., *Theory of the Moral Life.* New York: Holt, Rinehart and Winston, Inc., 1960

DRIESCH, HANS, *Ethical Principles in Theory and Practice,* trans. by W. H. Johnston. New York: W. W. Norton and Co., Inc., 1931

DUNCAN-JONES, AUSTIN, *Butler's Moral Philosophy.* Baltimore: Penguin Books Inc., 1952

EBY, L. S., *Quest for Moral Law.* New York: Columbia University Press, 1944

EDEL, ABRAHAM, *Ethical Judgment: the Use of Science in Ethics.* Glencoe, Ill.: Free Press, 1955

EDWARDS, PAUL, *Logic of Moral Discourse.* Glencoe, Ill.: Free Press, 1955

EWING, A. C., *The Morality of Punishment.* London: George Routledge and Sons, Ltd., 1929; *The Definition of Good.* New York: The Macmillan Company, 1947; *Ethics.* New York: The Macmillan Company, 1953

FAGOTHEY, AUSTIN, *Right and Reason: Ethics in Theory and Practice*, 2nd ed. St. Louis: C. V. Mosby Company, 1959

FLÜGEL, JOHN C., *Man, Morals and Society*, 2nd rev. ed. New York: International Universities Press, Inc., 1958

FROMM, ERICH, *Man for Himself: an Inquiry Into the Psychology of Ethics*. New York: Rinehart and Co., Inc., 1947

GREEN, T. H., *Prolegomena to Ethics*. London: Oxford University Press, 1890

HAMBURGER, MAX, *Morals and Law: the Growth of Aristotle's Legal Theory*. New Haven: Yale University Press, 1951

HAMPSHIRE, STUART, *Thought and Action*. New York: Viking Press, Inc., 1960

HARE, R. M., *Language of Morals*. New York: Oxford University Press, 1952

HARTMANN, NICOLAI, *Ethics*, trans. by Stanton Coit, 3 vols. New York: The Macmillan Company, 1932

HILL, THOMAS E., *Contemporary Ethical Theories*. New York: The Macmillan Company, 1950

HOBHOUSE, L. T., *The Rational Good: a Study in the Logic of Practice*. New York: Henry Holt and Co., Inc., 1921; *Morals in Evolution: a Study in Comparative Ethics*, 7th ed. New York: The Macmillan Company, 1951

HOCKING, WILLIAM E., *Human Nature and Its Remaking*, rev. ed. New Haven: Yale University Press, 1923

HUME, DAVID, *Essays, Moral, Political, and Literary*. New York: Longmans, Green and Co., Inc., 1912; *Moral and Political Philosophy* (Hafner Library of Classics, No. 3), ed. by Henry D. Aiken. New York: Hafner Publishing Co., 1948; *Inquiry Concerning the Principles of Morals*, ed. by Charles W. Hendel. New York: Liberal Arts Press, Inc., 1957

KANT, IMMANUEL, *Lectures on Ethics*, trans. by Louis Infield. New York: Century Company, 1931

KELSEN, HANS, *What is Justice? Justice, Law, and Politics in the Mirror of Science*. Berkeley: University of California Press, 1957

LAIRD, JOHN, *A Study in Moral Theory*. New York: The Macmillan Company, 1926; *Enquiry into Moral Notions.* New York: Columbia University Press, 1936

LAMPRECHT, STERLING P., *Nature and History.* New York: Columbia University Press, 1950

LA ROCHEFOUCAULD, FRANÇOIS DE, *Maxims,* trans. and ed. by Louis Kronenberger. Modern Library, New York: Random House, Inc., 1959

LEWIS, CLARENCE I., *An Analysis of Knowledge and Valuation.* La Salle, Ill.: Open Court Publishing Company, 1946; *The Ground and Nature of the Right.* New York: Columbia University Press, 1955

LIPPMANN, WALTER, *A Preface to Morals.* Boston: Beacon Press, Inc., 1960

LOCKE, JOHN, "Some Thoughts Concerning Education" in *On Politics and Education,* ed. by Howard R. Penniman. New York: D. Van Nostrand Company, Inc., 1948

LODGE, R. C., *Plato's Theory of Ethics* (International Library of Psychology, Philosophy and Scientific Method). New York: Humanities Press, Inc., 1953

LOTZE, HERMANN, *Outlines of Practical Philosophy.* Boston: Ginn and Co., 1885

MANDELBAUM, MAURICE, *The Phenomenology of Moral Experience.* Glencoe, Ill.: Free Press, 1955

MELDEN, A. I., ed., *Ethical Theories,* 2nd ed. Englewood Cliffs, N.J.: Prentice-Hall, Inc., 1955; ed., *Essays in Moral Philosophy.* Seattle: University of Washington Press, 1958

MOORE, G. E., *Ethics.* New York: Oxford University Press, 1947; *Principia Ethica.* New York: Cambridge University Press, 1959

NIETZSCHE, FRIEDRICH, *The Philosophy of Nietzsche.* Modern Library, New York: Random House, Inc., 1937; *The Portable Nietzsche,* trans. and ed. by Walter Kaufmann. New York: Viking Press, Inc., 1954

NOWELL-SMITH, PATRICK, *Ethics.* Baltimore: Penguin Books Inc., 1954

PATON, H. J., *The Good Will: a Study in the Coherence Theory of Goodness.* New York: The Macmillan Company, 1927

PAULSEN, FRIEDRICH, *A System of Ethics*, trans. and ed. by Frank Thilly. New York: Charles Scribner's Sons, 1899

PEPPER, STEPHEN C., *Ethics*. New York: Appleton-Century-Crofts, Inc., 1960

PERRY, RALPH BARTON, *General Theory of Value*. Cambridge, Mass.: Harvard University Press, 1950

PIAGET, JEAN and others, *The Moral Judgment of the Child*, trans. by Marjorie Gabain. Glencoe, Ill.: Free Press, 1948

PLUTARCH, *Selected Essays on Love, the Family, and the Good Life*, trans. by Moses Hadas. New York: New American Library (a Mentor Book), 1957

PRATT, JAMES BISSETT, *Reason in the Art of Living: a Textbook of Ethics*. New York: The Macmillan Company, 1949

PRICE, RICHARD, *A Review of the Principal Questions in Morals*, ed. by D. D. Raphael. New York: Oxford University Press, 1949

PRICHARD, H. A., *Duty and Interest*. New York: Oxford University Press, 1928; *Moral Obligation*. New York: Oxford University Press, 1950

PRIOR, A. N., *Logic and the Basis of Ethics*. New York: Oxford University Press, 1949

RAPHAEL, D. D., *Moral Judgement*. New York: The Macmillan Company, 1955

REYBURN, HUGH A., *The Ethical Theory of Hegel: a Study of the Philosophy of Right*. New York: Oxford University Press, 1922

RICE, PHILIP BLAIR, *On the Knowledge of Good and Evil*. New York: Random House, Inc., 1955

ROSS, W. D., *The Right and the Good*. New York: Oxford University Press, 1930; *Foundations of Ethics*. New York: Oxford University Press, 1939; *Kant's Ethical Theory: a Commentary on the Grundlegung zur Metaphysik der Sitten*. New York: Oxford University Press, 1954

ROYCE, JOSIAH, *Studies of Good and Evil: a Series of Essays Upon Problems of Philosophy and of Life*. New York: D. Appleton and Co., 1915; *The Philosophy of Loyalty*. New York: The Macmillan Company, 1908

RUSSELL, BERTRAND, *Education and the Good Life*. New York:

Boni & Liveright, 1926; *The Conquest of Happiness*. New York: Liveright Publishing Corp., 1930; *Marriage and Morals*. London: George Allen and Unwin, 1961

SANTAYANA, GEORGE, *The Life of Reason, or the Phases of Human Progress*, 2nd ed., 5 vols. New York: Charles Scribner's Sons, 1922

SCHLICK, MORITZ, *The Problems of Ethics*. New York: Prentice-Hall, Inc., 1939

SELLARS, WILFRID and JOHN HOSPERS, eds., *Readings in Ethical Theory*. New York: Appleton-Century-Crofts, Inc., 1952

SENECA, LUCIUS ANNAEUS, *The Stoic Philosophy of Seneca*, trans. by Moses Hadas. New York: Doubleday Anchor Books, 1958

SETH, JAMES, *A Study of Ethical Principles*. New York: Charles Scribner's Sons, 1895

SPENCER, HERBERT, *The Data of Ethics*. New York: A. L. Burt Co., Inc., 1879; *The Principles of Ethics*. New York: D. Appleton and Co., 1898

STEVENSON, CHARLES L., *Ethics and Language*. New Haven: Yale University Press, 1960

TAYLOR, A. E., *The Problem of Conduct*. New York: The Macmillan Company, 1901

TEALE, A. E., *Kantian Ethics*. New York: Oxford University Press, 1951

TOULMIN, S., *Reason in Ethics*. New York: Cambridge University Press, 1960

TSANOFF, RADOSLAV, *Ethics*, rev. ed. New York: Harper and Brothers, 1955

URBAN, WILBUR MARSHALL, *The Fundamentals of Ethics*. New York: Henry Holt and Co., Inc., 1930

VANN, GERALD, *Morals and Man*, rev. ed. New York: Sheed & Ward, Inc., 1960

VIVAS, ELISEO, *The Moral Life and the Ethical Life*. Chicago: University of Chicago Press, 1950

WESTERMARCK, E., *Ethical Relativity* (International Library of Psychology, Philosophy and Scientific Method). Paterson, N.J.: Littlefield, Adams & Co., 1960

C. Religious Ethics

BEACH, W., and H. R. NIEBUHR, eds., *Christian Ethics: Sources of the Living Tradition.* New York: Ronald Press Co., 1955

BENNETT, JOHN C., *Christian Ethics and Social Policy.* New York: Charles Scribner's Sons, 1946

BONHOEFFER, DIETRICH, *Ethics*, ed. by Eberhard Bethge, trans. by N. H. Smith. New York: The Macmillan Company, 1955

BRUNNER, EMIL, *The Divine Imperative*, trans. by Olive Wyon. Philadelphia: Westminster Press, 1947

BUBER, MARTIN, *The Way of Man: According to the Teachings of Hasidism.* Chicago: Wilcox and Follett Co., 1951; *Good and Evil: Two Interpretations*, trans. by R. G. Smith and M. Bullock. New York: Charles Scribner's Sons, 1953

CAMPBELL, C. A., *On Selfhood and Godhood.* New York: The Macmillan Company, 1957

COHEN, ABRAHAM, ed., *Everyman's Talmud.* New York: E. P. Dutton and Co., Inc., 1949

DE BURGH, WILLIAM G., *From Morality to Religion.* London: Macdonald and Evans, 1938

DEMANT, VIGO A., *Religion and the Decline of Capitalism.* New York: Charles Scribner's Sons, 1952

FANFANI, AMINTORE, *Catholicism, Protestantism and Capitalism.* New York: Sheed & Ward, Inc., 1955

JAEGER, WERNER, *Early Christianity and Greek Paideia.* Cambridge, Mass.: Harvard University Press, 1961

JAMES, WILLIAM, *Essays on Faith and Morals.* New York: Longmans, Green and Co., Inc., 1943

KIERKEGAARD, SØREN, *Stages on Life's Way*, trans. by Walter Lowrie. Princeton: Princeton University Press, 1940; *Fear and Trembling*, trans. by Walter Lowrie. New York: Doubleday Anchor Books, 1954; *Either/Or*, 2 vols. New York: Doubleday Anchor Books, 1959

LEWIS, C. S., *The Problem of Pain.* New York: The Macmillan Company, 1944

LEWIS, H. D., *Morals and Revelation.* New York: The Macmillan Company, 1951

LEWIS, JOHN, KARL POLANYI, and DONALD K. KITCHIN, eds., *Christianity and the Social Revolution*. New York: Charles Scribner's Sons, 1936

MARCEL, GABRIEL, *Homo Viator: Introduction to a Metaphysic of Hope*, trans. by Emma Craufurd. Chicago: Henry Regnery Co., 1951

McLAUGHLIN, TERENCE P., ed., *The Church and the Reconstruction of the Modern World: the Social Encyclicals of Pope Pius XI*. New York: Doubleday Image Books, 1957

MUZZEY, DAVID S., *Ethics as a Religion*. New York: Simon & Schuster, Inc., 1951

NELSON, BENJAMIN N., *The Idea of Usury: From Tribal Brotherhood to Universal Otherhood*. Princeton: Princeton University Press, 1950

NIEBUHR, H. RICHARD, *Christ and Culture*. New York: Harper and Brothers, 1956

NIEBUHR, REINHOLD, *An Interpretation of Christian Ethics*. New York: Harper and Brothers, 1935

OTTO, RUDOLF, *The Idea of the Holy*, 2nd ed., trans. by John W. Harvey. New York: Oxford University Press, 1950

PIEPER, JOSEF, *Fortitude and Temperance*, trans. by Daniel F. Coogan. New York: Pantheon Books Inc., 1954; *Prudence*, trans. by Richard and Clara Winston. New York: Pantheon Books Inc., 1959; *Happiness and Contemplation*, trans. by Richard and Clara Winston. New York: Pantheon Books Inc., 1958

RAMSEY, PAUL, *Basic Christian Ethics*. New York: Charles Scribner's Sons, 1950

ROUGEMONT, DENIS DE, *The Devil's Share*, trans. by Haakon Chevalier. New York: Pantheon Books Inc., 1945

TAWNEY, R. H., *Religion and the Rise of Capitalism*, new ed. New York: Harcourt, Brace and Co., Inc., 1947

TAYLOR, ALFRED E., *The Faith of a Moralist*, 1 vol. ed. New York: The Macmillan Company, 1937

THOMAS, GEORGE F., *Christian Ethics and Moral Philosophy*. New York: Charles Scribner's Sons, 1955

TODD, JOHN M., ed., *Springs of Morality: a Catholic Symposium*. New York: The Macmillan Company, 1956

TOLSTOY, LEO, *On Life, and Essays on Religion,* trans. by Aylmer Maude. New York: Oxford University Press, 1934

TROELTSCH, ERNST, *The Social Teaching of the Christian Churches,* trans. by Olive Wyon, 2 vols. New York: Harper Torchbooks, 1960

VON HILDEBRAND, DIETRICH, *Christian Ethics.* New York: David McKay Co., Inc., 1953;——and Alice Jourdain, *True Morality and its Counterfeits.* New York: David McKay Co., Inc., 1955

WARD, LEO R., *Christian Ethics.* St. Louis: B. Herder Book Co., 1952

WAXMAN, MEYER, *Judaism: Religion and Ethics.* New York: Thomas Yoseloff, Inc., 1958

WEBER, MAX, *The Protestant Ethic and the Spirit of Capitalism,* trans. by Talcott Parsons. New York: Charles Scribner's Sons, 1948

D. Scientific and Evolutionary Ethics

BERGSON, HENRI, *Creative Evolution,* trans. by A. Mitchell. Modern Library, New York: Random House, Inc., 1944

BRONOWSKI, J., *Science and Human Values.* New York: Harper Torchbooks, 1959

CHARDIN, PIERRE TEILHARD DE, *The Phenomenon of Man,* trans. by Bernard Wall. New York: Harper and Brothers, 1959

CLIFFORD, W. K., *The Ethics of Belief, and Other Essays.* London: C. A. Watts & Co., Ltd., 1947

CONKLIN, EDWIN GRANT, *The Direction of Human Evolution,* new ed. New York: Charles Scribner's Sons, 1922; *Man, Real and Ideal.* New York: Charles Scribner's Sons, 1943

DOBZHANSKY, THEODOSIUS, *The Biological Basis of Human Freedom.* New York: Columbia University Press, 1956

DRUMMOND, HENRY, *The Ascent of Man.* London: Hodder and Stoughton, Ltd., 1894

FISKE, JOHN, *The Destiny of Man.* Boston: Houghton Mifflin Co., 1884; *Through Nature to God.* Boston: Houghton Mifflin Co., 1899

HUXLEY, JULIAN, *Knowledge, Morality and Destiny.* New York: New American Library (a Mentor Book), 1960

HUXLEY, THOMAS H., *Evolution and Ethics and Other Essays.* New York: D. Appleton and Co., 1898;———and Julian Huxley, *Touchstone for Ethics, 1893-1943.* New York: Harper and Brothers, 1947

KEITH, ARTHUR, *A New Theory of Human Evolution.* New York: Philosophical Library, 1949

OTTO, MAX, *Science and the Moral Life.* New York: New American Library (a Mentor Book), 1949

SIMPSON, GEORGE GAYLORD, *The Meaning of Evolution.* New Haven: Yale University Press, 1956

THOMSON, J. ARTHUR, *What is Man?* New York: G. P. Putnam's Sons, 1924

E. Political and Social Ethics

BAKUNIN, MIKHAIL ALEKSANDROVICH, *The Political Philosophy of Bakunin,* ed. by G. P. Maximoff. Glencoe, Ill.: Free Press, 1953 (Part I)

BELLOC, HILAIRE, *The Servile State,* 3rd ed. London: Constable & Co., Ltd., 1927

BOSANQUET, BERNARD, *Social and International Ideals.* New York: The Macmillan Company, 1917; *The Philosophical Theory of the State.* New York: The Macmillan Company, 1920

BRUNNER, EMIL, *Justice and the Social Order,* trans. by Mary Hottinger. London: Lutterworth Press, 1945

BUBER, MARTIN, *Between Man and Man,* trans. by Ronald Gregor Smith. Boston: Beacon Press, Inc., 1955; *Paths in Utopia,* trans. by R. F. C. Hull. Boston: Beacon Press, Inc., 1958

CARRITT, E. F., *Ethical and Political Thinking.* New York: Clarendon Press, 1947

CASSERLEY, J. V., LANGMEAD, *Morals and Man in the Social Sciences.* New York: Longmans, Green and Co., Inc., 1951

CHILDS, MARQUIS W. and DOUGLASS CATER, *Ethics in a Business Society.* New York: Harper and Brothers, 1954

DEWEY, JOHN, *Individualism, Old and New.* New York: Minton, Balch & Co., 1930

EDEL, ABRAHAM and MAY, *Anthropology and Ethics*. Springfield, Ill.: Charles C Thomas, 1959

GINSBERG, MORRIS, *Essays in Sociology and Social Philosophy*, 3 vols. New York: The Macmillan Company, 1957-61

HIRST, E. WALES, *Ethical Love: Its Basis and Expression*. London: George Allen and Unwin, 1928

HOBHOUSE, L. T., *The Elements of Social Justice*. New York: Henry Holt and Co., Inc., 1922

JASPERS, KARL, *Man in the Modern Age*, trans. by Eden and Cedar Paul. New York: Doubleday Anchor Books, 1957

JOAD, C. E. M., *Guide to the Philosophy of Morals and Politics*. New York: Random House, Inc., 1948

JOUVENEL, BERTRAND DE, *The Ethics of Redistribution*. London: Cambridge University Press, 1951

KROPOTKIN, PETER, *Mutual Aid*. Boston: Porter Sargent, Publishers, 1955

LIPPMANN, WALTER, *The Good Society*. New York: Grosset & Dunlap, Inc., 1956

MANDEVILLE, BERNARD, *The Fable of the Bees; or, Private Vices, Public Benefits*, ed. by F. B. Kaye, 2 vols. New York: Oxford University Press, 1924

MARCEL, GABRIEL, *Man Against Mass Society*, trans. by G. S. Fraser. London: Harvill Press, Ltd., 1952

MARCUSE, HERBERT, *Soviet Marxism*. New York: Columbia University Press, 1958 (Part II)

MARITAIN, JACQUES, *The Person and the Common Good*, trans. by John J. Fitzgerald. New York: Charles Scribner's Sons, 1947; *The Rights of Man and Natural Law*, trans. by Doris C. Anson. New York: Charles Scribner's Sons, 1951

MEAD, GEORGE HERBERT, *Mind, Self and Society: From the Standpoint of a Social Behaviorist*, ed. by Charles W. Morris. Chicago: University of Chicago Press, 1934

MOUNIER, EMMANUEL, *A Personalist Manifesto*. New York: Longmans, Green and Co., Inc., 1938

NIEBUHR, REINHOLD, *Moral Man and Immoral Society*. New York: Charles Scribner's Sons, 1932

PIEPER, JOSEF, *Leisure, the Basis of Culture*, trans. by Alexander Dru. New York: Pantheon Books Inc., 1952

RIESMAN, DAVID and others, *The Lonely Crowd: a Study of the Changing American Character*. New Haven: Yale University Press, 1950

RIEZLER, KURT, *Man: Mutable and Immutable; the Fundamental Structure of Social Life*. Chicago: Henry Regnery Co., 1950

RUSSELL, BERTRAND, *Human Society in Ethics and Politics*. New York: Simon & Schuster, Inc., 1955

SCHELER, MAX, *The Nature of Sympathy*, trans. by Peter Heath. New Haven: Yale University Press, 1954

SCHWEITZER, ALBERT, *The Philosophy of Civilization*, trans. by C. T. Campion. New York: The Macmillan Company, 1949

SOREL, GEORGES, *Reflections on Violence*, trans. by T. E. Hulme and J. Roth. Glencoe, Ill.: Free Press, 1950 (Chapters 6-7)

STIRNER, MAX, *The Ego and His Own*, trans. by S. T. Byington. New York: Modern Library, Inc., 1918

TANNENBAUM, FRANK, *A Philosophy of Labor*. New York: Alfred A. Knopf, Inc., 1951

TAWNEY, R. H., *The Acquisitive Society*. New York: Harcourt, Brace and Co., Inc., 1946

WALLAS, GRAHAM, *The Great Society*. New York: The Macmillan Company, 1914

WHYTE, WILLIAM H., JR., *The Organization Man*. New York: Doubleday Anchor Books, 1957